In

Island Sunrise by Laur...

Accustomed to makin... ...lation-
ships based on the bottom line, Ashley Simmons is in way
over her head when she meets oceanographer, Rick Adams.
Rick is forthright about his Christianity, and soon Ashley
knows this man has depths that dollar signs cannot measure.
God brought them together for a brief island vacation—
how can He part them now, when the sand beneath her feet
is shifting?

Matchmaker 911 by Wanda E. Brunstetter
Wendy Campbell doesn't trust men. A sour relationship
and putting up with rude clients at her barbershop caused
her self-doubts to escalate. In the hope of finding Wendy
a good Christian man, her father decides to take matters
into his own hands. Can the paramedic who answers a 911
call help Wendy overcome her struggles and allow God's
love to transform her?

Wellspring of Love by Pamela Griffin
When a woman literally drops into his arms, firefighter
Blaine Carson cannot help wondering if God placed her
there for a reason. Beneath her fiery independence, he senses
a woman in need of God's touch. Can the Lord use Blaine's
patience and courage to restore Cat McGregor's heart?

Man of Distinction by Tamela Hancock Murray
When wealthy Veronica Van Slyke teaches a Bible study at a
homeless shelter, she gets more than she bargained for. Can
she fall in love with a man who has nothing to offer but his
courage and companionship? As time passes, truth threatens
to destroy her relationship with Caspar. Only Christ's example of forgiveness and humility can rescue their love.

RESCUE

Four Contemporary Romance Stories
with Life and Love on the Line

Lauralee Bliss
Wanda E. Brunstetter
Pamela Griffin
Tamela Hancock Murray

BARBOUR
PUBLISHING, INC.
Uhrichsville, Ohio

Island Sunrise ©2001 by Lauralee Bliss.
Matchmaker 911 ©2001 by Wanda E. Brunstetter.
Wellspring of Love ©2001 by Pamela Griffin.
Man of Distinction ©2001 by Tamela Hancock Murray.

Illustrations by Mari Goering.

ISBN 1-57748-973-X

Scripture verses in *Island Sunrise* and *Man of Distinction* are taken from the King James Version of the Bible unless otherwise noted.

Scripture verses in *Matchmaker 911* and *Wellspring of Love* are taken from the HOLY BIBLE: NEW INTERNATIONAL VERSION®. NIV®. Copyright © 1973, 1978, 1984 by International Bible Society. Used by permission of Zondervan Publishing House.

Published by Barbour Publishing, Inc., P.O. Box 719, Uhrichsville, Ohio 44683 http://www.barbourbooks.com

 Member of the
Evangelical Christian
Publishers Association

Printed in the United States of America.

RESCUE

Island Sunrise

by Lauralee Bliss

Dedication

To Steve—my scuba diver, salesman,
and sweetheart all rolled into one!
Thanks for bearing with me
through my writing adventures.

*For the LORD seeth not as man seeth;
for man looketh on the outward appearance,
but the LORD looketh on the heart.*
1 SAMUEL 16:7 (KJV)

One

Excuse me, but where are you going? This isn't the right way!"

The drums from an island jingle blaring through the radio rattled Ashley Simmons's brain. Tension filled the muscles of her neck and shoulders. "Hello? Are you listening to me?" She tapped the man on the arm. "Hey, do you speak English? Where are you going?"

Through the rearview mirror, the cab driver grinned at her with a set of teeth that appeared not to have seen a toothbrush in months. She fought off the chill racing through her. "This isn't the right way," she complained again, scanning the map before her. "You're taking some coastal road and not the most direct route to the resort."

At that moment, the cab veered around a sharp bend in the road. She slammed against the door, knocking her head into the window. A bag fell to the floor, dumping possessions onto the soiled carpeting. The tension in her muscles now turned into a full-blown headache.

"Sorry." He grinned again before erupting into a song native to the island.

Ashley righted herself before picking up magazines,

a cosmetic bag, a hairbrush, and camera and stuffing them back inside the bag. "Obviously this guy thinks he can take advantage of a tourist," she mumbled, shaking back her shoulder-length blond hair. "I've got news for him." She inhaled and announced, "I guess I'm going to have to report you to your boss."

The grin grew even wider, spreading from one side of the rearview mirror to the other. "George the boss." He patted the dashboard. "This is George's cab."

"Then I'll complain to this George and tell him how you rip off visitors by taking them on some out-of-the-way route." Ashley gritted her teeth and stared out the window. She had not been on this island more than an hour, and she already had mixed feelings. Nothing had gone right since that morning when the phone jarred her awake from a sound sleep. It was her sales manager, Todd Alderman, calling from an inflight phone, inquiring of her whereabouts. Ashley dashed to the itinerary lying on the kitchen table, only to discover that she'd missed the early morning flight to St. Thomas in the U.S. Virgin Islands.

"How could I have done this?" she groaned. "I've never been late for anything in my life!" As a successful businesswoman in the area of sales, Ashley prided herself in her accomplishments that stemmed from an orderly life. Everything had to be just right, including her clothes, her hair, and her schedule for the day. The car was always neatly packed for a day of sales, with brochures and samples stored away in crates and bags. To Ashley, missing the flight was like dropping an expensive crystal goblet on a cement floor. It shattered her image.

Her manager, Todd, had taken it all in stride, joking that Ashley must already be in vacation mode to have overslept. He booked her on another flight and called back with the new schedule, promising to meet up with her at the resort when she arrived.

"If there's a penalty with the airlines, just dock it from my pay," she'd told him.

"No way. You earned this trip, Ash. I promised everyone in the sales force that if they exceeded their sales goal, I would foot the bill for this vacation. That's what you did. You, Sylvia, Troy, and Mac made our group number one in the company."

"We should really thank all those sweet kids in the schools for selling like they did," Ashley had mused. "And the teachers for signing me on to help with their fund-raising. Too bad they can't get the free trip to St. Thomas."

"Someone had to be behind their success. You motivated them to sell once you had the contract in hand. You did it all. At this rate, you'll make President's Club by the national meeting for sure. You know how prestigious that is."

Ashley twisted a thin strand of blond hair around one finger, pondering Todd's words, which made her glow with confidence. She enjoyed her job as a sales representative, initiating fund-raising programs in which students sold items off slick sales brochures to earn money for trips, scholarships, equipment, and necessities the teachers required. The kids and teachers were great to work with, and their enthusiasm showed in the vast amounts of money they raised. Ashley owed much of her success to the knowledge that Todd imparted to her. She thought for a moment about tall, dark-haired Todd and his winning smile. She'd learned a great deal since the company chose him to be her sales manager two years ago. Without him, she wouldn't be enjoying the success that helped her purchase her own home with the proceeds from last year's bonus. Many times, Todd had left his own sales territory to attend fund-raising kickoffs with her. He'd stood with her during the presentations before teachers and students, helping her initiate the programs. Not only was he a valuable teacher, but a selfless friend.

A bump in the road jarred her back into the reality of the never-ending cab ride. She breathed a sigh of relief when the cab finally turned into the long drive of the resort hotel. It was lined with waving palm trees and tropical flowers. A fountain sprayed water high into the air. The cab pulled to a stop before the lobby doors. The man turned in his seat, displaying a grin that reminded her of a ripe banana.

"We're here," he said in glee.

"It's about time," Ashley muttered, sliding out of her seat to fetch her bags from the trunk. Golden rays of bright Caribbean sunlight pierced through the sunshades she wore. She already felt her skin reacting to the intense heat and made a mental note to slather on the suntan lotion as soon as she could find it in her bag.

The cabbie held out his grimy hand. "Thirty dolla, lady. Thirty dolla, please."

Ashley gaped at him. "Thirty dollars for a cab ride? Are you crazy?"

"Thirty dolla," he repeated.

"Look, that so-called ride wasn't worth a dollar. A trip from the airport is only supposed to take twenty minutes. It's been nearly an hour. Not only that, but you hit every pothole and flew around the curves." Ashley flipped her hair with a huff. "If I'd wanted a roller coaster ride, I would've taken my vacation at an amusement park. I'll give you ten bucks. That's it."

The cheerful face of the cabbie deteriorated into a snarl. "Thirty dolla," he repeated.

"And I told you that—"

"Trouble?" asked a friendly voice behind Ashley. She whirled to find a tall man standing behind her, decked out in shorts, a baby blue polo shirt, and sunglasses. He gripped an overnight bag. Ashley exhaled a sigh of relief, thankful the inquirer was only a fellow vacationer, until he walked up and peered into the cab window. "Hey, George, I thought that was you. What's up?"

The grin appeared once more. "They send you back again, Rick?"

"Back again, into the deep blue sea. Didn't get enough of it the last time I was here. I tried to hire your cab at the airport, but they said you'd already left. So what's the problem, George?"

He pointed a finger of accusation at Ashley. "Lady won't pay the fare."

"How much did you tell her, George?"

"She's a classy lady of the mainland. First time here. Thought she'd like the nice route by the ocean and the nice views, so. . ."

"How much, George?"

The cabbie blinked. "Thirty dolla."

The man smiled. "Now, George, you know it's not more than twenty from the airport to the resort."

"But I got a family to feed."

"I know all the stories, George, and I know you. You'll hand over the twenty to your boss and keep the ten for yourself. But if you insist, let the young lady pay you twenty and I'll give you the ten." The man named Rick reached into a back pocket for his wallet and pulled out a ten-dollar bill. "Make sure you spend it on something decent and not a bottle of island rum."

Ashley watched the exchange in bewilderment, unable to believe what was happening until both men focused on her. She opened her purse and pulled out a twenty-dollar bill, keeping one eye trained on Rick, who was now removing her luggage from the trunk of the cab.

The cabbie cheerfully waved the bills before starting the engine. "Bye, Rick."

Rick slammed the trunk closed. "Take care, George. And I'm leaving Friday. Flight's at two in the afternoon, so pick me up at twelve noon."

"Okay. Twelve o'clock, Friday." The cab sped away, leaving an incredulous Ashley staring in disbelief, first at the cab disappearing down the palm-lined drive, then at the man named Rick, who held her luggage in tow.

"Hey, look, I can take it from here," she said, "unless you want a huge tip like everyone else."

"No tip necessary." Warm ocean breezes ruffled his light brown hair. His tanned skin displayed the many hours he had basked in the island sun.

"Thanks for your help. I appreciate it. Glad you

knew that guy was trying to rip me off."

"No problem."

He continued to stare at her, his bag in one hand, as if frozen in place. Ashley wondered if he expected her to pay him back the ten dollars. With a sigh, she picked up the handle to her luggage only to find an eager bell-hop ready to whisk her luggage into the lobby. A spacious room, decorated with overstuffed chairs and indoor plants, met her curious gaze. The room opened up to a view of the ocean. Ashley walked over for a glimpse at the waters. Never before had she seen such a sight, as if green and aqua paint had been poured into various parts of the ocean. Waves lapped at the beach sprinkled with vacationers playing in the sand. She inhaled a breath of delight.

"I'm about ready to dive right in there," acknowledged a familiar voice.

Ashley whirled to find Rick behind her. His shades were propped on top of his head, revealing a pair of stark green eyes that focused intently on the ocean view.

"You dive?"

He nodded. "Scuba dive, that is. This is the place for it. I've done many Pacific dives, especially in Hawaii. I only started diving here in the last year or so. The species of fish and coral found in the Atlantic are quite different from the Pacific."

"I've never been diving," Ashley commented.

"What about snorkeling?"

"Once, when I was a kid. Not a pleasant experience. My goggles fogged up and my feet cramped in the fins. I didn't see a thing."

Rick nodded, plopping his bag into an overstuffed chair. "There are a few tricks to it, but snorkeling is a great way to be introduced to the ocean." He propped a foot on the cushion and rested his arms on one knee. "The first time I looked beneath the ocean, I thought I was visiting an alien world. The spectacular color of the fish, the living coral and plant life. . . I couldn't help but thank God for making such a beautiful place. Few people get the opportunity to see it unless they put on the right gear and go."

Ashley fiddled with the strap to her purse before sidestepping her way to the hotel desk. "Uh, excuse me, but I'd better check in. Nice meeting you." She made her way to the front desk, casting a quick glance over her shoulder at the man who remained where she had left him, drinking in the ocean scenery.

"A bellhop will take you to your room," the clerk informed her, handing over a plastic card key once Ashley checked in. "Wait by the front doors and he will be by momentarily. Enjoy your stay at the Grand Beach Resort."

"Thanks," Ashley said, walking toward the revolving doors. Out of the corner of her eye, she scanned the lobby for the man named Rick, but he had vanished. She sighed and headed outdoors to await the transport vehicle, when she noticed Rick walking toward her with a travel bag in his hand.

"You waiting for transportation?" he asked.

She nodded. "I guess this is a big place. I didn't realize I would need a lift to my hotel room."

"It is quite spread out, with three restaurants, two

pools, and an exercise area. They rent boats here and even have their own dive shop on the premises."

Ashley raised an eyebrow. "I guess you would know all about that, being a diving fanatic."

"It helps having everything in one area. Besides the fact that just up the road there," he said, pointing beyond a row of palm trees to a narrow road that snaked up a hill, "is the best coral reef on this side of the island. Coki Beach. The fish and coral are fantastic."

"I don't see what's so wonderful about coral," Ashley muttered, more to herself than to the man standing beside her. "The only coral I've ever seen is in my friend's saltwater aquarium. It looked like a hunk of yellow rock with holes in it. Ugly, if you ask me."

His mouth curved upward into a faint smile. "There are many species of coral. Elkhorn and staghorn coral make formations that look like the antlers of a deer. Fire coral feels like a red-hot ember if you accidentally brush against it. . .and then there's brain coral."

"Brain coral!" Ashley repeated. "Don't tell me an animal left its brain behind."

"No." He chuckled. "Coral is actually an animal made up of polyps that look like miniature jellyfish or sea anemones. They live together in colonies and secrete calcium carbonate—the same substance found in limestone. It builds up to make different types of coral. When a large amount of coral is deposited, it forms a reef where fish live."

Ashley pondered this new information with interest until a vehicle, reminiscent of a golf cart but twice the size, zoomed to a stop before them. Ashley stared in amazement when Rick forged ahead and picked up her bags from the bellhop's cart, carefully placing them in the rear of the vehicle. "After you," he said, gesturing to a seat with a wave of his bronze-colored hand. He then occupied the seat directly in front of her, draping a long, muscular arm across the back of the seat. "By the way, I'm Rick Adams."

"Ashley Simmons."

"So are you here on vacation?"

"Yes. A reward from my manager. I had a great year in sales. Fund-raising projects, like everything else, seem to be reaping the benefit of this great economic boom."

"You like being in sales?"

"Love it. I get to meet lots of fascinating people. The kids can be obnoxious at times, though."

Rick raised an eyebrow. "Kids?"

"I help organize fund-raising projects for area schools," she explained. "So that means traipsing into schoolrooms and getting kids to sell candles, candy, and wrapping paper."

"Oh, that kind of sales. I've had a few kids knock on my apartment door in recent years."

"I'm the one to blame. I'm guessing you're here to play with fish and brains, right?"

He laughed with a heartiness that sent tingles shooting through Ashley. "Would you believe that I'm paid to play with fish? I'm a marine biologist. I study the oceanic environment, note the habitats, and examine aquatic behavior. Over the last year or so, I've come here to dive in the Caribbean. Most of my previous dives were in the Pacific."

"So you dive to find out if the fish are good or bad—is that it?"

"Right. Also to see if pollutants are affecting reproduction or the life span of the fish."

"Sounds like a one-in-a-million job. At least you get to enjoy a tropical paradise while you're at it."

"It does have its benefits."

"Room 101," the driver announced, slipping out of his seat to help with the baggage.

"That's me," Ashley said.

"I got the bag," Rick told the driver. He leaped from the vehicle and offered Ashley his hand. Ashley was taken aback by the gesture, then placed her hand in his and jumped out of the vehicle.

"Chivalry is not dead, even among fish lovers," she teased.

He said nothing but took out all the bags, then tipped the driver. Ashley blinked when Rick picked up his own bags, wondering where he was going. "Well. . . uh, thanks for your help."

"Sure. Anytime. Have fun on your vacation."

"Have fun with your fish and that brain. . .whatever." Ashley headed for the door of her room. Rick followed before swerving to the right at the last minute and inserted his key card into Room 102. Ashley nearly lost her breath when they disappeared into their respective rooms. She hardly took the time to examine the amenities of the room before flopping down on the luxurious queen-size bed to mull over the encounter. "What a guy," she murmured, "and he's staying right next door to me!" At that moment, she imagined herself with

Rick, skimming the ocean surface in snorkeling gear, examining the depths below. Fish would bob up from the deep to nibble at their fins. Rick would laugh heartily before sweeping her into his bronze arms and holding her close.

Just then the phone in her room shrilled.

"You made it, finally," came a hearty voice.

"Oh, Todd. Yes, I made it, amazingly enough."

"You're just in time for a welcome dinner. The five of us are meeting at the Smugglers' Grill in about half an hour. You up for it?"

"Sure, I'll be ready." Ashley replaced the receiver, still thinking about Rick and wondering what it would be like to play tag in the ocean with the creatures of the deep. The mere thought of a gigantic brain coral, pulsating with life, sent chills racing up her spine. "No way would I ever be caught diving or snorkeling," she began out loud, "or maybe I would. Just how many brains does one get to see in a lifetime?"

Two

Y ou look like you're a million miles away," Todd observed as he stirred cream and sugar into his coffee.

Dinner had been a loud affair, with everyone but Ashley engaged in boisterous conversation, talking about the various activities they planned to do while on St. Thomas. When dinner was served—broiled mahimahi with a side order of lemon sauce, Ashley took one look at it and imagined the fish swimming around in the ocean. Perhaps Rick had even studied the thing before it was scooped up in a net and served on a platter. She pushed the plate aside and ate her salad instead.

"I also didn't realize you had become a vegetarian," Todd noted with a raised eyebrow after the others left, leaving the two of them alone in the dining room. "You didn't eat one bite of the mahimahi. I thought it would be a nice entree."

"I'm not a vegetarian. It's just that I met this guy in the hotel who studies fish for a living. Guess all the talk made me realize I was about to eat one of his friends."

"You start thinking about your food walking or

swimming, Ash, and you'll never eat anything again."

"I guess." She sat back in her chair, aware of Todd's dark eyes probing her own.

"So have you made any plans yet?"

Ashley righted herself in her seat. "Plans? Afraid not. I just arrived at my room then ran to this dinner invitation—but I realize it's my fault, missing the flight and all. I wouldn't feel so stressed out right now if I'd been a good girl and made the original flight."

"Don't worry about it. I'm just glad you made it here. Would've been a shame to miss out after all your hard work. Just remember—you're here to enjoy yourself. You deserve it."

"I guess."

"By the way, I have some great news. I was doing some calculations, and it looks like you're in for another huge bonus, come summertime. Any ideas what you would like to use the money for this year? It always helps to keep a goal set in your mind. Last year, it was the house. Maybe this year a new car?"

"I hadn't thought that far. I don't think I have enough for the kind of car I want."

"Which is?"

"A Lexus."

"You're joking."

She winked. "Of course."

"Anyway, I've been doing the figures, Ash." He took a small notepad from the pocket of his sports coat. "If you do well during the cheerleading season, which starts up as soon as we get back, your chances improve greatly. I see you knocking on the door of the

President's Club and maybe getting your baby Lexus. Pretty exciting, eh?"

Any other day, the idea of money would send tingles of excitement shooting through Ashley and fire dreams about how she would spend the money. Somehow, the brief meeting with Rick had mellowed her thinking, leading her to consider the simpler things in life—like the world he described beneath the ocean.

When she stayed silent, Todd stared at her quizzically. He rose to his feet and stuffed the notepad into a pocket. "Maybe this is the wrong time to be discussing success. How about an evening stroll along the beach instead?"

"That would be great," Ashley agreed, following him outside. She tried to clear her thoughts enough to concentrate on the beauty of the place. Tall palm trees waved their feathery fronds in the stiff island breeze. The scent of the salty ocean filled the air. The sun had just begun to dip below the horizon. Ashley slipped off her sandals and ambled barefoot in the soft sand. Couples walked hand in hand along the shoreline with the ocean water bathing their feet. Watching them, Ashley grew warm, wondering if Todd would dare try to hold her hand. To her relief, he only walked beside her and commented on a trip to Florida he'd once made, including several sailing ventures down in the Keys.

Listening to his conversation, Ashley noticed the many boats tied to the dock in the distance, bouncing gently with the waves that rolled into the shore. "So you've gone sailing?"

"It's been awhile, but I know how. Maybe we can rent one of the boats and take a trip around the cove."

"I wouldn't mind snorkeling again," Ashley piped up, recalling Rick's love for the ocean depths. "There are supposed to be great reefs or something where the fish hang out—even brain coral and stuff that looks like a deer's antlers. That's what Rick says, anyway."

"I take it Rick's the guy who studies fish for a living."

"Right."

Todd chuckled. "Not a great way to get ahead in this world, talking to creatures with goggly eyes and gills—but I guess if you're that kind of environmental fanatic. . ."

"I don't think Rick's an environmental fanatic," Ashley said, swinging her sandals with one hand. "He just likes to study fish and brains."

"So he didn't tell you how he's trying to protect marine life from us diabolical humans?"

"He did mention something about studying environmental hazards to fish."

Todd paused to face the ocean. "You see, Ash? He is one of those fanatics. Probably cruises in those boats that blocks ships from fishing in the seas, holding up a sign that reads, 'Save the Whales'. They're always looking for a publicity stunt."

Ashley fell silent, confused by Todd's reaction to Rick's work.

"Anyway, I like our job," Todd went on. "We help people help themselves. We help them make money and reap the benefits at the same time. I personally think it's better to help mankind than some lower species on the evolutionary scale. I never heard of fish carrying on a decent conversation, myself. But enough of that." In an afterthought, he took up her hand and gave a gentle squeeze. "I just want you to enjoy yourself, okay? What do you say we head to Charlotte Amalie in the morning and check out the shopping? Interested?"

"That would be great," Ashley agreed, allowing the image of Rick to fade into oblivion with the idea of scanning boutiques. "I hear the shopping on St. Thomas is wonderful, especially in the main city."

He released her hand. "Good. There's a breakfast buffet at the Baywinds Restaurant. Meet you around nine o'clock?"

"Sounds good, Todd," Ashley said with a smile. "See you." When she retreated to her hotel room, she heard a soft greeting from the adjoining patio. Rick sat in a lounge chair with a book lying open on his lap.

"Studying about fish?" Ashley joked.

"Actually, there are a few passages in here about fish. Even about diving and sailing." Rick flipped through several pages and cleared his throat, squinting to see in the diminishing light. " 'They that go down to the sea in ships, that do business in the great waters; these see the works of the LORD, and his wonders in the deep.' "

"Weird textbook."

Rick lifted up the book. "Actually, it's the Bible."

Ashley hesitated. "You mean the Bible talks about diving?"

"Sure. It talks about doing business in the waters and seeing the wonders in the deep. I believe it. I've been there. The ocean is like another world."

Ashley managed a weak smile. "That's very nice," she said saucily.

"The Bible talks about many things, even dinosaurs. It's really amazing. Everyone—including scientists—tries to make sense out of this world we live in. They don't realize that the manual to the world is right here." He waved the Bible. "They can buy it in any bookstore."

"Cute. Gotta run." Ashley headed for her room, confusion welling up within her. While Rick appeared like a normal guy on the outside, on the inside he was different. He talked about religion as if it were the most natural thing in life. Ashley shook her head. She could not remember the last time she'd opened a Bible. To her, the Bible was a boring piece of literature; yet Rick made the vague passage teem with life, as if his heart and soul depended on it. The only printed words Ashley found directing her life were quotes from sales books and magazines, all of them motivating her to get out and make it on her own. Rick did not live for himself. He lived for this God and the Bible that lay open in his lap. The mere notion seemed unbelievable and maybe even crazy.

※

Ashley awoke the next morning after a fitful night spent dreaming of the strange brain coral that grew with each passing moment until it filled her hotel room. When she opened the patio door, the sun had just risen, bathing the beach in rays of tangerine and gold. A warm breeze caressed her face, bringing with it the scent of freshly brewed coffee.

"Good morning," came a cheerful voice behind the partition separating the two patios. "Isn't it great out here?"

Ashley occupied a lawn chair. "I like seeing the sun

reflecting on the ocean. The water looks like it's on fire."

"It does. Have you had your morning coffee?"

"No, actually, I just woke up and. . ." She paused when a brawny figure came around the partition, his hand extending a mug of coffee. Steam swirled in the air. Ashley rose and took the cup. Watching Rick scurry back to his hotel room, she called out, "Hey, I don't bite."

"Forgot the cream and sugar," he answered, returning to dump a few packets of sugar and a handful of creamers on the white wrought iron table.

Ashley smelled the scent of soap when he passed by, dressed in a black nylon warm-up suit with his damp hair slicked back. She stirred in a cream and two packets of sugar while admiring his features, quickly forgetting the incident last evening with the Bible. "You're an early riser."

"I just got back from a dive," he said. "Had time to hit the shower while the coffee was brewing."

"You went scuba diving already? Are you kidding?"

He pulled up a chair and plunked himself down. "It was great. An early morning dive is my favorite. During the return trip by boat, you get another treat—watching the sun rise over the island."

"How can you see anything underwater when it's still dark?"

"You carry lights. Some species don't even venture out unless it's dark, much like land animals such as raccoons and skunks. In the ocean it's lobsters, sea horses, octopi. I like to go in the predawn hours because it's a transition time in the ocean. When the sky brightens, the night crew leaves and the day crew comes on. You get an opportunity to see both worlds."

Ashley giggled between sips of coffee. "So you hang out and watch the ocean change shifts. What a life."

"Actually, it's fun and educational. You learn a lot about life that few people get the opportunity to explore. You descend into the depths like a modern-day Columbus, searching for new discoveries." He placed a hand across his stomach. "And right about now, I'm ready to eat like an explorer. You going to breakfast this morning?"

"Actually, I'm going to the buffet."

"Mind if I tag along? I'll fill you in on what I saw during the dive."

Ashley nodded. "I guess it wouldn't be too much of a bother to talk about diving during breakfast. After everything you said yesterday, I couldn't eat my fish for dinner. All I could think about were those critters you like to study. My appetite went south."

Rick snickered. "I know what you mean. I find it difficult to eat any kind of seafood with the work I do. Once you see lobsters walking along the ocean floor or feed scraps of food to a school of fish, it's pretty hard to turn around and find it on your fork."

"But we do have to eat," Ashley remarked, recalling Todd's words the previous evening. "I hope you're not one of those people who condemns anyone who eats meat and fish."

"Of course not. Whether one is vegetarian or a meat eater is a personal matter. I admire the water world; I don't worship it. Creatures like fish and coral only point to the existence of God. Man, on the other hand, is made in the image of God. Man must have great value to God to be made in His image. Pretty amazing stuff when you think about it."

Ashley gasped for air as if her breath had been forced out by a fist. A strange sensation overcame her. She leapt to her feet. "Look, I just remembered that I'm supposed to meet some fellow employees for breakfast."

His expectant face grew crestfallen at the news. "Oh."

"Maybe we can get together some other time. Thanks for the coffee." She managed a lopsided grin before trotting into her hotel room and shutting the blinds. Again, Rick's words cut to the core. He appeared so much like an ordinary guy with his athletic build, good looks, and interest in aquatic sports. His words, though, spoke of someone who thought differently than the average joe she had come to know. Ashley realized then what was meant by the saying, *Don't judge a book by its cover*. She only hoped she could still admire Rick's handsome features and not be sucked into his strange ideology.

Three

Ashley stared blankly at the map Todd had picked up from the hospitality desk. While they ate breakfast, he tried to interest her in several of the shops in the town of Charlotte Amalie that sold expensive perfumes and glass figurines. All Ashley could think about was Rick in his black warm-up suit and his passion for the ocean.

"Hello in there," Todd said in her ear. "Anybody home?"

Ashley jumped. She picked up a fork to begin eating the slices of honeydew melon arranged on the plate before her. "Yes, what were you saying?"

"I was saying, if you're interested in these figurines, you might want to check out this shop." Todd's dark eyebrows narrowed. His lips twisted into a frown. "Ash, you haven't been right since you got here. Is something wrong? Are you sick or something?"

"Well, I. . ." She paused, her mouth open to reply, when she saw Rick enter the restaurant. Their eyes met briefly before he went to the buffet to help himself to the food. He then settled down at a far table to eat his meal.

Beside his plate rested the Bible he had been reading the night before.

Todd followed her gaze to the far corner where Rick sat. His teeth ground in response. "Hey, we've got a taxi to catch. Let's get moving, shall we?" He took her by the arm and propelled her to her feet.

Ashley slipped the strap of her purse over one shoulder and allowed Todd to guide her out of the restaurant. Before leaving, she stole another glance at Rick solemnly eating his breakfast with his head buried in the Bible. She wondered at that moment if he had discovered anything else about marine life within the passages of that Book.

Ashley quickly forgot about Rick and his Bible once inside the taxi with Todd. When she launched into her difficulty with the cabbie who had driven her to the hotel, thoughts of Rick again drifted into the forefront of her mind.

"I hope you only paid ten dollars to that cabbie after the way he treated you," Todd was quick to say.

"Actually, Rick paid part of my fare. I couldn't believe it. Right out of the blue he helps a perfect stranger, and he wasn't even looking for brownie points as far as I could—"

Todd interrupted her to point out the scenery. "Hey, look at how the houses seem attached to the cliffs; and down below, you can see the village of Charlotte Amalie, sitting right beside the water's edge. Neat view." He took up her hand and gave it a squeeze. "We're going to have a great time. No more talk about rude cab drivers or wacko fish lovers. Let's just relax and enjoy the day."

Ashley was in all her glory, browsing in the wonderful shops. Todd was soon helping her carry the shopping bags laden with goods. At a toy store, she paused to view the trinkets displayed in the windows, including a brightly colored beanbag fish, nestled in an ocean box depicting pictures of the antler coral once described by Rick. Her feet propelled her into the store and to the display. She examined the cuddly beanbag fish that conformed to the palm of her hand, then brought it to the counter and paid for it.

"You have a niece or someone who likes stuffed animals?" Todd asked when he saw her purchase.

"I just like it," she said, slipping the small bag into a larger sack. "I'm hoping to see some real fish while I'm here." She yawned. "Wow, this has been a fun morning, but do you mind if we head back? I think I need a nap."

Todd nodded, promptly waving down a taxi to take them back to the hotel. Along the way they sat quietly, observing the scenery the island was known for. When they arrived back, the beach was filled with guests taking a dip in the warm waters, relaxing in lounge chairs, or building sand castles. Todd said he was due to swim with a few of the other employees. Ashley returned to her hotel room and flung the bags on the bed. In an afterthought, she rummaged for the small plastic bag from the toy store and took out the beanbag fish with its fur-covered fins. Feeling the softness of the critter beneath her fingers, she again thought of Rick. She couldn't dismiss an attraction for him and his love of the ocean, despite his strange ideology. With the toy in her possession, she unlocked the patio door and tiptoed around the partition to gaze at his patio. The chair and table were in the same position as they'd been in that morning when he rose to fetch her a cup of morning coffee. The blinds to his room were closed. Summoning up the courage, she marched up to the patio door and rapped on the glass. Silence met her friendly call.

"Probably diving again," she mused, retreating to her room. She returned the beanbag fish to its box and placed it on the bureau beside pamphlets outlining various activities found on St. Thomas. Her eyes fell on a brochure describing Coral World—a marine aquarium for visitors, adjacent to an area called Coki Beach.

"Rick talked about Coki Beach," she murmured, glancing out the patio door to see the road that wound its way to the famous beach. "He said I could find fish in the water near there." Stuffing the pamphlet and a towel in a beach bag, Ashley put on her bathing suit beneath a pair of shorts and a T-shirt. "Might as well see what all the hubbub is about."

After locking the patio door, she walked over to the dive shop in the direction of the road and paused to peer inside. Several men had congregated in the rear of the store, discussing aspects of diving. She moseyed on in to find an assortment of gear for sale, from fins and masks to swimsuits and suntan lotion.

"Can I help you?" asked a clerk.

"I heard from someone that there's great snorkeling at Coki Beach."

"Sure, it's right up the road there, about half a mile. You need to rent some gear?"

"Uh. . .I guess so."

The man sized her up with a practiced eye and placed a pair of fins, a snorkel, and a mask on the counter. "The rental fee is eight dollars a day."

Ashley promptly paid for the gear, wondering what she would do with it once she reached the beach, when a familiar voice filled her ears.

"You going snorkeling?"

She looked up to find Rick staring down at her with his moss green eyes and a smile on his face. In an instant, her heart skipped a beat. "I thought I would give it a try."

"By yourself, or are you going with your friends?"

"I, uh. . . ," she hesitated. "Actually my friends are back at the resort. I wanted to check out Coki Beach, myself."

"Mind an escort?"

Ashley opened her mouth to agree when she recalled the lecture on the Bible received that morning. "That's okay. I can handle this myself."

"Maybe, but it's wise to snorkel in pairs." Rick acknowledged the clerk behind the counter. "Isn't that right, Larry?"

Larry winked. "Sure, Rick. Especially if you've never done it before."

"I really don't need a—" Ashley began.

"It's more fun this way. Besides, you told me that snorkeling was a disaster the last time you tried, so let me teach you a few of the basics."

Rick grabbed a bag of gear stowed away behind the counter and followed her. They walked along a pebbled path and onto a small road that led out of the resort. As they walked, Ashley stared at the run-down shacks lining the road, belonging to the island inhabitants. She swallowed hard at the simple structures slapped together with rotting boards. Many of the shacks had broken windows. A few children sat on the wooden steps to the homes and stared. A lone dog, tied by a rope to a tree, barked continuously at them. Just then, a small boy ventured up to them and tugged on Rick's polo shirt.

"Bet I know what you want," Rick said with a smile, giving the boy a dollar out of his pocket. "Now you spend it on food, okay?"

The boy grinned and dashed off to a shack to show his friends.

"We'd better get a move on, or he'll have the whole neighborhood after us."

"You seem to know a lot about this place," Ashley commented. "And you're quite generous with your money."

Rick shrugged. "This area reminds me of downtown L.A.," he said, gesturing to the shacks. "It isn't all mansions of celebrities there, you know. Some of the neighborhoods are in pretty bad shape. I try to help out with renovation projects, Big Brother programs, things like that. That's not to put me on a pedestal or anything, because I wouldn't give a hoot about people if it weren't for God."

Ashley kicked at several stones. "You talk an awful lot about God. Are you also a part-time minister besides being a marine biologist?"

"Not really a minister. I guess you could say I try

to reach out. When people become desperate in life, they're ready to hear some good news. All I do is give them Good News."

"Like lectures about fish from the Bible?"

Rick glanced at her and smiled. "More like about God."

"So besides fish, you're also into religion."

To her surprise, he laughed. "I'm not into anything. If you mean I'm hooked on God, you'd be right. Just like fish to bait." He winked. "And what about you? What are you into?"

"Shopping. I did plenty of it at Charlotte Amalie this morning. Great place." In an instant, she regretted her words. How could she compare shopping to the self-less acts he had just described? She lowered her head and continued kicking at the pebbles.

He only responded, "The shopping is pretty good there."

Silence enveloped them. They approached Coki Beach, crowded with people setting up chairs or spreading colored beach towels on the sand. Others were already swimming around in the water or decked out in headgear and fins for a snorkeling adventure. Ashley walked to the shoreline, scanning the sand for any shells washed up with the morning tide.

"Here's a piece of conch shell," Rick said, placing the shell, smooth and cool to the touch, in her hand. "It looks like mother-of-pearl on the inside."

Ashley picked up another shell to examine the pretty colors as it lay in her hand. Rick followed while she combed the beach for more unusual shells or pieces of driftwood, and he explained about the creatures that once used the shells for their homes. With these explanations, her gaze wandered out to the bay. Swimmers, floating on the waters with snorkels high in the air, perused the depths. "So is that what snorkeling's about?"

"That's pretty much it. You want to give it a try?"

Ashley nodded, dropping a handful of shells into the sand. She shed her T-shirt and shorts, then proceeded to remove the fins, snorkel, and mask from the net bag, wondering if she could really go through with this.

"Did you bring socks to wear?" Rick asked.

"Socks? I didn't know I would need socks."

"They protect your feet in the fins, but it won't matter. We won't be out that long."

Ashley sat down in the sand and slid her foot into the rubbery material of the fin. She tried lifting her leg and nearly fell backwards. "They're heavy!"

Rick chuckled. "A little. Now this." He gave her the mask with a tube attached to it. "The snorkel helps you breathe while your face is in the water. Watch me. First, spit into your mask and rub it around. Saliva keeps your mask from fogging underwater. Then you bite down on the mouthpiece." Rick spit into his mask before slipping it over his eyes and nose and positioning the tube upright beside his face.

Ashley laughed. "You look like a sea monster."

"You take deep breaths through the mouthpiece," his muffled voice explained. She could hear the stridor within the pipe. "Feel the air escaping through the snorkel as I breathe?"

Ashley held her hand over the top of the pipe. "Okay, I see."

"All right, now you try. Don't forget to spit into your mask."

"Pretty disgusting, if you ask me, but I guess it's necessary." Ashley lubricated the mask as delicately as possible, then placed it over her eyes and nose. "I can't breathe with this thing on!" she cried, panting through her mouth.

"You're supposed to breathe through the mouthpiece attached to the snorkel," Rick said. "That's the whole point. The snorkel sticks up in the air, allowing you to breathe while your face is in the water."

Ashley bit down hard on the mouthpiece that tasted like seaweed and saltwater, mixed with rubber.

"Now try breathing."

She did so, awkwardly at first, before taking off the mask to inhale the fresh ocean air. "That takes some getting used to."

"It's the only way you can view the fish through a mask without holding your breath. Now you're all set. Let's head on out and see what we can find."

Ashley watched several other swimmers, with their fins and masks intact, meander to the shore and drift out into the aquamarine waters. She pressed her lips together in determination, picked up her mask, and followed Rick, who had already begun to wade into the water. The fins slowed her progress as she tried to keep her balance. Once she entered the cove, the warm waves felt soothing. When the water came up to her waist, Rick directed Ashley to spit into her mask and put it on. She adjusted the strap that pressed it tight around her cheeks and nose, then placed the mouthpiece between her lips.

"Okay, let's take a few practice breaths," he instructed.

Ashley did so with her face in the water. At first, she refused to open her eyes, for fear the saltwater would rush in and blind her. Blinking rapidly, she forced her eyes open, only to find sand and rocks below.

"It's okay." Rick's soothing voice encouraged her when she came up and removed the mask. "Like everything, it takes practice. You want to give it a try out in the deeper water?"

"Just don't leave me." She curled her hand tightly around his forearm, terrified at the thought of being left alone in the waters, unable to breathe.

The rough lines of his face softened in response. "I won't leave you, Ashley. I'll be right by your side every step of the way. If it makes you feel better, once we're out in the bay, just hold onto my arm. That way, we won't drift apart."

Ashley nodded and reapplied the mask. She continued wading to where others were swimming about, floating on the water's surface with their heads down and snorkels erect, examining the wonders of the ocean. Ashley clung to Rick's arm until she felt him begin to float. She did the same, trying to calm herself enough to look through her mask to the waters below.

Finally, she found a pattern of breathing and opened her eyes to behold a world she had never seen in her life. Brightly colored fish floated just below her as if oblivious to her presence. Some had large snouts or growths like moles sprinkled across their bodies. Others were flat, reminiscent of floating pancakes bobbing in the water. Some were a bright yellow with black stripes like tigers, while others sparkled purple and blue. Ashley gasped at the sight. Never had she seen anything so beautiful. Her hand tugged on Rick's arm as she pointed out one spectacular sight after another. She felt like a little kid acknowledging her discoveries to an adult. She rose to the surface and pushed the mask up on her forehead. "It's gorgeous down there! It's just like you said."

Her heart quickened at the smile on his face. "Once you get the hang of this, Ashley, I'll take you diving."

"I don't know about diving. . . ."

"C'mon, there's more to see." He tugged on her arm. They took off again to examine the ocean depths, exclaiming joy over every discovery. Seaweed waved majestically in the fine water current. They spouted giggles of air and water through their snorkels at a fellow swimmer, surrounded by striped fish while he threw pieces of bread into the water. When they rose once more to the surface, Ashley was laughing so hard she could barely tread water.

"Did you see that guy? He must've had five dozen fish swimming around him! You only see that at a city park when people throw bread crumbs to the pigeons."

"It was pretty funny," Rick agreed, treading the water with her. For several moments, they stared at each other while arms and legs churned the ocean to keep them afloat. An attraction began to build. Even in the water, Ashley felt perspiration dot her forehead, and her neck flush under his steady gaze. Rick began to drift toward her, his eyes locking with hers, his face melting into a picture of tenderness. He appeared ready to kiss her. Her heart began to race at the thought. How she hoped he would take her in his strong arms and kiss her, with the tropical fish darting around their fins in the waters below.

Suddenly he turned to the shore. The moment vanished. "We'd better get back. It's not wise to be out for too long. You don't want to get fatigued—then you start cramping up."

Ashley followed him silently until they returned to the beach. She removed the fins and wrapped a towel around herself. "So how did I do for my first day?"

"Fine," he said brusquely, keeping his face averted while gathering up the equipment and placing it inside the net bag. "Look, I need to get back. I've got some things to do."

Ashley wiped away the seawater trickling down her face, observing his aloofness in confusion. She followed him back down the road, trying to think if she had done anything to make him uncomfortable. When they arrived at the dive shop, Rick took her gear.

"Thanks for taking me, Rick. I had fun."

"Sure. Glad you enjoyed it." He whirled and retreated into the dive shop, leaving a bewildered Ashley to wonder what had spawned the distance between them.

Four

Ashley let out a yawn before returning her attention to the strands of angel-hair pasta coated in a marinara sauce. She spun the pasta around the fork before allowing it to slither into a heap on the china plate. Once she had arrived back to the hotel room after spending the afternoon at Coki Beach with Rick, the phone rang. The caller was Todd, inviting her out to dinner and another late night stroll on the beach.

"Are the others going to be there?" she had asked him.

"Not unless you want them to be. I figure we deserve a quiet dinner without all the loud talk."

Ashley was touched by his consideration, especially after what happened with Rick. Just when she thought they might have something going, Rick had suddenly turned away. Ashley pondered his response while showering and dressing for dinner and finally came to the conclusion that since she wasn't religious, he found her unworthy of a relationship. Unless she quoted the Bible and talked about God like a best friend, Rick would never hold her in his arms, let alone kiss her. Ashley stood before the mirror and brushed out her blond hair before her gaze fell on the toy fish she'd purchased at the shop. Even if Rick would have nothing more to do with her, she owed him a great deal for introducing her to the wonderful world beneath the surface of the ocean.

An irritated sigh drew her out of her contemplative mood. Todd dropped his fork with a loud clink. "Ash, we can't go on like this," he said slowly. "You act like you're in another world. Does this have anything to do with that Rick character?"

Ashley straightened in her seat as if she'd been reprimanded. "Why do you say that?"

"I saw you walk back to the dive shop this afternoon with a guy I assume was Rick. Look, I'm concerned that you're setting yourself up for a big fall, getting involved with someone like him. After a few days, you'll each go your own way—you and I back to Virginia, and he'll go to. . .where does he live?"

"I think California. He mentioned L.A."

"The opposite ends of the country."

Ashley continued to wrap the noodles around her fork. "You're probably right. Rick does all these helpful things for people, like Big Brothers, for example. He probably builds homes for Habitat for Humanity. I don't know, but somehow I feel like I'm not on his level."

"You're not. You're way above him. He's low on the simple evolutionary scale, especially with this fish fascination of his. Just because this guy performs a few good deeds in life doesn't mean you and I do any less. You've come so far in your sales and who you are as an individual. Don't let some kook who's hooked on fish make you lose everything you've gained."

Ashley raised an eyebrow at his insistence. Todd seemed concerned for her well-being. Perhaps it was wrong to consider a relationship with a guy she might never lay eyes on again. "I know what I do is just as important as what he does. I shouldn't be comparing myself to him. It's just that. . ." She paused. "Todd, I don't know if I should be asking you this, but I consider you a good friend, and you're a guy. What does it mean when you think you have something going with a guy, the sparks are beginning to fly, then suddenly he gets cold feet?"

"It's a signal to get out fast, before you get burned," he said, reaching for her hand. "You have to look for a genuineness in a relationship. Two people who get along well and help each other. Two people who are the best of friends."

Ashley began to laugh. "You make it sound like us."

Todd removed his hand and bent over his plate to finish his meal. "Maybe. You never know."

She shook her head. "But we have an employer-employee relationship. We've only been friends, and it should stay that way."

"In my opinion, nobody is more compatible than we are. We like to do the same things. We have fun together, and I won't turn away from you, Ash, just because you may not fit a personal mold like fish lover."

"I wish you wouldn't call Rick a fish lover. He showed me some great reefs this afternoon. He taught me how to snorkel and everything."

Todd again bent his head, this time scraping his

fork against the plate in agitation. "I suppose you've been sailing, too?"

"No, I haven't."

"Good. Then I'll show you an even better time. We'll go sailing tomorrow, and I'll take you to the best reefs."

Ashley leaned forward, her eyes wide in anticipation. "Oh, Todd, could you find me a place that has a brain coral? I'm dying to see one."

"I'll ask at the dive shop. The people there would know where the best reefs are." He nodded his head. "Yes, that's just what we'll do."

Ashley jumped to her feet. "Let's check it out now. The dive shop is still open. I know someone there can help us."

"Sure," Todd agreed, smiling with enthusiasm. He offered his arm, which she took. Together they strolled out of the restaurant and to the small dive shop. Inside, a crew was preparing for an evening dive. Ashley sucked in her breath, staring at the equipment they used, including vests with weights and large oxygen tanks that lined the floor. Her eyes grew even wider when she noticed the man leading the expedition. Rick Adams stood in front of the group, outfitted in diving gear, explaining the difference between a shore dive and a dive from a boat. Suddenly their eyes met. Rick paused in his instruction and stared.

"What's the matter?" Todd asked.

"That's Rick," she murmured. "He's the one I've been telling you about."

"Really. The infamous fish man himself—doing

what he does best, I see. C'mon, let's go find someone who can help us."

"Rick would know where to find a brain coral, Todd. In fact, he was the one who described it to me." Ashley pushed her way through the small group of divers. "Hey, Rick."

"I'm leading a diving expedition right now, Ashley," Rick said, looking off to one side.

"We just want to know where to find one of those huge brain corals, like the one you described to me."

"Excuse me," Rick said to the group before striding to the opposite corner of the shop. "Look, this isn't a good time. I'd have to show you on a chart where to find it, and even then, you'd have to take a boat out there. You can't just swim to it."

"Todd is going to take me sailing in the morning," she said with a smile, waving Todd over. "Todd, this is Rick. He's a marine biologist."

The two men stared at each other until Rick extended his hand in a friendly gesture. "Glad to meet you."

Todd shook it once and dropped his hand, his eyes staring fixedly at the man. "Who else would know about this brain coral of yours?" he asked. "Then you can proceed with your fishing expedition."

"Larry would know, but he's on break. Look, I really need to get back to this group. They all paid a lot of money for this dive and. . ."

"C'mon Ash," Todd said, gripping her hand. "We'll find out what we need to know elsewhere."

Stunned by Rick's brusqueness, Ashley felt the tears swim in her eyes. She followed Todd numbly into the cool of the night. "I had no idea he would. . . ," she began.

"What have I been saying, Ash? You get yourself all worked up for a big letdown." He wrapped an arm around her. "I don't think you have your eyes open to what's good for you. That's why you need me to watch out for you."

"I guess," she said while her feet shuffled through the sand. She turned once to see the parade of divers march behind Rick, heading for a van that would take them to Coki Beach for the night dive. She bit her lip, remembering the wonderful time they had spent in the water and the tender expression he had given her. Maybe it was wrong to have fallen for some guy she'd only met two days ago—one who had flung some money in her direction and showed her how to spit in a mask. The man interested in her welfare stood right by her side as he had all along, helping her with her sales and counseling her in times of difficulty.

"I've been a real fool," she whispered.

"Ash, you're no fool." Todd gave her a squeeze. "Just remember, you're mine. No one else's."

Sleep refused to come that night. Ashley tossed and turned, finally accepted defeat in the venture, and rose out of bed. She dressed and opened the patio door to gaze at the night. A full moon lit up the sky, casting a brilliance across the waters. The moonlight appeared like fine lace covering the sand and the ocean. Boats of all shapes and sizes bobbed in the waters. In only a few hours, she and Todd would be in one of them, heading for the horizon in search of more ocean treasures. Ashley plunked into a chair. The mere thought of finding treasures in the deep made her think of Rick. Ashley trembled inside her sweater jacket. No, she would not think of Rick. Todd was the only one who truly cared about her.

Just then, Ashley heard a cough next door. A chair scraped across the concrete patio. She rose to her feet and peeked around the partition to find Rick seated at the small table, his head in his hands. The picture of him bent over, as if caught in the throes of some sickness or grief, stirred her heart. "Rick, are you okay?"

Her voice jarred the silence. "Huh? Oh, Ashley. Yeah, I'm okay."

"How was the dive?"

"Okay."

"Mind if I sit?"

He shrugged. Ashley slid into a chair opposite him. The sparkle she'd seen in his moss green eyes appeared muted this night, despite the full moon shining overhead. His eyes drooped in sadness. Wrinkles creased his face. His mouth did not portray the easygoing smile that had warmed her heart. "You look like you've just lost your best friend," she remarked.

"I'm having a rough time."

"With your work?"

Again he shrugged his broad set of shoulders. "It's kind of complicated. I'm not sure if I can talk about it."

"I'm a good listener."

"I'm sure you are." He blew out a sigh and stared up into the moonlit night. "Look, I'm sorry I couldn't help you at the dive shop tonight. It's just that. . ."

Ashley chuckled. "Is that why you're upset? Don't be. I'm used to people telling me to be quiet and mind my own business. You should see some of the teachers I try to sign up for fund-raising projects. I've had phones slammed in my ear, teachers renege on projects signed months in advance, and others who put me off until their project has no hope of succeeding. I'm used to being put out. My friend, Todd, just wants us to have a good trip. I think he's trying to impress me."

Rick centered his gaze on her with a look that renewed a soothing warmth within her. "I'm sure he is. Guys like to impress a girl. I was trying to impress you, too. Maybe too much."

"You do some wonderful things, Rick. I'm glad you took the time out of your busy schedule to show me how to snorkel." She picked out a strand of blond hair and wrapped it around her finger. "In a few days, we'll both be returning to our own separate worlds."

He traced a finger across the table. "I guess I saw you as a student, eager to learn whatever you could. I was glad to oblige. At least you'll leave here learning a few new things about this world we live in. Speaking of which, did you locate the position of a brain coral for tomorrow's trip?"

"We asked around, but it looks like it may be too far out. We'd planned to sail around the bay and not into open water."

Rick appeared ready to say something, then nodded.

Ashley rose to her feet and yawned. "I'm glad we had a talk, Rick. I sure didn't want us to leave everything the way we did in the dive shop."

"Thanks for stopping over." He rose and bid good night before retreating to his hotel room.

Ashley lingered on his patio a few moments longer, allowing the moon's rays to bathe her face. The air smelled delicious, scented with tropical flowers and the faint odor of the ocean. She turned at that moment, just in time to see the blinds in Rick's room fall back into place. Had he been looking at her? The mere thought made her tingle inside.

Five

Rick paced the length of his hotel room, scooping up strands of light brown hair with his fingers. *Ashley*, his mind reverberated in singsong fashion. He loved her name, her face, her smile. Everything about her mesmerized him. He paused by the sliding glass door. How could he fall in love with someone like her? She knew nothing about the God he served or him, for that matter. Yet the two of them had been drawn together in some mysterious fashion. Her childlike fascination for the wonders of the deep that day at Coki Beach had stirred him. He nearly kissed her while they were together, treading the waters among the beauty of God's creation. Even an hour ago, when she'd sat so demurely on the patio, asking about his troubles—which involved her, though she didn't know it—he'd wanted to kiss her. He fought against the sensation with everything in him, but it was like trying to push back a tidal wave already flooding his heart.

"This isn't right," he said aloud. "We both have our own lives to live. She's a successful saleswoman. I'm just a guy who likes fish. We live on opposite ends of the world, so to speak. God, how can this possibly work?"

Rick paused in his tirade. He knew better than to try to rationalize it. Wasn't God greater than all this? If he couldn't figure it all out, perhaps he would do better to release it and go on. Rick spent the next half hour pouring out his heart to God—praying that Ashley's heart might somehow open up to His ways. He also prayed that if it was not God's will for Ashley and him to be together, that God would take her out of his life.

When he rose the next morning, he remembered that this was the day Ashley and that friend of hers were to set sail on their own private excursion. He frowned at the thought, wishing he had taken the initiative of offering Ashley a sailing excursion around the island. Rick felt a pang of jealousy toward this man who stood poised to sweep her away and fill her head with all sorts of worldly knowledge. Rick scuffed a foot along the carpet of his hotel room. How he wished he had treated yesterday differently. It was his own fault that he appeared preoccupied with his dive class. The truth be known, he couldn't have cared less about the diving class with Ashley standing there, watching his every move. Now it was too late. He had cast off Ashley as a helpless prey to the man named Todd.

Rick decided to forgo an early morning snorkeling adventure to watch the couple prepare for their journey. He picked up a pair of binoculars, wondering if it was the mark of a good Christian to spy. "I'm only looking out for Ashley's welfare," Rick told himself, slinging the binoculars over one shoulder. "Who knows if this guy even understands how to navigate a sailboat?

I trust him about as much as a barracuda."

Rick stiffened when he heard the swish of the patio door next to his room. *Ashley*. He peeked between the blinds to see her striding across the beach toward the dock. Her blond hair glimmered like strands of spun gold against the bright morning sun. She swung a bag containing personal belongings for the day. Rick slipped out of his own room and into a chair, then focused the binoculars on her. Sandals kicked up the sand, and her legs appeared tanner than when she first arrived. She paused to gaze out into the bay, staring at the view with a hand cupped over her eyes to protect them from the glaring sun.

"I could show you everything out there, Ashley," Rick murmured, focusing the binoculars on her face. "Anything you want to see, even the brain coral." He chuckled at the thought. Ashley held a fascination for the brain coral from the very beginning. If only he could make her wish come true.

Now the man Ashley had introduced as Todd strode out to meet her. He looked like a tennis player, clad in white shorts and a polo shirt with sunglasses propped on his head. In one hand he held a basket, in the other, a nylon bag containing snorkel gear. Rick nearly bloodied his lip from biting down on it. Ashley and Todd stood chatting for a bit, pointing to the boats and laughing.

"That should be me out there," he grumbled. "I should be taking her out." He rose to his feet. "But I can't. God, please, show me what to do before I lose myself completely over this."

For the next fifteen minutes, Rick endured the sight

of Todd leading Ashley over to the boat they had selected for the morning ride. He watched Todd exchange words with the proprietor of the boat, pointing to the sailcloth that the proprietor held in his hands. "This I gotta see," Rick noted, watching through his binoculars while Todd took up the sailcloth and began rigging it. "Ha! That character doesn't know what he's doing. He's already got it rigged incorrectly." Rick lowered the binoculars and chuckled. "What a great trip this will be. Betcha they make it a hundred yards before they'll have to turn around." He watched Todd extend his hand to Ashley and help her into the boat. "I give them ten minutes before the trip is over. That's it. Ten minutes, and they'll call it quits." He added silently, *Then in ten minutes, I can whisk Ashley away on a sailing trip she'll never forget.*

To his surprise, Todd was able to direct the sail enough to pick up a bit of crosswind, sending the boat adrift into the bay. Rick took to his feet and headed for the beach, watching the little boat sail across the waters. "For having it on wrong, he's not doing too badly." He stared, unblinking, until his eyes fell on a small Sunfish the proprietor had just rigged with sail. He felt a gentle nudging in his heart. Despite his distaste for Todd, he knew it would be wrong to let them wander away with an improperly rigged sail when he could do something to help.

"Hey, can I take that Sunfish out for an hour?" Rick inquired. "I'm a guest here at the hotel."

"Sure. Rental is free for guests."

Rick waded into the water, pushing the small craft with him. He climbed in, took hold of the line, and directed the sail to catch the wind that fanned across the bay. Soon the craft was off, tacking along the gentle waves. Up ahead he could see Ashley's boat, floating aimlessly in the water. Todd stood looking over the sail, trying to pinpoint the problem. "You got it rigged wrong, Pal," Rick muttered, steering in their direction. He maneuvered the boat alongside their craft, to be met by Ashley's astonished gaze. Just the sight of her face and her hair blowing in the breeze made his heart leap.

"Rick, what are you doing here?" she asked.

"Looks like you're having a bit of a problem. Can I help at all?"

Todd whirled. Even through the sunglasses obscuring the tall man's features, Rick could sense the eyes staring him down. "I've got a handle on it, thanks."

"I'm Rick, by the way. We met at the dive shop."

"I know," Todd said dryly, "probably more than I care to."

Rick ignored the remark. "Do you know what's wrong?"

"Of course. The wind's died down. Just have to wait for it to pick up again."

Rick shook his head. "It's more than just the wind. You've got that sail rigged incorrectly. I can show you what the problem is."

Todd turned. "Oh, really? What makes you the expert? I thought playing with fish was more your style."

"I've sailed quite a bit in my days. I also helped out on many boats in Hawaii. I can tell you for a fact that you've got the sail on wrong."

"Thanks for the feedback, but I can take care of this."

"Look, it won't take anything for both of us to fix it," Rick suggested. "Then you'll be on your way."

"Todd, let Rick help," Ashley echoed.

"Ash, I know what I'm doing," Todd told her. "I don't need this guy following us around, watching our every move. We make an awesome team together, you know."

"Todd, this has nothing to do with—"

"It most certainly does."

Rick heard the makings of an argument falling into place and quickly opened the sail to his craft. "I'm sorry I came by," he said. "I didn't mean to interrupt your trip."

"Thanks, but you already have," Todd answered through clenched teeth.

Rick said nothing. He maneuvered the sail and made for the opposite end of the bay. He could barely hear the sounds of Ashley and Todd arguing on the breath of wind that drifted by his boat—words that spoke of the friendship that had begun during the few days they had been here. He sighed, thumping his sandal on the floor of the boat. He could do nothing but head back to the dock and proceed with his day, yet the yearning to be with Ashley rose up like a mighty wave within him. He glanced back several times to find their craft still in the same position on the water. "God, I can't break through a thick skull," he murmured. "I just pray they both get back safely, and I pray You will guide me concerning Ashley."

"You're being totally unreasonable," Todd said as Ashley forced her foot into a fin.

"I'm being unreasonable? You're practically accusing me of being associated with a criminal. Rick and I talked a few times and just happened to hit it off."

"That's the whole point. Now he feels he can cruise out here to be with you. If you want to know the truth, I don't care to have you interested in anyone but me."

Ashley stared at him in shock. "Are you crazy? You're my business manager. That's as far as our relationship is supposed to go." She jammed her foot into the other fin. "Maybe you had other ideas for this vacation. I came because I believed in what you said—that I'd earned it. Now it looks like you just wanted me here for some other purpose."

"Ash, I wouldn't have paid for the others to come if I had some ulterior motive. Of course, you earned it with your sales. Don't start psychoanalyzing me."

She picked up a mask and snorkel. "Well, I'm going snorkeling. As long as you can't get this boat to do anything, I'm not wasting my time getting a sunburn."

"Ash, c'mon," he said soothingly, reaching out a hand to her. "Don't ruin our trip. I've got this great picnic here. We can have a quiet time, just the two of us." He curled his hand around her shoulder and drew her towards him. "What's wrong with spending time together?"

"Todd, this isn't right. You're my manager and. . ." She sensed her rationale falling on deaf ears. Something else controlled Todd at that moment, overshadowing any thought of business ethics.

"Look, I'll play it straight with you: I'm madly in love with you. I have been for a long time. I'm sure you've felt it, too. We have the right chemistry. We do everything so well together."

When he pulled her close, his lips seeking hers, Ashley pushed him away. "I'm not doing this, Todd. It's unprofessional and goes against everything we've been taught."

He inhaled sharply. "But you don't mind fish lover cruising over here, wanting to spend time, do you? What's so special about him, anyway? What's he done that I haven't? Tell me, has he ever helped you get your feet on the right track in life? Has he ever driven hundreds of miles to help you in your work and make you what you are today?"

Ashley felt her vexation rising. "Forget it. I'm going snorkeling. We can't even have a rational discussion right now. Maybe when I get back we can have a *professional* picnic as associates, the way it should be."

With a huff she entered the water, swimming as far away as she could from Todd and the boat. At that moment, she was thankful the sail had been rigged incorrectly so he couldn't follow her. She shook her head, recalling his words the other night that now rang loudly in her ears. *You're mine and no one else's.* "How could I have been so blind?" she muttered to herself. "I should have seen this coming. All the signs were there, but I ignored them. I thought Todd was being nice because that's his personality. Guess I was dead wrong."

Ashley breathed out slowly, trying to control her anger enough to do what she had come here for—

exploring the deep. She slipped the mask off, spit into it as Rick had instructed, then put it back on. Her breathing became erratic as she tried to calm herself enough to go snorkeling. At last, she found a pattern of breathing comfortable enough to open her eyes and behold the world that so intrigued Rick.

It's beautiful down here. No wonder Rick loves it. And I'm loving it, too. Straightening in the water to gulp a lungful of air, Ashley then slipped the mask back over her nose and eyes. She skimmed the surface, examining the multitudes of fish swimming about, unaware of how far she had drifted from Todd and the boat until she came up out of the water. "I'll take one more look, then tell Todd we can have a professional picnic and keep a professional distance. If he can't play by the rules, then that's the end of it." Ashley shook her head, again putting on her mask, wondering if that would really happen after the events on the boat. Yet, she felt she had to make amends. No matter what had occurred between them, he was still her manager.

When she placed her face in the water, the snorkel filled with salty seawater. Ashley gagged and rose to the surface. "What's the matter with this thing?" She searched for a blockage in the snorkel, adjusted the headpiece, and tried once again. This time she did not place the mask correctly over her face. Saltwater filled her nose and mouth. The mask began to fog up. She choked and coughed. "What's wrong?" Ashley cried, treading the water furiously to keep herself afloat while trying to assess the situation. The fins soon felt like lead weights that dragged her below the surface. She moved her arms, trying to swim back to Todd's boat that now appeared like a dust speck on the vast waters.

Exhaustion rapidly overcame her. "Oh, no," she sputtered, her voice betraying her panic. Painful spasms gripped her legs and feet. "Help! Oh, God, please, I need help! Todd!" She began to pant. "Relax, relax." Again, she tried to paddle her way back to the boat, but found her muscles unresponsive.

"Help!" she cried, spitting out the saltwater that filled her mouth. "I'm not going to make it. Oh, God." She slipped beneath the surface, still calling for help. Bubbles churned the water. *Oh, God, is this what it means to drown?*

Suddenly, an arm grabbed her around the waist and hoisted her to the surface. "Relax," said a male voice. "I've got you. I won't let you go."

"I—I can't. I can't make it. I'm gonna drown!" She coughed violently, clawing at the muscular forearm that held her in a firm grip.

"You won't drown. I have you."

Ashley tried to help, but her legs refused to move. "My feet hurt so bad," she cried, her hands slipping on his wet forearm. "I—I can hardly breathe." She coughed again, spitting up ocean water.

"Hold on," he said. "We're almost there." The rescuer's face pressed against her head, his free arm lunging into the water; his feet kicking furiously. When they reached the boat, she felt him nuzzle her wet hair before helping her aboard the tiny craft. Ashley coughed and cried at the same time, even as she felt the warmth of a towel encircle her, and gentle hands working to remove the fins from her feet. "Oh, my feet! They're all twisted."

"They cramped up."

Ashley blinked, her eyesight blurry from the contact with the saltwater. When her vision began to clear, she found herself staring into Rick's face. "Oh, Rick!" Sobs filled her throat. "Oh, thank You, God. I—I almost died."

"You're okay," he said, clasping her hand in his while using the other to direct the boat toward land. "We'll get you checked out when we reach the shore."

Silent tears cascaded down her cheeks. *It's not okay. I would have drowned. . .were it not for Rick.*

Six

Ashley rested comfortably in her hotel room after being checked at the medical facility in Charlotte Amalie. She still sneezed and coughed up seawater from her lungs. Visions of the water closing over her head and her body drifting out to sea sent her into another round of quiet weeping. "I was never so scared in my life," she whispered, flicking tears from her face. "How did Rick know I was drowning? I don't understand. No matter where I am or what situation I'm in, he's always there." She blinked at the view outside the patio doors, of the fading rays of sunlight kissing the shore farewell before dropping below the horizon. "Just like the rising and the setting of the sun, I can count on him to be there."

A knock on the door disturbed her thoughts. Ashley rose slowly, still dizzy and weak from the harsh encounter with the ocean, and peeked through the security hole. The image of Rick standing before the unopened door sent strength surging through her. With a shaky hand, she unlocked the door. "Rick," she breathed.

"Hi. I just wanted to check and see if you needed anything."

"I'm okay, thanks. Please come in."

He looked rather uncertain about her request before stepping inside. "Okay, but just for a few minutes. I know you need your rest. How are you feeling?"

"My head feels like it's splitting apart." She sighed. "I'm coughing up saltwater, so I must have swallowed half the ocean. Other than that. . .I guess I'm lucky to be alive."

He nodded, averting his gaze to a lone chair in the corner of the room where he sat down. Ashley occupied the edge of the bed and observed him for a moment. She recalled his powerful arm that had plucked her from the sea, and the impression of some tender contact on her head before she entered the boat. *Like a kiss,* she thought. *Did he kiss me as he was helping me aboard the boat? Do I dare ask?* She shook her head. *I can't ask him something like that—but, oh, how I would love to know!*

His voice interrupted her thoughts. "What's the matter? You have a funny expression on your face."

Ashley coughed. "Still got some seawater in my lungs. I–I need a heavy dose of Tylenol, too." Ashley hurried off to the bathroom to find the medicine in her toiletry kit, sensing Rick's eyes perusing her from the other room. How she wished he would care for her as she did for him. Maybe the incident in the ocean would help. Ashley swallowed down the tablets with a glass of water and returned to the room. "That's better."

"Look, I'll let you get some rest," he said, rising to his feet. "I've got a few things to do, anyway."

"Sure. And Rick, thanks for all you've done."

Rick offered a faint smile and nod before heading for the door. When it shut behind him, Ashley fell back onto the bed, rested a hand across her forehead, and declared, "I love that man."

Rick had shut the door to Ashley's room, yet his fingers remained clasped around the knob. He closed his eyes, envisioning her safe and sound in the room, thankful he had hung around the bay in his boat after being chased away by Todd. A shudder raced through him at the image of her frail being bobbing helplessly in the waters. "God, thank You for using me to protect her," he whispered. "I only wish she could see Your hand in all of this. God, please help her see." He shuffled off, his lips moving in silent prayer, when a figure approached him from the opposite direction.

"Did you see Ashley?" came a concerned voice. "Is she okay?"

Rick noticed at once it was Todd—the man who had driven Ashley into the ocean. "Yes," he said shortly.

Todd dug his hands deep into the pockets of his shorts. "I doubt she'll want to see me after what happened today. She's always talking about you, you know. Guess I saw you as a threat or something. She got mad at me and took off."

"I'm no threat to you. There's nothing going on between Ashley and me. Besides, I'll be leaving the day after tomorrow. We won't see each other again." Rick moved to his room before Todd's voice stopped him short.

"Anyway, thanks for what you did today. The boat wouldn't move. I couldn't get over there to help her out. Guess you were right about that sail. I'm glad you were there." He walked off with his head down.

Rick stared after Todd, questioning the conversation. *Am I a threat?* he mused. *Is there anything going on between Ashley and me?* "Of course not," he said aloud. "There is nothing. There can't be anything. She's nice, yes, and good-looking, but we can never have a life together." Yet the mere thought of Todd getting his hooks into her irritated him to no end. Perhaps there was something going on, after all. "God, I'm so confused. I feel like I love her, yet I know we can't be together. God, only You can make it happen, if You want it to."

A few hours later, Rick heard a knock on his hotel door. He threw aside the magazine on scuba diving and rose to open the door, hoping for a second it might be her. To his surprise, he found a deliveryman holding a box of pizza.

"Are you Rick Adams?"

"Yes, but I didn't order a pizza."

"Another customer paid for it. Enjoy." The pizza man handed him the box and promptly left, leaving Rick standing there with the pizza in his hands, inhaling the fragrant aroma. He glanced through the blinds to see someone moving about on the back patio. He opened the door to find the patio converted into a dining area. Cups and paper plates were arranged on the table. A single flower stood in a drinking glass filled with water. "Ashley?" he whispered, scratching his head in puzzlement. "Is that you?"

"Surprise!" she said in glee, jumping out from behind the partition. She shook back her blond hair in a gesture that drew him like a magnet. "I thought you deserved dinner after your heroism this day. Too bad I couldn't hire a band and have a trophy made up. Hail, Rick, hero of the deep!"

"You should be resting," he admonished, setting the pizza box down on the table.

"I'm fine now. Headache's gone. You must have been praying for me."

The comment sparked hope that perhaps she was beginning to acknowledge God in her life. "I pray for lots of people," he said quickly, unwilling to reveal how he had been interceding for her these past few days. When he bent his head to pray over their meal, he noticed Ashley praying along with him. They both helped themselves to the pizza and ate silently, neither one sure of what to say.

After a bit, Ashley drew a napkin across her lips and managed a smile. "I guess you didn't expect your time here to turn out quite the way it has, huh?"

"You never know, I guess."

Ashley stared down at her unfinished pizza. "It's pretty amazing how everything worked out, in the ocean, I mean. I've been wondering all afternoon how you knew I was in trouble. The last I saw of you, you were sailing back to the resort."

Rick intertwined his fingers. "This may sound kind of strange to you, Ashley, but God told me to turn around. I was on my way back to the beach, but I felt I should go back. I didn't know why, but I had a feeling that something was wrong. When I heard your cry for help, then I knew." He closed his eyes before snapping them open again. "I'm glad I found you. A minute later and you might have. . ."

Ashley shivered. Tears pooled in her blue eyes. "I–I don't understand how God could tell you something like that. I mean, does His voice speak to you or something?"

"It's like a firm nudge, an ache, you might say, that doesn't go away. Sometimes even a tingly feeling. It's hard to describe. I can't say I've heard an audible voice, but I know it's Him when He speaks. When you hear Him often enough and obey the voice, you know when He's talking."

"I never thought that God could speak like that," she mused. "It makes Him seem so real."

"God is real, as real as you or me. He came to earth as a real Man and saved us from our sin. In fact, sin is a lot like the ocean out there." Rick waved his hand toward the beach and the view of the ocean waters, rapidly fading into the dusk. "I nearly drowned in it, myself, but Jesus came floating along on that cross at Calvary and plucked me right out of it. He rescued me."

Ashley stared at him, her eyes wide. "I never heard it explained that way, despite all the Sunday school lessons I listened to when I was little. It makes so much sense after what I went through today. Oh, I never want to experience that again." She bit her lip and turned away. "I really thought I was going to die. I thought to myself—this is it. I'm going to experience that dark tunnel and the brilliant white light everyone talks about. And what have I to show for my life? Nothing. I just lived my life for one person: me."

"God cares about you," Rick said softly, leaning over the table in his eagerness to have her understand. "I think this is just His way of showing you that He cares and that He wants you to think about living your life for Him. With God, you can't lose in life. You can only win."

"Maybe. I'll have to really think about all this. Oh, but I can't believe tomorrow's my last day here." Ashley sighed before standing to gather up the plates and napkins. "What do you plan on doing? I heard you tell that cabbie named George that you're leaving Friday. I leave then, too. Time flies when you're being rescued."

Rick chuckled. "I was thinking of going for an early morning snorkel. Care to join me?"

Ashley laughed. "Oh, really. . .after what happened today? I don't think you need to perform another ocean rescue, thank you."

"The only way to learn snorkeling is to keep doing it."

Ashley paused to consider this. "All right, I will—if you don't mind lugging me along."

Would I mind? Ashley, I would lug you anywhere, just to be with you. Rick only rose to his feet, his face a huge smile filled with anticipation. "Meet you here at six-thirty."

"Six-thirty," she said with a smile of her own. She quickly cleaned up the table and waved good-bye before heading to her room.

Rick slipped into a chair. Tomorrow would be their

last day on St. Thomas. He wished there were a thousand tomorrows left to spend with her, yet he had to settle for one final day. He prayed it would be their best.

Ashley waited patiently by the patio door, trying to stifle the yawn that rose up from within. She'd slept little that night, thinking about the meeting with Rick and the words he had shared. She had opened the Bible inside her hotel room and leafed through it, looking up Scriptures and ruminating on the words for the first time in years. She wanted to know all about this Person who had spoken to Rick and why Rick served Him. She wanted to experience the things he had experienced, but found her heart filled by the cares of the world—her job, her lifestyle, her friends. Now as she waited patiently for him to appear out of his room, she wished she had the ears to hear and the eyes to see like he did.

To her surprise, Rick bounced up from the direction of the dock. "Come on," he waved.

"Where are we going?" she asked, following him to a small Sunfish, already rigged with a sail.

"I thought it would be great to see the sunrise this morning."

Ashley settled down gingerly in the boat to find snorkeling gear at her feet, along with two life preservers and a cooler. Rick unwound the rope anchoring the Sunfish to the dock and directed the sail to catch the breath of wind fanning across the bay. In no time, the boat sailed out into the pristine waters. The sky above erupted into a myriad of colors with the approaching sunrise.

"Look," he pointed.

Ashley followed his finger to see a semicircle of sun rising above the island of St. Thomas. Her heart nearly flipped within her. "It's beautiful."

"Isn't it? I had to see it again, especially after the first dive I took here. When I see the sunrise, it means another new beginning in my life, just like the new day."

"What kind of new beginning?"

He did not elaborate, but only concentrated on guiding the boat through the churning waters. Ashley looked over at him, but he stayed focused on the ocean with the rudder in hand, guiding the boat to its destination. She considered their many meetings over the course of the last few days. Gazing back at the sunrise now in full bloom over the island, she wondered if this, too, might be a signal of new beginnings in her life.

Rick maneuvered the boat to a small outcropping of rock. "We passed this during the dive. I thought we could do a little snorkeling along the reef here, then have some breakfast on the rocks."

"Is that what's in the cooler? Breakfast?"

He nodded and threw the equipment onto shore before giving her his hand. When his fingers clasped hers, she sensed a tingle spread through her arm and straight to her heart. The feeling left her light-headed. Once on shore, she proceeded to slip on the fins with confidence and even spit into her mask as he once instructed.

"You remembered!" Rick said with a laugh.

"I'd better remember. I have a pro with me. Pro diver, that is." Ashley readied herself by the rocks, waiting for Rick to descend into the water first. He extended his hand. For a moment, Ashley stared at the ocean waters surrounding him, envisioning yesterday's near calamity.

"Ashley?"

Rick's voice seemed miles away, caught in a hazy cloud of fear that swept over her. She shook her head. "I–I can't."

"Yes, you can. I'm right here. I won't let go of you. Trust me."

His words were like a soothing balm. Slowly, she gave him her hand. The contact again brought forth a familiar tingle that swept through her. He continued to hold her hand as they swam out from the shore, sharing in the beauty of the deep. He pointed out the multicolored fish and the living coral. When they came up for a breath of air, smiles lit their faces.

"I'm so glad I came," Ashley admitted. "The ocean is beautiful. It's like I jumped on board a spaceship and traveled to another planet."

He grinned before placing the mask over his eyes and returning the snorkel to an upright position. "C'mon, there's more to see."

They continued to skim the ocean surface, searching the nooks and crannies of the reef. Suddenly she saw it and gave a yelp. A huge yellow coral, contorted into the perfect shape of a brain, met her astonished eyes. She spoke through the snorkel, jostling Rick's arm, nearly jumping out of the water. When they came up for air, she tore off her mask. "Oh, Rick, it was my brain coral! You found my brain coral! It's exactly like you said it would be."

A smile spread across his face. "Just for you."

Ashley leapt into his arms. Suddenly they were kissing, enjoying the taste of saltwater on their faces. His arms held her tight, his lips hungering after hers. Then he pulled away.

"Rick? Is something wrong?"

"Let's go back to shore." He grabbed her hand and said nothing more.

Once they were safely on the rocky bank, Ashley anticipated him embracing her again. Instead, he shook his head of wet hair and proclaimed, "I think this calls for some breakfast." He opened the cooler and took out containers of fruit, croissants and jelly, and a carafe of juice. When he had the breakfast laid out, Ashley bowed her head along with him and prayed for the meal.

At that moment, remembering all the many wonders that morning and the spectacular sunrise over the island, a prayer rose up from within. "Thank You, God, for showing me all Your beauty. I don't know You personally like Rick does, but I pray I might be able to hear Your voice, and that You will continue to show me Your wonders. Thank You for Rick's companionship and his care, even though I took it all for granted. And thank You most of all for this wonderful vacation. Amen."

When she lifted her head, Rick's face shone like the sunrise she had witnessed over the tiny island. He broke a croissant in half and gave it to her. "That was a great prayer, Ashley."

"I feel like I just woke up," she said. "It's like I've been walking around in a daze for most of my life. I could have never appreciated everything I've seen or the people I've met if it weren't for the knowledge of God's existence. Most of all, I found out that He really does care about me."

"He cares very much, more than you or I could ever understand." Rick put down the croissant. Ashley held her breath when he embraced her. "You probably know that I care, too."

"I–I hoped you cared," she whispered. "We're so different, yet there are ways we're alike." She began to relax in his arms that held her close, like the arm that cradled her when she found herself sinking into the ocean depths. He nuzzled her wet hair.

"I must smell like fish," she complained with a laugh.

"Not at all," he said, his voice muffled in her hair that streamed around her shoulders. He kissed the top of her head, then proceeded to one ear, which elicited a giggle. The tender expression showed his concern for her well-being. Ashley hungered after his attention. She turned in his arms and they kissed once more. When they parted, his eyes were wide, his facial muscles taut as if he struggled with something internally.

"Ashley, I care so much about you. I hate to leave you, but I have to go back to California. That's where God wants me right now."

"It's okay," she said with a sigh. "I just wanted to let you know in some small way that I care about you, too."

They packed up the breakfast in silence, each contemplating what had transpired on the rocky shore. The trip back to St. Thomas was likewise clouded by silence. Yet when Ashley departed from the boat, with the sun shining full in her face, she could not help but thank the Lord for bringing her to this island and to Rick Adams.

Seven

Ashley stood on the curb beside her bags, feeling as though she were leaving all that she loved for the real world. The mere thought left her depressed. Beside her stood Todd, who had said very little since the near drowning. Ashley was grateful he had kept his distance for the remainder of the trip. She cast him a look or two out of the corner of her eye and noticed his gaze drifted to a distant palm tree. Things would never be the same again.

Just then, a cab pulled up to the curb. To Ashley's surprise, George the cabbie sat behind the wheel. She ran to the driver's window. "Hi, George, remember me?"

George shook his head before giving a loud whistle when Rick came running up, dragging his heavy bags with him. "You almost missed me, Rick," the cabbie noted, rising out of his seat to help him load his gear into the trunk.

Ashley stood watching before marching to the rear of the taxi and throwing in her bags alongside his. "We are going in the same direction," she explained. "The airport."

"Ashley, don't make this any more difficult than it already is," Rick told her in a low voice. "You know we have to go our separate ways."

"Can't we spend a little more time together, even if it is in a dirty cab on the way to the airport? There's no harm in that, is there?"

Shrugging, Rick opened the passenger door for her. Once they were on their way, George and Rick chattered about his time on St. Thomas. Ashley stared out the window, trying to think of a way to draw him into a meaningful conversation. Perhaps this was Rick's way of letting go. Maybe she would do well to follow his lead.

All at once she felt his hand close around hers. "I'm really going to miss you," he whispered in her ear.

Ashley sighed, grateful that he still possessed feelings for her, despite their imminent separation. "Me, too. Look, I want to give you something before I forget." She rummaged inside her handbag. "Here's my business card. We can e-mail each other. My phone number is on there, too, if you ever want to talk. You can tell me about the gorgeous weather in California. In Virginia, we're just beginning to enjoy spring."

Rick took the business card with her picture and the words, *Fund-raising Consultant*. His finger traced her smiling image before tucking it into his shirt pocket.

"So you got a girlfriend now, Rick?" George asked from the driver's seat.

"She's just a friend, George."

"Ha! That's what they all say. I know you and her good for each other, the way you pay her fare when she first come here. And see what I get with the money?"

George snapped the red suspenders he wore over a plaid, short-sleeved shirt.

"Good for you, George. I like those suspenders much better than a liquor bottle. They don't knock your senses for a loop like booze can."

"I get off the rum like you told me, Rick. I promised the wife I would."

Ashley stared admiringly, first at George, then at Rick. "That's wonderful news."

"Rick a good man," George said, grinning at Ashley from the rearview mirror with the same set of yellow teeth. "You shouldn't let him get away."

Ashley thought on the cabbie's words as the taxi pulled into the airport. *I don't want to let Rick go,* she confessed, *but what other choice is there? I have my work in Virginia, and he has his work in California. There's nothing else I can do but let go.*

Soon they were standing on the curb, surrounded by baggage. The time had come to say farewell. "Well, Rick, it's been a wild time," Ashley managed to choke out. "Thanks for everything, and I do mean everything."

"Ashley, I. . . ," he began before falling silent. Instead he picked up his bags and turned to leave.

Tears filled her eyes, watching him stride off toward the opposite end of the airport. Suddenly she took off after him and caught his arm. "Rick."

"I have to go. My flight leaves soon."

"I know." Ashley hastily unzipped her carry-on bag. "I have a present for you." She pushed the beanbag fish, nestled in its ocean box, into his hands. "Just a reminder of the good times we had. I–I'll never forget our snorkeling trips. . .especially seeing that brain coral."

Rick opened his mouth to speak, but instead, wrapped his arms around her and pulled her close. His kisses were sweet. With a shake of his head, he withdrew; his arms struggling to let go as if agonized by the decision he had to make. He choked out a good-bye and strode off to the gate.

The tears slowly trickled down her cheeks. "Bye, Rick."

Once inside the airplane heading back for Virginia, a great heaviness fell over Ashley. For the first time in her life, she didn't relish walking into a cold, dark home to be greeted by the houseplants sitting on the windowsills. She closed her eyes and leaned her head against the glass. If there were only some way she and Rick could be together. It didn't seem possible. He had a life in Los Angeles and she had her job in Roanoke, Virginia. They lived at opposite ends of the country, with opposite goals and dreams in life. The time in St. Thomas had been a sweet memory, but now she must face reality.

The flight home went smoothly. Ashley soon reached her ranch home, which she proudly called her castle before the events in St. Thomas made her consider other avenues in life. She began attending church and committing herself to living a Christian life rather than being caught up in her own little world. Not a day would go by when she did not think of the rocky shore where she and Rick kissed, or the times they held hands while exploring the wonders of creation. She sent him E-mails and even tried to call him, but heard nothing. As the months trickled by, Ashley came to the realization they were not meant to be together. God had sent Rick to her on St. Thomas so she might understand Him. Rick had exemplified Christianity, right down to the moment when he saved her from the ocean depths. Their relationship meant nothing more than this.

One day, Ashley arrived home from work to find a visitor lounging on her front porch, reading a book. When she stopped on the sidewalk and stared, the figure rose to his feet. He held up a hand in greeting.

"Rick?" she said in astonishment.

"Hey, I'm on my way back from Norfolk. They have a marine center there where I've been doing some research."

"Wow, this is a surprise." Fumbling for the keys, she dropped the purse on the porch, spilling the contents. He helped her scoop up the accessories before giving her back the bag. "Sorry," she mumbled.

"Guess I kind of shocked you."

"Well, yes," Ashley admitted. She finally managed to unlock the door. "I'm not used to men hanging around my doorstep, waiting for me."

"That's a relief," he remarked before venturing inside. Immediately he paused at a large framed print on the wall. "Where did you get that?"

Ashley giggled at the huge underwater mural, complete with coral and fish, including the brain coral. "I found it at an art shop and I couldn't resist it. Isn't it fabulous?"

"I should say." He strode up to the picture with his

hands stuffed in his pockets, studying it. "I can name practically every species on this mural. Elkhorn coral, sergeant major fish, yellowtail damselfish. . ." His gaze drifted to the display shelf of shells gathered on Coki Beach. He picked up the conch shell that he had given to her. "I remember this."

"It's beautiful," she sighed. "I've been talking to a friend who has a saltwater aquarium. He's telling me how to set one up. I'm going to use my bonus money this year to get myself a nice setup. Maybe even some live coral to go in it."

Rick turned, his face mere inches from hers. "I guess you really like this stuff now, don't you?"

Her gaze was unflinching. "I had a good teacher who taught me all about our underwater world."

She trembled beneath the touch of his finger that swept her chin. "You amaze me," he said gently. "Now I know why I couldn't get you out of my mind."

Ashley stepped back. "I just figured if I need to be here in Virginia, then I could bring a bit of your world into mine. C'mon into the living room." He followed her and occupied a seat on the sofa. Soon they were engaged in lengthy chatter about their respective work.

"So how long will you be in Norfolk?" she asked.

"Actually, I just finished up there." His finger traced the rosy print fabric of the couch. "It was hard, though."

Ashley lifted an eyebrow in concern. "Why? Did they make you do all sorts of strange things?"

"No. I couldn't get you out of my mind. Just the idea that you were living in the same state. . .I had to come see you."

"I'm glad you did. Life here has certainly changed since I got back. Todd has moved on to supervising other salespeople down in North Carolina, so I have a new manager."

"I'm glad to hear that," Rick was quick to say.

"Work is going well. But I missed you, too." Her gaze traveled to the underwater mural in the hallway. "That's why I bought the mural. When I look at the picture, I think of us snorkeling together, staring at all that beauty. I like to show members of the home group the mural and tell them what we saw."

"Home group?"

"Oh, the home group from church. We meet every other week in someone else's home." She went on, explaining her church's activities, never noticing his face blossom into a grin wider than the ones he used to flash so brightly on St. Thomas. Only when he took her hands in his did she cease in her conversation.

"This must be God," he said softly.

"What do you mean?"

"I heard Him again, Ashley, loud and clear, while I was in Norfolk. That's another reason I couldn't get you out of my mind. When God puts someone on your heart, it's pretty hard to forget. He said you were ready. That's why I came here."

Ashley blinked. "I'm ready? For what?"

Before she could inquire further, he leaned over and kissed her. His hands sifted through her hair. "You don't know how much I wanted you by my side while I was in California."

She nearly laughed. "I've thought about being with

81

you, too," she confessed, "but I knew you wanted to be in California. There wasn't anything I could do but go on with my life here in Virginia."

"We've each had our seasons," he confirmed. "I felt such an attraction for you on St. Thomas, but I knew there were things God had to accomplish in both our lives. I knew if the attraction was from Him, He would bring us together in His timing."

"Does that mean you're leaving California?"

"I was hoping you might want to come with me. I could use a new scuba partner."

Ashley stared at him. "You want me to go to California?"

"I know it's a lot to ask. You'd have to sell your home, leave your job. . ."

"I can always get a sales territory in California." She glanced around at her home. "This house has been nice, but it reminds me of another life I once lived. The day I left St. Thomas, I knew I had changed. The person who bought this place was into her career, her money, and her singleness. Now I'm 'into God,' like you once said to me. Things like this house and a career don't mean as much to me anymore."

His hand gently caressed her cheek. "So you'll come?"

Ashley nodded. "I'll go wherever you take me. . .if you will show me the sunrise over California."

"Gladly," he said before they fell into each other's arms, thanking God for kindling an everlasting love that would never fade.

LAURALEE BLISS

A former nurse, Lauralee is a prolific writer of inspirational fiction as well as a home educator. She resides with her family near Charlottesville, Virginia, in the foothills of the Blue Ridge Mountains—a place of inspiration for many of her contemporary and historical novels. Lauralee Bliss writes inspirational fiction to provide readers with entertaining stories, intertwined with Christian principles to assist them in the day-to-day walk with the Lord. Aside from writing, she enjoys gardening, cross-stitching, reading, roaming yard sales, and traveling.

Matchmaker 911

by Wanda E. Brunstetter

Dedication

To my daughter-in-law, Jean—
a sweet, petite barber—
and to my daughter, Lorine,
friend, Lauralee, and others
who gave me so many helpful ideas.

One

Y a know what?" croaked an aging, gravelly-sounding voice. "I was six months old before I even saw the light of day!"

In the past four years of cutting customers' hair, Wendy Campbell had listened to more ridiculous jokes and boring stories than she cared to admit. Clyde Baxter sat in her antique barber's chair, and she was quite certain she was about to hear another joke or two from him. Barbering was her chosen profession, and as long as it wasn't an off-color joke, she would play along.

"Why's that, Clyde?" Wendy prompted, knowing if she didn't make some kind of response, the elderly man would probably tell her anyway.

"Well, Darlin', my mother, God rest her soul, was a bit nearsighted. So the poor woman kept on diaperin' the wrong end!"

Wendy's muffled groan did nothing to deter the amicable man, and with no further encouragement, he continued. "Now, I don't want to say I was an ugly baby or anything, but I hear tell that the doctor who brought me into this ol' world took one look at my homely mug and promptly made a citizen's arrest on my daddy!" At this remark, Clyde roared with laughter.

Wendy grimaced. The joke was respectable enough, but thanks to Clyde's interruptions by moving around each time he laughed, this haircut was taking much longer than it should. It was only ten o'clock, and she still had several more clients scheduled in the next two hours—including four-year-old Benny Jensen, the kid who hated haircuts and liked to kick and scream. That didn't take into account any walk-ins who might happen by, either.

Wendy could hardly wait for lunchtime when she could run home, grab a quick bite to eat, and check up on her father. At least *Dad* had sense enough not to tell a bunch of lame wisecracks and off-color stories. Wendy didn't mind cutting hair, and now that Dad couldn't work, she certainly needed the money. There were days like today, though, when she wondered if a woman working in a predominately man's world was really such a good idea.

"Why, I'll never forget the day I graduated from grammar school," Clyde continued, with a silly grin plastered on his seventy-year-old, weathered face. "I tell you, I was so nervous I could hardly shave!" The old man laughed so hard this time that his whole body shook, and he had tears running down his wrinkled cheeks.

Wendy rolled her eyes toward the plastered ceiling and feigned a smile. "You'd better quit laughing and hold still, Clyde. If you don't, it might be your ear that comes off and not those sideburns you've finally decided to part with."

Clyde slapped his knee and let out another loud guffaw, ending it on a definite pigsnort. "Tell ya what, Honey, you could probably take my ear clean off, and it wouldn't make much never mind to me. I can only hear outa one ear anyways, and I ain't rightly sure which one that is!"

Without making any reply, Wendy took a few more snips and followed them with a quick once-over on the back of Clyde's stubbly neck with her clippers. She dusted him off with a soft-bristled brush and announced, "There you go, Clyde. That ought to hold you for at least another month."

Wendy was already moving toward her antiquated cash register, which had to be manually opened by the use of a handle on one side. Due to the hour, she sincerely hoped her joke-telling client would take the hint and move on.

Clyde finally stood up and ambled slowly over to where she stood, smiling through clenched teeth and waiting impatiently for him to pay. "You sure ain't much for fun today, are you, little lady?"

Before Wendy could think of an intelligent reply, Clyde added, "Nothin' like your old man, that's for sure. Why, good old Wayne used to tease like crazy all of the time. He could tell some jokes that just kept ya in stitches, too!"

Clyde appeared thoughtful, with a faraway look clouding his aging eyes. "I sure do miss that guy. It's been two years now since he took a razor to my chin or shortened my ears a few inches with them clippers of his. Such a downright shame that your daddy can't cut hair no more."

Wendy nodded, causing her short, blond curls to

bounce. "Dad's been battling arthritis a long time. After two knee replacements and even having the joints in his fingers surgically repaired, I'm afraid the disease has finally gotten the best of him. He hardly gets out of the house anymore, unless it's to go to the hospital for his regular physical therapy appointments. Once in awhile, he still stops by here, if the weather is good enough and he's not in too much pain. He likes to sit right there and reminisce." She pointed with the tip of her scissors to her dad's old barbering chair in the corner of her early American shop and swallowed the impulse to shed a few tears.

Clyde clicked his tongue noisily. "Wayne sure could cut hair."

Wendy brushed some of Clyde's prickly gray hair off the front of her blue cotton smock. "Yes, he was a great partner. Even when all Dad could do was sit and give me instructions, he taught me a whole lot that I never learned in barber's school."

The old man gave Wendy a quick wink. "Don't get me wrong, little lady. I wasn't tryin' to say you can't cut hair. For a little whip of a gal, you're a real whiz at scissor snippin'."

"Thanks—I think," Wendy said with a grin, as Clyde handed her eight dollars for his haircut. She pulled sharply on the handle of the cash register, dropped the bills inside, then snapped the drawer shut. Wendy moved toward the front door, assuming Clyde would follow.

"You know what a little gal like yourself really needs?" Clyde asked, obviously not in much of a hurry to leave.

Wendy drew in a deep breath, then let it out in a rush. "No, Clyde, what *do* I need?"

Playfully, the old man poked her on the arm and laughed. "You need a man in your life, that's what you need. Maybe someone like that good-looking fellow, Gabe Hunter."

Wendy bit down firmly on her bottom lip. She was trying so hard to be patient with Clyde, but if he didn't head for home soon, there was a good chance she might say something she would probably regret. Clyde didn't understand what it was like for her. No one did, really. She had a deep hurt from the past which affected her response to men. Having so many guys at the shop trying to make a play for her only made things worse.

"Dad is the only man I need," she affirmed, opening the front door and letting in a blast of chilly air. "I have all I can do just to take care of him and keep this little barbershop running."

Clyde shrugged and slipped into the heavy jacket he'd hung on one of the wooden wall pegs near the door. "Suit yourself, Girly, but I think a little romance might be just the ticket."

With that, he crammed his hands into his pockets and strolled out of the shop.

After Wendy swept the floor clean of hair one more time and said good-bye to her final customer of the morning, she leaned heavily against the door and let out a low moan. Her stomach rumbled with hunger, and a feeling of weariness settled over her like a heavy blanket of fog. She licked her lips in anticipation of going home, where she could have something to eat, prop her feet up for awhile, and get in a short visit with the only man in her life. Dad always seemed so anxious to hear what was going on at the barbershop, often plying her with questions about who came in today, what they said or did, and whether Wendy was sure she could handle things on her own. Her father seemed to pride himself on being in total control. He'd run a barbershop for more than twenty years and sent her to barber's school so she could be his partner in this small Northwest town.

However, there were at least two things Wendy knew he hadn't been able to control. First, he'd had no control over his wife's untimely death, when she was killed by a drunk driver nearly ten years ago. That terrible accident had left him a widower with a young daughter to care for. Yet in all these years, she'd never heard him complain. Nor had her fifty-year-old father been able to control the doctor's diagnosis of severe rheumatoid arthritis many years ago. Wendy knew it had been a terrible blow, especially when he'd tried so hard to keep on working. Eventually, he had to turn the shop over to her and retire his barbering shears.

"Why did it have to happen? Sometimes life seems so unfair," Wendy lamented, as she reached for her coat. As she closed the door, a chilling wind blew against Wendy's face, stinging her eyes and causing her nose to run. "I'll be so glad when spring finally comes," she murmured. "At least then Dad will feel more like getting out."

Wendy's house was just a block from Campbell's Barbershop, so she always walked to and from work. The exercise did her good, and it only took a few minutes to get there. As usual, Wendy found the front door of their modest, brick-faced home open. In a town as small as Plumers, everyone knew each other. The crime rate was almost nonexistent. Leaving doors and windows unlocked was one of the fringe benefits of small town living.

Dad sat in his vibrating, heat-activated recliner, staring out the living room window. He offered Wendy a warm smile when she came though the door. Tipping his head, the dark hair now thinning and streaked with gray, he asked the proverbial question. "How's business?"

"About the same as usual, Dad," Wendy answered. "How was your morning?"

"About the same as usual." He chuckled. "Except for one thing."

She draped her coat over the back of the couch and took a seat. "Oh, and what was that?"

"Clyde Baxter phoned. We had quite a talk."

Wendy leaned her head back against the cushions. "Clyde was in the shop this morning. Of course, I'm sure he told you."

He lifted himself from the recliner and reached for his walking cane. "Clyde didn't tell any of his off-colored jokes, I hope. I'll have a talk with him about that, if it's a still a problem."

Wendy shook her head. "He was a perfect gentleman today. Just told a few clean jokes." She propped her feet on the coffee table and sighed deeply, choosing not to mention the fact that the elderly man's stories were repeats from other times he'd been in the shop. "So, what else did Clyde have to say to you, Dad?"

"He thinks you need a man in your life," he said, grunting as he sat down beside her.

Wendy gritted her teeth. "Clyde doesn't know what he's talking about."

Her father reached out to lay a gnarled hand on her jean-clad knee. "You do spend most of your time running the barbershop and taking care of me. A young woman needs a social life. She needs—"

"You're all I need, Dad," Wendy interrupted. She gave his hand a few gentle pats, then abruptly stood. "I don't know about you, but I'm starving. What would you like for lunch?"

He shrugged. "I'm not all that hungry. I thought we could talk awhile."

"If it's about me finding a man, you can forget it." Wendy started for the kitchen but turned back just before she reached the adjoining door. "Dad, I know you have another physical therapy appointment this afternoon. Would you like me to close the shop and drive you over to the hospital in Grangely?"

Her father shook his head. "I've already called People for People, and they're sending a van out around one-thirty."

Wendy nodded. "Okay, if that's what you want." She closed her eyes and inhaled sharply. At least she had managed to successfully change the subject. She headed for the kitchen, wondering, *Now why does everyone suddenly think I need a man?*

Paramedic Kyle Rogers and his partner, Steve, had just

brought an elderly woman to the hospital. She'd been doing some laundry and slipped going down the basement steps. The physicians determined a possible broken hip. Kyle left the woman in the emergency room and was heading to the cafeteria. Steve was parking their vehicle and planned to join him for a much-needed lunch after he checked their supplies.

I sure hope we don't get any more calls for awhile, Kyle thought. *It's only three o'clock, but I'm completely beat!* The morning hours had been full, with several 911 calls coming from the three smaller towns surrounding Grangely. This afternoon they'd already had two local emergencies. Kyle would be the first to admit that the life of a paramedic was often grueling. A few good men and women burned out even before they reached their mid-thirties. Some became harsh and callous from witnessing so many maladies, too.

One of the worst tragedies Kyle had ever seen was a young college student who'd committed suicide by jumping out his dorm room window. The mere image of the distorted man made him cringe. Kyle knew he would never be able to handle such abhorrent things without Christ supporting him.

As he entered the cafeteria, Kyle saw a middle-aged man using a cane with one hand, trying to balance a tray filled with a cup of coffee and a donut with the other. It looked as if the poor fellow was about to lose the whole thing, as it tipped precariously this way and that. Before Kyle could respond, the cup tilted slightly, spilling some of the hot coffee onto the tray.

"Here, let me help you," he said to the red-faced

man. "Where do you plan to sit? I'll set the tray on the table."

The man nodded toward the closest table. "Right there's fine."

Kyle put the tray down and pulled out a chair. "Here you go, Sir."

The man's hand trembled as he reached it toward Kyle. "The name's Wayne Campbell, and I sure do appreciate your help, young man."

Kyle smiled warmly, and being careful not to apply too much pressure, he shook the arthritic hand briefly. "I'm Kyle Rogers, and I'm just glad I happened to be in the right place at the right time." Unconsciously, he reached up to place one finger against the small *WWJD* button he wore on his shirt pocket. Just thinking about the man's gnarled hands filled him with compassion. *I bet those hands used to be hardworking. Probably cradled a baby at one time, or maybe stroked a wife's cheeks with ease. The poor man has lost so much normal function that he couldn't even balance a tray with one hand.*

"Are all paramedics this helpful?" Wayne questioned, breaking into Kyle's thoughts.

Kyle shrugged and ran his fingers through his thick, dark hair. "I can't speak for all paramedics, but I try to do whatever God asks of me."

Wayne nodded and took the offered seat. "You're welcome to join me. In fact, I'd appreciate the company."

Kyle nodded. "Sure, why not? My partner's meeting me here for a late lunch, so if you don't mind sitting with a couple of tired paramedics, we'd be happy to share your table."

Wayne smiled in response. "No problem a'tall. I just finished with physical therapy and was planning to gulp down a cup of coffee and inhale a fattening donut before I head for home."

"I guess I'll go get myself a sandwich," Kyle said. "How about if I get you another cup of coffee?"

Wayne reached into his jacket pocket to retrieve his wallet. "Here, let me give you some money then."

Kyle waved the gesture aside. "Don't worry about it." He grinned and moved over to the snack bar before the older man even had a chance to respond.

A short time later, Kyle joined Wayne at the table, carrying a tray with one jelly donut, two cups of coffee, and a turkey club sandwich.

"You said this was your lunch?" Wayne asked as Kyle took a seat at the small table.

Kyle nodded. "We've been busy all day. There was no time to stop and eat at noon."

He bowed his head and offered a silent prayer of thanks for the food. When he opened his eyes and started to take a bite of sandwich, he noticed the arthritic man looking at him curiously.

"You rescue guys sure do keep long hours, don't you?" Wayne asked, slowly reaching for his cup of coffee.

"Sometimes our days can go anywhere from eight to twenty-four hours," Kyle admitted.

"Wow!" Wayne exclaimed. "That must be pretty hard on your family life."

Kyle shrugged. "I'm single, and it's probably a good thing, too. I don't have to worry about unpredictable hours causing my wife to burn dinner."

With a trembling hand, Wayne set the coffee cup down, spilling some as he did so. Kyle reached across the table and mopped up the mess with a few napkins.

Wayne frowned deeply. "Not only do I manage to nearly dump my whole tray, but I can't even drink a cup of coffee without spilling it all over the place." He shook his head and grumbled, "It's not bad enough that I've messed up my own life, but I'm afraid my only daughter will be strapped with me til the day I die."

Kyle glanced toward the cafeteria door. *Still no Steve. He must have gotten sidetracked along the way. Probably ran into one of those cute little nurses he likes to flirt with. Well, Lord, maybe my mission for the moment is to let this poor man unload some of his woes.* He gave Wayne Campbell his full attention. "What makes you think your daughter will be strapped with you?"

Wayne bit down on his bottom lip. "I'm a widower. My daughter Wendy not only works full-time, but has had the added burden of taking care of me for the last few years."

Kyle rubbed his forehead, praying for the right words of encouragement. "Does she complain about her situation?"

Wayne shrugged. "Not in so many words, but no matter how brave a front she puts on, I can tell she's unhappy." He bumped his hand against the edge of the table and winced. "Her attitude at home is fine, but at work—well, the last time I observed things, she seemed kind of testy."

Kyle patted Wayne's arm gently. "Maybe all your daughter needs is more love and understanding."

Wayne nodded. "You know, you might be right about that, Son. I think Wendy could use a little bit of romance."

Two

Today was Tuesday, the first day of Wendy's workweek. She'd just closed up shop for lunch and was heading down the street toward home when the piercing whine of a siren blared through the air. It was all Wendy could do to keep from covering her ears and screaming. Sirens reminded her of that fateful day when her mother was killed. Clare Campbell had always been a crusader, and keeping the roadside free of litter was one of her many campaigns. She'd been walking just outside of town, picking up garbage as she went.

Wendy, only fifteen at the time, had been at the barbershop that Saturday morning, flirting with all the teenage boys who'd come in for a haircut and watching her father work. She heard the eerie sirens as they whizzed through Plumers, wondering what had happened. Sirens in their small town usually signaled some kind of serious mishap. A fire truck was sent from nearby Grangely for fires, and the paramedic vehicle came for accidents and serious ailments.

Wendy could still see the shocked expression on her

dad's face when a police officer arrived at the barbershop and gave him the news that Mom had been hit by a car. Those sirens had been for her, only it was too little, too late. Clare Campbell was dead—killed instantly by a drunken driver who'd veered off the road.

The blaring sound drew closer now, pulling Wendy from the past and causing her to shiver. As the rescue vehicle flew past, she saw that it was the paramedic truck. Something serious must have happened. Someone would probably be taken to the hospital in Grangely.

Wendy began to walk a bit faster, broke into a cold sweat, then ran at full speed when she saw the vehicle stop in front of her house. It couldn't be! "Please God, don't let anything happen to Dad," she prayed.

Two paramedics were already on the front porch when Wendy bounded up the stairs.

"It's open," she cried. "My father never locks the front door."

One of the men turned to face her. "Did you make the call?"

Wendy shook her head. "No, I just got here." She yanked open the front door and dashed into the living room.

Her father sat slumped over on the floor. His cane, one leg, and both hands were badly tangled in a long piece of fishing line. A well-used rod and reel were connected to the other end of the line, lying at an odd angle against the front of the couch. The phone was on the floor by his hip. Its cord was wrapped around the twisted mess.

"Dad, what on earth happened?" Wendy dropped to her knees beside him, and the paramedics moved swiftly toward their patient.

"Mr. Campbell?" Kyle Rogers could hardly believe it. This was the same man he'd spoken to in the hospital cafeteria just last week.

"You remember me?" Wayne inquired as Kyle donned a pair of surgical gloves.

"Of course. We met at the Grangely Hospital last week," Kyle replied. "You seem to have a bit of a problem, Sir. Are you hurt? You didn't get a fishhook stuck in your hand or anything, did you?"

Wayne groaned and shook his head. "I don't think so, but I'm so glad you're here. I was trying to tie some flies, but I sure made a mess of things, didn't I?" He glanced over at Wendy, who was white-faced and wide-eyed. "Don't look so serious, Wendy girl. I met one of these young men at the hospital," he said, nodding toward Kyle. "He was nice enough to help me with some spilled coffee, and—"

"Dad, I'm concerned about you," Wendy interrupted. "How in the world did you get all tangled up like this?" Her forehead wrinkled. "And why didn't you call me instead of 911?"

Wayne shrugged. "Guess I thought you wouldn't know what to do." He glanced over at Kyle again. "Do you think you guys can get this stuff untangled? It's starting to cut off my circulation—what little I have left, that is," he added with a grimace.

Kyle turned to his partner. "Let's see what we can do to help the man, Steve."

As the two men began to work, Wayne smiled at his daughter and said, "Wendy, this is Kyle Rogers."

Kyle's full attention was focused on the job at hand as he tried to disengage the fishing line without causing Wayne too much discomfort. He did stop long enough to mumble, "Nice to meet you."

"Are you going to be able to get that line off Dad without breaking it?" Wendy asked, glancing at Kyle.

"That's what we're trying to find out, Miss Campbell," Steve answered. "If you'll just move aside so we can have more room to—"

"My daughter's name is Wendy," Wayne interrupted.

"I'm really sorry about all this," Wendy said apologetically. "I'm sure you busy men have better things to do than untangle a fishing line."

"That's okay, Wendy," Kyle said kindly. "We were free when the call came in, and this could have been a real emergency. What if that line had gotten tangled around your dad's neck?"

Wendy nodded and waited silently as the paramedics tried unsuccessfully to unwind the line. Finally, when their efforts seemed futile, Steve took out a pair of scissors from his belt pouch and began to cut.

After a few minutes Kyle announced, "There you go, Mr. Campbell. Freedom at last!"

Wayne smiled appreciatively as the paramedics helped him to his feet and onto the couch.

"Are you planning a fishing trip in the near future, Mr. Campbell?" Kyle asked, as he moved aside the fishing pole that was still leaning against the couch.

"No—no—not really," Wayne sputtered. "I mean, maybe—"

Wendy gave her dad a quizzical look, but when he

didn't acknowledge her, she turned to face Kyle. "If you think Dad's okay, then I'll excuse myself to go fix us some lunch. I need to get back to the barbershop by one."

"You're a barber?" Kyle asked, raising his eyebrows. *Wow! This really is a day full of surprises.*

She nodded. "I have been for the last five years."

"Wendy and I used to be partners," Wayne put in. "Then my rheumatoid arthritis got the best of me, and I finally had to hang up my shaving gear and retire the old scissors." He grunted. "Now I'm just a worthless, crippled widower who sits around wishing he could do something worthwhile with his life."

Steve was already moving toward the door, but Kyle wasn't in any hurry to leave just yet. He pulled out a chair from the dining room table and placed it directly in front of Wayne. He took a seat and leaned forward. "Look, Mr. Campbell, none of God's children are worthless. Just because you're a bit hampered by your arthritis doesn't mean you can't do something worthwhile or have an active social life."

Wayne's eyes lit up. "You really think so?" He turned to Wendy. "Did you hear that? This nice young man thinks I have potential."

Wendy opened her mouth, as if to comment, but was cut off when Steve held up the medication box and asked, "You about ready to head out, Kyle?"

Kyle waved one hand toward the front door. "You can wait for me in the truck. I'll just be a few more minutes."

Steve shrugged, grabbed the rest of their medical cases, and headed out the door.

"You know, Mr. Campbell—" Kyle began.

"Wayne. Please call me Wayne."

Kyle smiled and pointed toward the Bible, lying on the coffee table. "I see you have a copy of the Good Book over there."

When Wayne nodded, Kyle continued. "I hope that means you put your faith in God."

"I try to, but I don't get to church much these days."

"My father doesn't drive the car anymore," Wendy explained.

Kyle eyed her with speculation. "What about you? Don't you drive?"

"Of course I do." She frowned. "Why do you ask?"

Before Kyle could respond, Wayne cut right in. "I bought Wendy a new car for her twenty-fourth birthday last month, and she makes a great chauffeur."

"Dad!" Wendy exclaimed. "I don't think Mr. Rogers cares how old I am, or that you just bought me a car."

Wayne shrugged and offered her an impish, teasing smile. "He did ask if you could drive."

Wendy drew in a deep breath and blew it out with such force, Kyle gave her a concerned look. "Are you all right, Miss Campbell?"

"I'm perfectly fine," she insisted. With a dimpled smile she added, "Thanks so much for rescuing Dad. I'm relieved there was no fishing hook involved and that it wasn't anything really serious. If you'll excuse me, I do need to fix lunch so I can get back to work."

Wendy started for the kitchen, but she stopped in her tracks when her father called, "Say, why don't we ask the paramedics to join us for lunch? You wouldn't mind fixing a little extra soup and some juicy roast beef sandwiches, would you, Honey?"

Kyle glanced over at Wendy. She seemed a bit flustered, and he had a sudden desire to put her at ease. "I'm meeting someone for lunch, but thanks, anyway," he said quickly.

Wendy's ears were burning like a three-alarm fire. *What would possess Dad to invite someone for lunch without conferring with me first? It's just not like him to do something like that.* She shook her head, trying to make some sense out of this whole scene. One minute she had been frightened out of her wits by the sound of a siren, only to see the rescue truck stop in front of her house. The next moment, she was paralyzed with fear at the thought of her father being seriously hurt. Then she felt relief flood her soul when the paramedics were able to get Dad free and discovered that he hadn't been injured in any way by the fishing line. Now, Dad was inviting strangers to lunch! What was going on here, anyway?

"You take care, Mr. Campbell, and remember—God loves you," Kyle said, breaking into Wendy's disconcerting thoughts. "I'm sure if you pray about it, you can find something worthwhile to do." He smiled at Wendy. "It was nice meeting you."

Wendy's heartbeat picked up slightly, but she merely nodded and closed the door behind Kyle Rogers.

"Didn't you think those guys were great? Especially Kyle. What a nice young man he seems to be," her father said.

Wendy shrugged her shoulders. Kyle was nice, all

right. And good-looking, too. His dark, wavy hair looked like something she would enjoy cutting, and those eyes— the color of her favorite chocolate candy. She shook her head, as if to knock some sense into it. She couldn't allow herself to think such thoughts. What had come over her, anyway?

"Paramedics are supposed to be good, Dad, or else they wouldn't be in the rescue business." Wendy flopped onto the couch. She grabbed a throw pillow and hugged it close to her chest. Her hands still trembled from the scare she'd just had, not to mention her unexplained attraction to one *very nice* paramedic. She felt a humdinger of a headache coming on, too. All thoughts of food suddenly faded.

"I know all about what paramedics are trained for," her father said with a smile. "Allied Health Technical College in Grangely not only teaches emergency medical services but gives their students plenty of hands-on experience in the campus lab. The classroom training covers everything from cardiology basics to defensive driving of their emergency vehicles."

Wendy's mouth dropped open. "Just how in the world did you find out so much about paramedic training?" Before he could respond, she hurried on. "And why, Dad? Why would you need to know all that stuff?"

Her father smiled, causing his steel blue eyes to crinkle around the edges. "You know me. I'm always reading and doing some kind of research." He repositioned himself on the couch, then leaned his head against the cushions. "What else is there for a poor old cripple to do all day?"

Wendy shook her head. "You're only fifty, Dad. That's not old. And, while you're not filthy rich, you certainly aren't poor, either. I make an adequate living at the barbershop, and your disability benefits help quite a bit."

He pointed a knobby finger at her. "You didn't bother touching on the subject of me being a cripple though, did you? That's because it's true."

Wendy began to knead her forehead. "Listen, Dad, I know being housebound so much of the time is probably getting to you, but you can't start feeling sorry for yourself. It won't solve a thing."

"Who says I'm feeling sorry for myself?" he snapped.

"Dad, I apologize."

"No, I'm the one who needs to do that," he said in a more subdued tone. "I don't know what came over me. I shouldn't have barked at you." He frowned and reached down to massage one leg. "Guess I'm in a bit of pain right now. It's making me kind of touchy and out of sorts."

Wendy was immediately on her feet. "Oh, Dad, I'm so sorry! How thoughtless of me to forget about the aspirin you usually take with your meal." She started toward the kitchen but turned back. "Listen, about lunch—"

"Just a bowl of soup will be fine for me," he interrupted. "Forget about the roast beef sandwich. I'm not all that hungry, anyway."

She shook her head. "No, I wasn't going to ask that."

"What then?"

"I was wondering why you invited those paramedics to stay for lunch?"

"They looked hungry," he replied with a Cheshire cat grin.

"Yeah, right," she countered. "You're such a kidder, Dad."

"I just thought it would be nice if we had some company for a change," her father said, giving her a look that resembled a little-boy pout.

Wendy came back to kneel in front of the couch. "Dad, if you're really that bored, why not invite Fred, or even good old Clyde over for lunch one of these days? If you give me some advance notice, I might even be willing to whip up something really nice."

He scowled. "Fred and Clyde? You've gotta be kidding, Wendy. Why, those guys and their same old jokes are boring."

"Dad!"

He smiled sheepishly. "Well, maybe not boring exactly, but certainly not full of vim and vigor, like those nice paramedics seemed to be."

Wendy groaned inwardly. She just didn't understand what had come over Dad. Maybe he was in his second childhood or something. Maybe he thought he needed to be around younger people in order to feel youthful.

She gave him a weak smile. "I *am* going out to the kitchen now. I think a bowl of chicken noodle soup might help both of our moods."

Three

O h, brother," Wendy fumed, as she closed the door behind what she hoped would be her last Friday morning customer. She needed at least half an hour to repair the damage left in the wake of little Jeffrey Peterson. Maybe by the time she'd eaten and checked on Dad, her emotions would have settled down.

"If the rest of my day goes as badly as the last few hours, I may consider closing this shop and finding a *normal* job!" she said, leaning against the edge of the counter.

First thing this morning, the Miller brothers came in—without appointments, of course. Rufus and Alvin lived in an old shack just outside of town, and the mere sight of the tall, gangly men made Wendy's stomach churn. Their clothes were always grimy and smelled like week-old, dirty socks. The brothers' greasy, matted hair looked as if it hadn't been washed since their last cut, nearly eight weeks ago. It was a wonder they didn't have a head full of lice!

If that wasn't bad enough, both of the men sported the foulest breath she'd ever had the misfortune of smelling. To add insult to injury, Alvin spit his chewing tobacco into the potted palm sitting in one corner of the barbershop.

Jeffrey Peterson had been her next client, and what a time she'd had trying to get the active three-year-old to sit still! Even with the aide of the booster seat, he'd sat much too low. It was a miracle Wendy didn't take off an ear instead of the unruly mass of bright red hair, glued together by a hunk of bubble gum that could only be cut out. To make matters worse, Jeffrey managed to leave another wad of sticky gum on the arm of her barber's chair.

"Now wouldn't that give someone a nice bonus when they sit down, expecting a haircut or shave?" Wendy grumbled, scrubbing the gummy clump and wondering about the logic of buying that antique, claw-foot gum ball machine. "Maybe I should have gone to beauty school like my friend Sharon."

Suddenly, the bell above her shop door rang, indicating another customer.

She looked up from her gum-removal project and scowled. It was Gabe Hunter, the very man old Clyde Baxter wanted to link her up with. *That will never happen,* Wendy fumed. *Gabe acts like a conceited creep, and the guy thinks he's every woman's dream come true.*

A quick glance at the wall clock told her it was eleven-thirty. While she certainly wasn't thrilled about this particular customer, she knew she could manage to squeeze in one more haircut before lunch.

"Morning, Wendy," Gabe said with a wink. "You're lookin' as pert and pretty as always."

"Flattery will get you nowhere, Gabe," Wendy said through clenched teeth. "At least not with me."

Gabe removed his leather jacket and carelessly threw it over one of the old opera-style seats in the small waiting room. "Aw, come on. You know you find me irresistible. I mean, how could you not? I'm probably your best-looking customer, not to mention the fact that I'm a great tipper." Gabe plopped into the chair Wendy had been scrubbing and planted his hairy hand inches from hers.

"Why don't you sit in that chair?" she suggested, pulling her hand away and motioning to what used to be her father's barber chair. "As you can probably see, this one has recently been initiated."

Gabe shrugged and moved to the other chair. "You know what?"

"No, what?" Wendy shot back.

"I don't have to start work until two today. How about you and me going over to Pete's Place and sharin' a large pepperoni pizza?"

"I'm working."

"Well, you've gotta take a lunch break, right?" he persisted.

Moving away from the gummed-up chair, Wendy grabbed a clean, cotton drape and hooked it around Gabe's humongous neck. He'd been a star football player during high school, and now he worked as a mechanic for the only car repair shop in Plumers. Every time the brute came in for a haircut, he tried to come on to Wendy. Some of the town's young, single women might be fooled by his good looks and somewhat crass charisma, but not Wendy. She'd been burned once, and she couldn't let it happen again. Especially not with some six-foot-two, blue-eyed charmer who didn't have the good sense to know when to keep his mouth shut.

"Well, how about it?"

"How about what?" Wendy sidestepped.

"Lunch—with me." He gave her another wink.

"I'm going home for lunch so I can check on Dad," she said evenly.

Gabe threw both hands in the hair, nearly pulling the cotton drape off his neck. "Whatever!"

"How much do you want off?" Wendy ignored his childish antics and made a firm attempt to get down to business. If she didn't get this guy out of the chair soon, not only would she be late for lunch, but what was left of her sanity would probably be long gone as well.

"Same as usual," came the casual reply. Then Gabe added with a wide grin, "You sure do have pretty blue eyes, Wendy Campbell."

Wendy closed those pretty eyes briefly and offered up a pleading entreaty. *Oh, Lord, please give me strength.* It wasn't really much of a prayer, but it was the first one she'd petitioned God for since her father's 911 scare three days ago.

Wendy had accepted Christ as her Savior at an early age. She'd attended Sunday school and church for many years, too. Prayer and Bible reading used to be an important part of her life.

It wasn't until she began dating Dale Carlson while she was attending Bailey's Barber School in Spokane that things started to change. Dale had been the perfect

Christian. . .or so he'd let on. Dale's mask of self-righteousness came catapulting off when he began making sexual advances, asking Wendy to sacrifice her chastity. Not more than a week after putting Dale in his place, Wendy discovered he'd been sleeping with Michelle Stiles the whole time while coming on to her. The entire episode had shaken her faith in men and her own good judgment. Her relationship with Christ had suffered, as she was no longer sure she could even trust God.

"I don't think you're gonna get much hair taken off by just standin' there frowning like the world was about to end," Gabe declared, disrupting Wendy's reflections.

She shook her head, trying to reestablish her thoughts and get down to the business at hand. The sooner she got garish Gabe's curly, black hair trimmed, the better it would be for both of them.

Half an hour later, Wendy had just taken the clippers to Gabe's neck and was about to dust him off when he announced, "That's not quite how I want it. Could you take a little more off the sides?"

Exasperated with this big hulk of a man, Wendy gritted her teeth, forcing herself as always to comply with the customer's wishes.

"I wouldn't mind having one of those neck rubs you're so famous for," Gabe said when the haircut was finished. "Yep, it sure would feel great to have your soft hands work some of the kinks out of my neck."

Right here is where I draw the line with this guy, Wendy reasoned silently. "I just don't have time for that today, Gabe," she said through tight lips. "I barely managed to squeeze you in for a haircut."

"You're sure not very sociable." Gabe stepped down from the chair. "I've spent the last half hour telling you how great we'd be together, and all you've done is give me the silent treatment."

Wendy chewed on her bottom lip, trying to hold back the words that threatened to roll off her tongue. She moved toward the cash register, hoping he would follow.

He did, but as soon as he'd handed her the money, Gabe blurted out, "If your mood doesn't improve some, you might start to lose customers." He shrugged into his black leather jacket. "Seriously, most folks don't come in here for just a shave or a good haircut, you know."

Wendy eyed him speculatively. "Oh? Why *do* they come in, Gabe?"

"A barber is kind of like a bartender," he said with another one of his irritating winks.

"Is that so?" Wendy could feel her temperature begin to rise, so she took a few deep breaths to keep from saying the wrong thing.

"Yep," Gabe retaliated. "Many barbershops—especially ones that operate in small towns like Plumers—are noted as places where folks can share their problems, tell a few jokes, and let their hair down." He draped his muscular arm across her slender shoulders and smirked. "Get it, unfriendly Wendy? A good barber is supposed to be *friendly* and courteous to their customers."

Wendy grimaced. Gabe had stepped on her toes with that statement. She really did try to be polite to her customers, no matter how much they might irritate her.

115

With Gabe, it was different. She didn't need men like him trying to put her down or take advantage. And she certainly wasn't going to give him the chance to make a complete fool of her the way Dale had.

"Have a nice day, Gabe," Wendy said in a strained voice.

He nodded curtly. "Sure. You, too."

The door was closing behind Gabe when Wendy heard it—that ear-piercing whine of a siren. She shuddered and glanced out the window. An emergency vehicle sped past the shop and headed up her street.

"Oh, no," she moaned, "not again. Please God, don't let it be going to my house this time."

Kyle Rogers couldn't believe he was being called back to the same house he'd been to only a few days ago. The dispatcher said Wayne had called asking for help because he was in terrible pain. What really seemed strange was the fact that the 911 call had come in about the same time as three days earlier. He shrugged. *Probably just a coincidence.*

"Ready?" Kyle asked Steve, opening the door of their truck and grabbing his rescue case.

"Ready," Steve said with a nod.

Kyle rapped on the front door. A distressed sounding voice called out, "It's open. Come in."

When they stepped into the living room, they found Wayne lying on the couch.

"What is it, Sir?" Kyle asked, kneeling on the floor in front of the couch. He had just put on his gloves, when Wayne reached out to clasp his hand.

"I—I've got a cramp in my leg, and it's killing me! Wendy's not home from work yet, but she should be here soon." He drew his leg up and winced in pain as Kyle began probing.

"Is this where the cramp is, Mr. Campbell?"

Wayne shook his head. "No. I mean, yes—I think it's there."

"Do you get leg cramps very often?" Kyle inquired.

"Sometimes. It goes along with having rheumatoid arthritis, you know." Wayne glanced at the door. "Where is Wendy, anyway? She should be home by now."

Kyle gently massaged Wayne's contorted limb. "Is this helping any?"

Wayne thrashed about. "No, no, it still hurts like crazy. I think it's getting worse, not better!" He began moaning, then started gasping for breath. "I can't take it! I can't take anymore!"

"Calm down, Mr. Campbell," Steve admonished. "You're only making it worse."

"He's hyperventilating, Steve. Get a bag."

Steve reached into their supply case and quickly followed instructions, placing a brown paper sack over Wayne's nose and mouth. "Do you think he could be having a panic attack, Kyle?"

Kyle nodded. "It looks that way. Once he begins to relax, we can work on that leg cramp."

The uncooperative patient pushed the bag aside. "Wendy—she—"

"I don't think we should be concerned about your daughter right now," Kyle asserted. "Let's get you calmed down, then we'll see if we can't take care of that charley horse." Kyle took the paper sack from Wayne and held it to his face again. "Breathe as normally as you can, and please, no more talking until we say."

A red-faced Wayne finally complied, settling back against the throw pillows.

Steve had just started to massage the leg again when Wendy came flying into the house.

"What happened? Is my dad sick? He wasn't playing with his fishing line again, I hope." Her eyes were huge as saucers, and her face white like chalk.

Kyle eyed her with concern. "Steady now, Miss Campbell. Why don't you have a seat?"

With an audible moan, Wendy dropped into the rocking chair. "Please tell me what's wrong with Dad."

"He called 911 because he was in terrible pain. When we got here, he said his leg had cramped up," Kyle explained.

"What's the paper sack for?"

"He started hyperventilating," Kyle replied.

"What would cause that?" She leaned forward with both hands on her knees.

"Probably a panic attack, brought on by the stress of not being able to get the pain stopped," Steve interjected.

Wayne was trying to remove the sack again, but Kyle shook his head. "Let's keep it there for a few more moments, Mr. Campbell. It will help you calm down, then you'll be able to breathe better." Kyle turned to Wendy. "Does your father get many severe leg cramps?"

She shrugged. "Some, but nothing he can't usually work out with a bit of massage or some heat." She looked at her father with obvious concern. "Dad, when did the cramping start, and why didn't you call me instead of 911?"

Kyle pulled the sack away so Wayne could respond to his daughter's question.

"I didn't want to bother you," Wayne mumbled.

"Wouldn't it have been better to interrupt my day than to make these men answer a call that could have been handled with a simple heating pad?"

Wayne tipped his head to one side and blinked rapidly. "Guess I didn't think about that. I just wanted to get some relief, and it hurt like crazy, so—"

"When was the last time you had some aspirin?" Steve asked.

"He has to take it with food, or it upsets his stomach," Wendy put in. She glanced over at her father with another anxious look. "I'd better fix some lunch so you can take your pills."

Wayne nodded and pulled himself to a sitting position. "The leg cramp's gone now." He looked up at Wendy. "Some of that take-and-bake pizza you bought last night would sure be good."

"Okay, Dad, if that's what you want."

Wendy was almost to the kitchen when Wayne called, "Let's invite these nice young men to join us. How about it, Guys? It's lunchtime. Does pizza sound good to you?"

"Sure does," Steve was quick to say.

"Count me in, too," Kyle agreed. He cast a quick glance at Wendy. "That is, if it's not too much trouble."

Wendy smiled. "No trouble at all."

Wendy sat across the table from her dad, watching with

interest as he and the other two men interacted. *He really is lonesome,* she thought ruefully. *How could I have let this happen?* She began to massage her forehead. *I've got to figure out some way to help fill Dad's lonely hours.*

"Wendy, are you listening? Kyle asked you a question."

Wendy snapped to attention at the sound of her father's deep voice. "What was it?" She looked at Kyle, who sat in the chair beside her.

"I was wondering about your barbershop."

"What about it?"

"What are your hours? Do you only take appointments?"

"I do take walk-ins, but many of my customers make appointments. The barbershop is open Tuesday through Saturday, from nine in the morning until five at night, with an hour off for lunch at noon." Wendy eyed him curiously. "Why do you ask?" Her heart fluttered as she awaited his answer. Was she actually hoping he might come in for a haircut?

Kyle shrugged. "Just wondering."

"How did you become a barber?" Steve asked. "Isn't that kind of unusual work for a woman?"

"Actually, I've heard that some of the finest barbers are women," Kyle inserted before Wendy could answer.

"That's right," agreed her father, "and my Wendy girl is one of them. Why, she graduated in the top five of her barbering class."

"Spoken like a proud papa," Kyle said with a grin.

"Dad tends to be a little bit prejudiced," Wendy was quick to say. "After all, I am his only daughter."

"And the only breadwinner these days," her dad added, bringing a note of regret into the conversation.

"I served my apprenticeship under Dad," Wendy said, hoping to dispel the gloomy look on her dad's face. "He sometimes forgets that I wasn't always so capable." She shook her head. "If you had time to listen, I'll bet he could tell you some real horror stories about how I messed up several people's hair during those early years. Dad is a wonderful, ever-patient teacher, and if I do anything well, I owe it all to him."

Steve laughed, but Kyle seemed to be in deep thought. Finally, he reached for another slice of pizza and took a bite. "Umm. . .this is sure good." He washed it down with a gulp of iced tea, then changed the subject. "Say, Mr. Campbell, I know you were tying some flies the other day, and I was just wondering if you've done much fishing lately? I hear there's some pretty good trout in several of the streams around here."

Wendy's father rubbed his chin thoughtfully. "I used to fish a lot—back when I could still function on my own, that is."

"When was the last time you went fishing?" Kyle asked, leaning forward on his elbows.

"Well, let's see now," her dad began. "I guess it's been a little more than two years since my last fishing trip. My buddy, Fred, and I went up to Plumers Creek one spring morning. We sat on the grassy banks all day, just basking in the warm sun, shootin' the breeze, and reeling in some of the most gorgeous trout you'd ever want to see."

"Plumers Creek is a great place to fish," Steve put in. "I've been there a few times myself. How come you've never been back, Sir?"

"I don't really think Dad's up to any fishing trips," Wendy interjected. "You saw the way his leg cramped up." She grimaced. "I'm sorry, but there are times when I have to wonder if all men ever think about is hunting, fishing, and telling contemptible jokes."

Three pairs of eyes focused on Wendy, and her dad's face had turned as red as the pizza sauce.

"I, uh, think maybe we'd better go," Steve said, sliding his chair away from the table. "The pizza was great. Thanks, Miss Campbell."

"No, no, you can't leave yet!" Dad protested. "I mean, we were just beginning to get acquainted."

"Our lunch hour's not quite over yet, so we can hang out a few more minutes," Kyle said.

"I really do need to get back to work, Dad." Wendy stood up and grabbed the empty pizza pan. Not only was she going to be late for work if she didn't leave now, but she didn't care much for the direction this conversation was going. There was no point giving Dad false hopes, and besides, sitting next to ever-smiling Kyle Rogers was making her nervous.

"Since your cramp is gone and you seem to be feeling better," Wendy said, moving across the room, "I'll leave you in the capable hands of these paramedics."

Four

*T*wice in one week! Wendy fretted. *Was it a coincidence that Dad had called 911 so often, or did he really think it was an emergency? Was Dad merely "crying wolf" just to get some special attention?*

Wendy was glad they'd made it through the weekend without any more problems. Yesterday, she scheduled a doctor's appointment for her dad; today, right after work, she'd be taking him in for an exam. He didn't know she'd done it, though. He'd been so adamant about his leg feeling better and had assured her several times that there was no more cramping and no need to see Dr. Hastings until his regular checkup later in the month. She'd tell him about his appointment and try to make him see reason when she went home for lunch today.

Wendy's nerves felt all tied up in knots. Maybe that was why she'd been so testy the other day when the paramedics were talking to Dad about fishing. She didn't need any more chilling 911 calls to deal with, either. What she really needed was a little peace and quiet. Maybe she should close the shop for a few days and stay home with Dad.

"That's probably not the best solution, though," she murmured, as she put the "open" sign in the front door of the barbershop. "What I really need is to concentrate on finding some way to make him feel more useful and less lonely. If Dad won't take the initiative, then maybe *I* should give some of his buddies a call about lunch."

Wendy's first scheduled appointment wasn't until ten o'clock, so that gave her a whole hour. She drew in a deep breath and reached for the telephone.

After several rings, a gravelly voice came on the line. "Fred Hastings here. What can I do ya for?"

"Fred, this is Wendy Campbell, and I need to ask you a favor."

"Sure, ask away," Fred said with a deep chuckle.

"You and Dad are pretty good friends. Isn't that right?" Wendy drummed her fingers against the counter where the old rotary-dial phone sat.

"Yep. Right as rain. Why do ya ask?"

"When was the last time you paid Dad a visit?"

There was a long pause.

"Fred? Are you still there?"

"Yep, I'm still here. Let's see now. . .I think it was last month, when I dropped some fishin' magazines by your house."

Wendy grimaced. Fishing magazines? That was the last thing Dad needed, since he could no longer fish. What was the point of adding fuel to the fire by reminding him of what he couldn't do? No wonder he was trying to tie fishing flies.

"Your dad and me went fishin' a few years ago, and—"

A low moan escaped Wendy's lips as Fred began a

long, detailed narration of the last time he and her dad had gone up to Plumers Creek. She was trying to figure out the best way to politely get back to the reason for her call when the front door opened, jingling the bell and announcing an unscheduled customer. Wendy turned her head toward the door, and her mouth fell open. There stood Kyle Rogers, wearing a pair of blue jeans and a red flannel shirt. He looked so manly and rugged. Kind of like one of those lumberjacks who often came into the shop, only he was much better-looking. Another distinction was the fact that none of the woodsmen wore a religious pin on their shirt pocket, announcing to the world that they were trying to live and respond to others as Jesus would.

What would Jesus do right now? Wendy mused. She forced her thoughts back to the one-way phone conversation and cleared her throat loudly. "Um, Fred—someone just came into the shop. I'll have to call you back another time." She hung up and slowly moved toward Kyle.

He smiled softly and ran long fingers through his thick, brown hair. "Hi, Wendy. Do you have time to squeeze me in?"

"Squeeze you in?" she squeaked.

"For a shave and a haircut." Kyle rubbed his stubbly chin and chuckled. "I've heard through the grapevine that you not only cut hair well but can give a really close shave."

Was Kyle flirting with her? Well, why wouldn't he be? Gabe did, and a few other guys seemed to think they could make a play for the town's lady barber, too.

Why should Paramedic Rogers be any different? "I was trying to get some phone calls made, but I guess I could manage a shave and haircut," she said as politely as possible.

He started to move toward her, then stopped. "If this is going to be a problem, I could make an appointment and come back a little later. This is my day off, so——"

Wendy held up one hand. "No, that's okay. The rest of my day is pretty full, so it'll have to be now, I guess."

"Okay, thanks," Kyle said with a grin. "If I wait much longer for a haircut, I might get fired for looking like a bum."

Wendy reached for a cotton drape cloth and snapped it open, nodding toward her barber chair. "Have a seat."

Kyle quickly complied. When he was seated, with his head leaning against the headrest, Wendy hit the lever on the side of the chair, tipping it back so she could begin the shave.

"I'm sorry about the other day," Kyle said, while she slapped a big glob of slick, white shaving foam against one side of his face.

"Oh? What do you have to be sorry about?" she asked, keeping her tone strictly businesslike.

"For upsetting you." Kyle turned his head slightly so she could lather the other side as well. "You were upset when we started talking about fishing, right?"

Wendy shrugged. "Not upset, really. I just don't like it when someone gives Dad false hope."

"False hope? Oh, you mean about going fishing?"

Wendy nodded curtly. "You'd better close your mouth now, or you might end up with it full of shaving cream."

Kyle could only nod at this point, because she'd just placed a pleasantly hot, wet towel over his entire face. He drew in a deep breath, closed his eyes, and allowed himself to relax. Wow! This felt like heaven. Too bad the cute little blond administering all this special attention didn't seem to care much for him. She seemed distant, and if his instincts were working as well as usual, Kyle guessed her father might be right. Maybe Wendy did feel strapped, having to care for him and run a barbershop by herself. He couldn't even begin to imagine what it must be like for her to give shaves and cut men's hair five days a week. From what he'd witnessed in other barbershops, some of the clientele could be pretty crass and rude at times.

Kyle's forehead wrinkled. *I wonder if either Wendy or Wayne ever does anything just for fun. Maybe what they need is something positive to focus on. With God's help, maybe I can figure out some way to help them both.*

Wendy let Kyle sit with the warm towel on his face for several minutes, knowing that the procedure would not only cleanse the face, but also soften his bristly whiskers. When she lifted it off, he opened his mouth, as if he had to say something, but she quickly wiped his face clean and applied more shaving cream.

"Phase two," she explained at his questioning look.

He nodded.

Wendy began to use the straight razor on her client's appealing face. She'd shaved a lot of handsome faces during her years as a barber, but none had ever evoked quite the response from her as Kyle Rogers. It was unnerving the way he looked at her—with dark, serious eyes and a smile that actually seemed sincere.

That's just it, Wendy groaned inwardly. *He "seems" sincere. . .but is he really? Probably not,* she silently acknowledged. *Except for Dad, I can't think of a single man who is truly sincere.* She drew in a deep breath, bringing all the pain of the past right along with it. *Dale wasn't sincere, that's for sure.*

"Are you okay?"

She blinked. "Huh? What do you mean?"

"You look like you are distressed about something."

Wendy gave her head a slight toss. "Sure, I'm fine." She hit the lever on the side of the chair, and it shot into a sitting position with such force, Kyle's head snapped forward. "Oh! I'm sorry about that," she said, reaching for a bottle of aftershave lotion on the shelf behind her. "This chair's a genuine antique, and sometimes when the levers are messed with, it seems to have a mind of its own."

The spicy liquid penetrated Kyle's freshly shaven face as she patted it in place. He winced. "Do all your customers receive such treatment, or do you only reserve the rough stuff for guys like me?"

"Sorry," she said again. "Maybe your face is more sensitive than some."

"Guess so. That's what happens when you rely on an electric instead of a razor blade." He smiled up at her. "You sure have pretty blue eyes, do you know that?"

Oh, no. . .here it comes, she fumed. *That lay-it-on-thick, make-a-move-on-Wendy routine.* She should have guessed

Kyle was too good to be true. "How much hair do you want cut off?" she asked evenly.

He shook his wavy, dark mane. "Guess maybe you'd better take about an inch all the way around."

Wendy deftly began snipping here and there, never taking her eyes off the job at hand, trying to still the racing of her heart. Was she really dumb enough to be attracted to Kyle Rogers, or was her heart beating a staccato because she was irritated about his slick-talking ways and the silly, crooked grin he kept casting in her direction?

"Did you drive your dad to church on Sunday?" Kyle asked unexpectedly.

"No, I didn't. Why do you ask?"

"When I responded to Wayne's first 911 call, he made some mention of not getting out much," Kyle reminded her. "He said he can't drive to church anymore, so I was thinking maybe I could—"

"Well, don't worry about it," Wendy asserted. "If Dad wants a ride, he knows all he has to do is ask me."

"Do you go out much?"

"Huh?" Just where was this conversation leading? She stopped her work and turned his chair so she could see both of their reflections in the antique, beveled mirror. "Just so you know—I don't date—period."

He frowned. "Really? In your line of work, I thought you'd probably have a bunch of guys standing in line."

"I'm far too busy trying to keep this shop running," she stated. "And as I'm sure you must have noticed, Dad needs my help at home."

"I realize that, Wendy, but you do have a life of your own, and—"

"No, actually, I don't!" She gave the chair a sharp turn so she could resume work.

"Then I suppose you wouldn't be interested in attending a Christian concert at my church in Grangely tonight?" Kyle asked.

Wendy clenched her jaw so hard she could feel a dull ache. Never had she wanted to finish a haircut so badly. What was it about Kyle that affected her so?

"I plan to spend the evening playing a few games with my dad," she informed him. "I think he's bored and needs me to spend more quality time with him."

"Maybe he needs to get out of the house more," Kyle suggested.

Wendy stopped cutting again and held the scissors directly over her client's head. "I appreciate your concerns, Kyle, but my father's needs are really *my* business."

He shrugged. "I just thought Wayne might like to go to that concert with us, that's all. There's a very special widow who goes to my church, and since your dad said he likes to fish—"

"Fish?" She grimaced. "What's fishing got to do with a church concert?"

"Nothing," he admitted. "Maybe everything."

Wendy started cutting his hair again. "I don't follow you."

"Edna Stone—the widow I just mentioned—likes to fish," Kyle explained. "In fact, she goes fishing nearly every week. If we could get your dad and Edna to meet, they might strike up a friendship and maybe even go fishing together."

So it really wasn't a date he was asking her on after all. It was her dad he was trying to help. Wendy had obviously misjudged his intentions. However, that reality didn't make her feel much better. In fact, she wasn't sure how she was feeling about now.

"So what are you?" she asked. "Some kind of 911 matchmaker?" Before Kyle could respond, she rushed on. "Really, the last thing Dad needs is some fisherwoman." She made a few more scissor snips, then added, "And need I remind you, he is disabled?"

"I know that, Wendy, but it doesn't mean he has to stop living."

"He's gotten along just fine for the last ten years without a wife, and I don't think he needs, or even wants, one now."

Kyle held up one hand. "I wasn't insinuating that Wayne and Edna would soon be walking down the aisle together." He grinned. "Of course, I suppose that could happen if the two of them should hit it off."

Wendy placed her scissors on the counter, then stepped in front of the barber chair. "I'm only going to say this once, and I hope you understand."

Kyle nodded. "I'm all ears."

Wendy blinked back threatening tears that had unexpectedly filled her eyes. "Dad doesn't need a woman friend or a wife. He just needs me to help fill his lonely hours." She inhaled sharply. "And I'm already working on that."

As Kyle closed the door of his Bronco and started up the engine, he fought the urge to go back to Campbell's Barbershop. He dropped his head forward, until it rested on the steering wheel. *Am I treading on thin ice, Lord?* he prayed. *Am I interested in Wayne and Wendy Campbell because I see a real need, or am I merely experiencing some kind of unexplained physical attraction to the cute little blond barber?*

Kyle didn't date much, mostly because of his crazy work schedule. However, if he were completely honest, he'd have to admit that he was concerned about establishing any kind of serious relationship which might lead to marriage. The life of a paramedic was far from ideal, and trying to balance his career with a wife and children would be difficult, at best. He had no right to subject another human being to his "calling." He really should only date women he would never be apt to become romantically involved with.

"Wendy's father says he's a Christian, but I'm not so sure about Wendy," Kyle said, lifting his head from the steering wheel and turning on the ignition. She'd made no profession of Christianity, and apparently didn't attend church. "She doesn't seem to have any interest in men or dating, either," he murmured.

He pulled away from the curb with a slight smile tugging at the corners of his mouth. "Wayne Campbell needs some help, and I'm pretty sure Wendy does, too, Lord. So, if I am the one to help them, I'm asking for Your guidance in all this."

❧

Wendy was closing the barbershop at noon when she heard the distinctive whine of sirens in the distance. As the sound drew closer, she felt a funny feeling in the pit of her stomach. She uttered a quick prayer. "Not again, Lord. Please, don't let it be another false alarm."

Wendy grabbed her coat. "What am I saying? Do I want a real emergency this time?"

She jerked the door open just in time to see the rescue vehicle fly past her shop. Stepping onto the sidewalk, Wendy could see clear up the street. She watched in horror as the truck came to a full stop in front of her house.

"Oh, no!" she groaned. Not sure whether to be angry with her father or concerned for his welfare, Wendy made a mad dash for home. She stepped onto the porch just in time to meet Steve and an older paramedic who identified himself as Phil Givens. "What's the problem?" she asked breathlessly.

Steve shook his head. "Not sure. When we received the call, the 911 operator said she could hardly make heads or tails out of the man's frantic plea for help."

This had better be for real this time, Wendy fussed inwardly. But even as the words flew into her mind, she reprimanded herself. If Dad really was sick, he needed help, and she needed to be with him. She threw open the front door and spotted her father, sitting in his recliner. He didn't look one bit sick. In fact, Wendy thought he looked more anxious than ill.

"Where's Kyle?" her father asked, looking past Wendy and the two rescue men who had followed her inside.

"Kyle has the day off, Mr. Campbell," Steve explained. "Phil always fills in for him on Tuesdays."

Before Dad could say anything more, both men had opened their rescue cases and donned their surgical gloves.

"What seems to be the problem?" Phil asked, in a business-like tone. "I understand your call was pretty vague."

"I—uh—was feeling kind of dizzy," he stammered. "I'm much better now, though. Probably just got up too quickly."

"We're here, so we may as well check you out," Phil said with a curt nod.

"I agree," Steve put in. "It could be something serious this time."

Phil gave him an odd look. "What do you mean, *this* time?"

Steve shrugged. "This is the third call to this house in two weeks."

"And I just can't believe it," Wendy moaned. "What's the problem, Dad?"

He hung his head. "Nothing. I mean, I thought I was feeling kind of dizzy before, but now—"

"And now you're feeling just fine and dandy? Is that it?" Wendy lamented. She dropped to her knees in front of his chair. "Dad, do you know how bad you scared me?"

"We'll check him over, in case there is something really wrong," Steve said, before Dad could make any kind of reply.

Wendy turned to face the paramedic. "Just so you know, I have no pizza today."

Phil's expression revealed his obvious bewilderment. "Pizza? What's that supposed to mean?"

"Nothing. It doesn't mean anything at all," Wayne cut in.

"Maybe what you need is a cat, Dad," Wendy muttered.

Her father looked at her as if she'd completely lost her mind. "I think you men had better go now," he mumbled. "My daughter and I have a few things to discuss."

Steve hesitated. "But you said you were feeling dizzy. Are you sure you're all right?"

"I'm fine, really." Dad struggled to sit up again. "Sorry about the wasted trip to Plumers."

"You really should think twice about calling 911," Phil stated firmly. "We are extremely busy, and responding to unnecessary calls doesn't set very well with me."

Wendy gave the man an icy stare. "Dad *thought* he was sick."

Phil shot her a look of irritation in return, then nodded to Steve. "Let's get going."

"A cat or dog might not be such a bad idea," Steve whispered as Wendy saw them out the door.

"It's either that, or I may have to consider moving Dad to the Grangely Fire and Rescue Station," Wendy said with a faint smile. She closed the door and leaned heavily against it, wondering what she was going to say to her father, and how to say it without hurting his feelings.

"Look, Dad," she began, moving back to the living room, "I know you're probably lonely, and—"

He held up one hand, as if to silence her. "I'm afraid I have an admission to make."

"Oh, and what might that be?" she asked with raised eyebrows.

"All three of my 911 calls were trumped up."

Wendy waved both hands in the air. "No? You think?"

He laughed lightly, but she didn't respond to his mirth. Those calls had frightened her, and she saw nothing funny about calling out the paramedics for false alarms, either.

He motioned her to take a seat. "It's like this, Honey—I thought Kyle Rogers would be working today, so—"

"Kyle has the day off," Wendy interrupted. "He came into the barbershop for a shave and a haircut this morning."

Dad's face brightened considerably. "He did?"

Wendy nodded. "Yes, but it might be the first and last cut he ever gets at Campbell's Barbershop."

"Oh, Wendy! You didn't scare him off, I hope."

"Scare him off? What's that supposed to mean, Dad?"

"Kyle's a nice young Christian man, and I think he

would make good husband material."

Wendy moaned. "Husband material? Oh, Dad, please don't tell me you've been trying to set us up."

He shrugged, a smile playing at the corners of his mouth. "Okay, I won't tell you that."

"Dad! How could you?"

He hung his head sheepishly. "I thought you needed a man. I thought it might help—"

The rest of his sentence was lost on Wendy. All she could think of was the fact that everything had finally come into crystal-clear focus. Dad wasn't really that lonely, after all. The old schemer was trying to set her up. What in the world was she going to do about this?

⁓✣⁓

Right after lunch, Wendy convinced her dad to take a nap. He had seemed a bit overwrought ever since the paramedics left, and she thought he needed some rest. Besides, it would give her a chance to think things through more clearly.

Wendy closed the door to his bedroom and headed across the hall to her own room. She grabbed the telephone from the small table by her bed and dialed the Grangely Clinic. Since Dad was feeling fine, she saw no reason for him to see Dr. Hastings this afternoon, after all.

A few minutes later, the appointment she'd scheduled had been canceled, and Wendy hung up the receiver. At least, she thought it was hung up. Preoccupied with thoughts of Kyle, Dad, and her own self-doubts, Wendy missed fitting the receiver completely into the cradle. She left the room quickly and took a peek at Dad. He was sleeping like a baby, so she grabbed her coat and headed out the front door.

Outside the house, the air felt frigid. From the gray clouds gathering in the sky, it looked like it might even snow. Wendy stuffed her hands inside her pockets and hurried down the street toward her barbershop, hoping the storm wouldn't be too severe.

When she arrived at the shop, good old, joke-telling Clyde Baxter was waiting outside the door. He was leaning up against the building, just under the swirling, traditional candy-cane-style barber pole, blowing on his hands and stomping his feet up and down. "You're late," he grumbled, "and it's gettin' mighty cold out here. My eyes are sure smartin', too."

When Wendy apologized, his irritation seemed to vanish as quickly as it had come. He chuckled softly and said, "Say, here's a question for you, little lady. When are eyes not eyes?"

Wendy shrugged and opened the shop door. "Beats me."

"When the wind makes them water!" Clyde howled as he stepped inside, then slipped out of his heavy jacket and hung it on a wall peg.

Hanging up her own coat, Wendy let out a pathetic groan. "Sorry, Clyde, but I'm afraid I'm not in much of a laughing mood today. Things got a little confusing at home during lunch, and I ended up staying longer than usual."

"Everything okay with your dad?"

Wendy nodded. "Besides his arthritis, the only thing wrong with Dad is a very bad case of meddle-itis."

Clyde's bushy, white eyebrows shot up. "What's that supposed to mean?"

She shrugged. "Never mind. You probably wouldn't understand anyway."

"Try me," Clyde said, as he took a seat in Wendy's chair and leaned his head back in readiness for a shave.

Wendy drew in a deep breath and let it out in a rush. "For some reason, Dad thinks I need a man, and he's been making 911 calls in order to play matchmaker." She grabbed a handful of shaving cream, and was about to apply it to Clyde's face, when he stopped her.

"Whoa, hold on just a minute, little lady. I whole-heartedly agree with the part about your needin' a man, but what's all this about Wayne calling 911?"

Wendy bit her bottom lip so hard she tasted blood. Wincing, she replied, "In the past two weeks, he's called the Grangely Fire and Rescue Department three times, and they were all false alarms."

"Are you sure? I mean, maybe his arthritis is gettin' the best of him, and he just can't cut the mustard no more," Clyde defended.

Wendy shook her head, patting the shaving foam into place on the old man's weathered cheeks. "They were *planned* false alarms, believe me."

Clyde squinted. "Even if they were, what's that got to do with Wayne becomin' a matchmaker?"

"He's trying to pair me up with one of the para-medics who's been responding to his fake calls," Wendy replied. "It took awhile to learn the truth, but now that I know just what Dad's little game is, I've got a few games up my own sleeve." She shot him a playful wink.

"We'll just see who wins this war."

"I thought you said it was a game," Clyde mentioned as she dropped a hot towel over his face.

"It is," she said with a wry grin. "A war game!"

Six

Wendy lifted her weary head from the small desk where she sat. "When will the pain go away, Lord? Please make it go away." A nagging headache had been plaguing her for hours. She was grateful her workday had finally come to an end. Her last customer, a teenager named Randy, had nearly driven her to distraction. The pimple-faced juvenile had asked for a special designer haircut with the initials *PHS* for Plumers High School cut and shaped into the back of his nearly shaven head. This took extra time, of course, which meant she wasn't able to leave the shop until five-thirty.

Grabbing her coat and umbrella, Wendy stepped outside. It was snowing hard. A biting wind whipped around her neck, chilling her to the bone. Caught in the current, the umbrella nearly turned inside out. With an exasperated moan, she snapped it shut. "Can anything else go wrong today?"

Wendy shivered and tromped up the snowy sidewalk toward home. Today had been such an emotional drain. First, Kyle Rogers coming in for a shave and a haircut, which had evoked all sorts of feelings she'd rather not think about. Then another 911 scare, followed by her father's admission of the false calls. After she'd returned to the shop, there had been joke-telling Clyde waiting, then several walk-ins, ending with Randy Olsen, who had just about made her crazy expecting such a ridiculous haircut! It would be so good to get out of her work clothes and into a sweatsuit. After she fixed an easy supper of canned soup and grilled cheese sandwiches, she would collapse on the couch for a well-deserved rest. Hopefully, after a good night's sleep, she could come up with a game plan. She needed to figure out something that would keep Dad busy enough so he wouldn't have time to think about her needing a man.

As Wendy approached her house, she noticed there were no lights on inside. She thought this was a bit strange. Dad may not have been able to do many things, but he always managed to have several lights on in the living room.

As usual, the front door was unlocked. Wendy turned the knob and stepped inside. Everything was dark and deathly quiet. Believing Dad to still be asleep in his bedroom, she tiptoed quietly into the living room and nearly tripped over something. She bent down and snapped on a small table lamp.

Wendy let out a startled gasp as the sight of her father came into view. He was lying facedown on the floor, with one bloody hand extended over his head. "Dad! Can you hear me, Dad?" She dropped to her knees and shook his shoulder. "Dear Lord, please let him be okay."

Suddenly, Dad turned his head, and his eyes shot open. "Oh, Wendy, I'm so glad you're finally home," he rasped, attempting to roll over.

"What's wrong, Dad?" Wendy's voice shook with fear. "Why are you lying on the floor? What happened to your hand?"

"After my little stunt earlier today, I wanted to make amends," he said, wincing as she helped him roll over, then lifted his hand for inspection. "I was going to make savory stew for dinner, but I'm afraid the knife got the better of me."

"Knife?" she shrieked. "Dad, you know better than to try using a paring knife."

"Actually, it was a butcher knife," he admitted. "I couldn't get my stiff, swollen fingers to work with that little bitty thing you always use."

"So, what are you doing on the floor? Did the blood loss make you dizzy?"

He struggled to sit up. "I guess maybe it did."

"Let me get a towel for that hand, then I'll help you get to the couch," Wendy said as she stood up.

"It's a pretty deep cut," her father acknowledged. "I think it might need a few stitches."

"Just stay put until I get back," she insisted.

Wendy returned with a hand towel, which she quickly wrapped around her dad's hand. "Why in the world didn't you call me, or at least call—" She stopped in midsentence. "I guess after our little discussion earlier today, you weren't about to call 911 again, right?"

"Actually, I couldn't call you or the paramedics," he replied with a scowl.

"Why not?" she asked, leaning over so she could help him stand.

"No telephone."

Her head shot up. "No phone! What are you talking about, Dad?"

He nodded toward the phone, sitting on a small table across the room. "I never even considered calling 911 this time, but I did try to call you. The phone seemed to be dead, though."

Wendy led him to the couch, then moved to the telephone and picked up the receiver. She frowned. "That's funny. It was working fine when I used it earlier today." Before her father could open his mouth to comment, a light seemed to dawn. "I'll be right back."

"Where are you going?" he called to her retreating form.

"To check the extension in my room."

A few seconds later, Wendy returned to the living room, tears filling her eyes. When she knelt in front of the couch, Dad used his uninjured hand to wipe away the moisture on her cheek. "I'm gonna be okay, Honey, so please don't cry."

"The phone was off the hook," she wailed. "How could I have been so careless?" She blinked several times, trying to tame the torrent of tears that seemed to keep on coming. "What if you had bled to death? What if—"

"But I didn't, and I'm going to be fine, now that you're here." He gave her a reassuring smile.

"We'd better get you to the hospital. I'm sure that cut will require stitches."

"In a minute," he replied. "First I want to say something."

"What is it, Dad?"

"My actions over the past few weeks have been inexcusable, and I owe you a heartfelt apology, Wendy girl." He grimaced, as though he were in pain.

She nodded. "You're forgiven."

"I made those phoney calls so you could meet a nice man, but I was meddling," he acknowledged. "Matchmaking and matters of the heart should be left up to the Lord."

"You're the only man I'll ever need," Wendy said softly.

"I'm holding you back," he argued. "If you didn't have to take care of me, you'd probably be married and raising a family of your own by now. If it weren't for my disability, I'm sure you'd be going out on all kinds of dates instead of staying home and playing nursemaid to a fully grown man."

Wendy shook her head. "I'm not interested in dating—or men, Dad."

"Why the 'I-don't-like-men' attitude?" he pried. "You work on men's hair five days a week. I would think by now one of your customers might have caught your eye."

Wendy moaned. "Remember when I was away at barbers' school?"

Her father only nodded in response.

"I dated a guy named Dale Carlson for awhile. He treated me awful, Dad."

"Physical abuse?" he asked with raised eyebrows.

She shook her head. "No—uh—he wanted me to compromise my moral standards—if you get my meaning."

"You should have dumped that guy!"

"I didn't have to—he dumped me. When I wouldn't give in to his sexual advances, Mr. Self-Righteous, Phoney Christian dropped me for Michelle Stiles."

"I guess I must have had my head in the sand," her father said in obvious surprise. "I didn't know you were that serious about anyone, much less realize some knucklehead was treating you so badly."

"I really didn't want to talk about it," Wendy admitted. "I made up my mind after the Dale fiasco that I was done with men." She shrugged. "So many of the guys who come into the barbershop are either rude, crude, or lewd."

"I understand your feelings of betrayal and hurt," her father said, "but you're not right about your interpretation of all men. One bad apple doesn't have to spoil the whole barrel, you know. You can just pluck out the rotten one, and choose a Washington State Delicious."

Wendy smiled at her dad's little pun, then went to the hall closet, where she retrieved his jacket. "The roads are getting bad. I hope it won't take too long to get to the hospital."

"I don't think I'll bleed to death," he said with a sardonic smile. "If I thought it was really serious, I might have you call 911." His forehead wrinkled. "I don't think those paramedics would be too happy to get another call from here today, though."

"You're probably right," she agreed. "That older guy didn't respond to you at all like Kyle Rogers, did he?"

"That's putting it mildly. I think he was more than a bit irritated with me for wasting his precious time today."

"Well, just put it out of your head," Wendy said with a smile. "Tonight, *I'm* going to be your rescuer."

The roads weren't quite as bad as Wendy expected, and they made it to the hospital in twenty minutes. Fortunately, there weren't too many emergencies that evening, so her father was called to an examining room soon after filling out some paperwork.

"Would you like me to go along?" Wendy gave Dad's arm a little squeeze, as a young nurse began to usher him away.

He shook his head. "No, I'll be fine. Why don't you go out to the waiting area and try to relax?"

Relax? How on earth was she supposed to relax when her nerves felt taut and her stomach was playing a game of leapfrog? The headache, which she'd acquired around noon, was still pulsating like a jackhammer too. She would give anything for a cup of hot tea and an aspirin.

Wendy found a chair in the empty waiting room. She rested her elbows on her jean-clad knees and began to methodically rub her forehead. *At least Dad isn't seriously injured, and now that he's agreed to quit playing matchmaker, I don't have to wrack my brain to come up with any plan to steer him in some other direction, either.*

"What are *you* doing here?"

Wendy jumped at the sound of a deep male voice. Kyle Rogers stood a few feet away, smiling down at her. "Kyle! I—uh—Dad cut his hand."

"Another 911 call?" he asked with raised eyebrows.

She shook her head. "Not this time." She didn't bother telling him about the call her father had placed around noon. If the Grangely grapevine was as active as the one in her small town, then Kyle had probably already heard the whole story from the other paramedics.

"What then?" he asked, taking the seat beside her.

"Dad was trying to make supper, and the knife he was using slipped," she explained. "He has a pretty nasty cut on his left thumb, and it bled quite a lot."

"It's a good thing you were home when it happened."

Wendy blinked several times. "Actually, I wasn't. He did it while I was still at work. I found him lying on the floor."

Kyle grimaced. "You drove him to the hospital yourself?"

"Of course," Wendy replied. "After today, I wasn't about to call 911."

"What happened today?"

Wendy shrugged, realizing he must not have heard anything, after all. "It's not important."

She eyed him curiously. "Say, what are *you* doing here, anyway? I thought you were planning to take in a concert tonight. Shouldn't you be there and not here at the hospital?"

He chuckled. "I changed my mind about going. It didn't seem like such a good idea when I thought about attending it alone." He studied Wendy for several seconds, causing her mouth to suddenly go dry. Then he added, "I came here to check on a patient Steve and

I brought in yesterday."

I wish he'd quit looking at me like that, she mused. *What are those serious brown eyes of his trying to tell me? How do I know if Kyle is really what he appears to be? I misjudged a so-called Christian once, and I—*

"It was a little boy who'd been mauled by a dog," he said, interrupting her unsettling thoughts.

"What?" Wendy shook her head and shifted restlessly in her chair, trying to force her thoughts back to what Kyle was saying.

"The patient I came to see," he explained. "A five-year-old boy was playing at his neighbor's house and got in the middle of a cat and dog skirmish."

"How awful!" Wendy exclaimed. "Is he going to be all right?"

Kyle nodded. "He'll probably undergo extensive plastic surgery, but I think the little tyke will be fine."

"It's—uh—thoughtful of you to care so much about the patients you bring to the hospital," she stammered. "I think you go over and above the call of duty as a paramedic."

In a surprise gesture, Kyle reached for Wendy's hand. "I do care about my patients, but I also care about you and your father. In fact, I've been thinking that I might stop in and see you both from time to time—when I'm not on duty, that is."

She swallowed hard. "You've been thinking that?"

He nodded. "I really believe your dad could use some company, and since you're so opposed to me playing matchmaker—"

"Don't even go there," she warned.

He shrugged. "Okay, but I could sure use a good barber."

She pulled her hand sharply away. *So that's all he sees me as—just a good barber. In spite of my misgivings, I was actually beginning to think—hope, really—that Kyle was interested in me as a woman, and not merely someone to give him a shave and a haircut. I knew Mr. Perfect Paramedic was too good to be true. He's probably no different than Dale or Gabe, after all.*

Just when I'm beginning to make a bit of headway, Wendy pulls into her shell, Kyle thought, letting his head drop into his hands. *What's it going to take to break down her wall of mistrust and get her to open up to me?*

"Dad thinks you're perfect, you know," Wendy blurted out, interrupting his thoughts. "He wants us to get married."

Kyle's head jerked up. "What? Your dad wants *what?*"

"He tried to set us up." Wendy's face contorted. "That's why Dad kept calling 911."

Kyle chewed thoughtfully on his lower lip. "All the calls were phoney?"

She nodded. "Every last one of them. He even made a third call around noon today, saying something about feeling dizzy. I thought you might have heard about that one."

He shook his head. "No, I didn't. How do you know he was faking it?"

"He admitted it," she said evenly. "After Steve and Phil left this afternoon, Dad confessed that he'd been trying to play matchmaker all along."

Kyle sucked in a deep breath and expelled it with force. "But today was my day off. I didn't even respond to his 911 call, so—"

"I know," she interrupted. "He was really upset when you didn't show up. That's when I began to get suspicious. Up until then, I just thought he was trying to get attention or simply needed someone to talk to."

Kyle mopped his forehead with the back of his shirtsleeve. "Whew! This is pretty heavy stuff."

She nodded. "My feelings exactly!"

"And here I was trying to come up with some way to fix your dad up with Edna Stone." Kyle shook his head slowly. "Wayne was one step ahead of me all the way, wasn't he?"

"Dad's a pretty slick operator, all right," Wendy admitted. "Guess that's why he did well in business for so many years."

Kyle's eyebrows shot up. "Are you saying that Wayne was dishonest in his business dealings?"

Wendy waved one hand in the air. "No, no, of course not. I just meant—"

"You can see your father now, Miss Campbell," a woman's soft voice interrupted.

Kyle and Wendy both turned to face the nurse who had just entered the waiting room. "Would you like me to go with you?" Kyle asked.

Wendy shook her head. "No, thanks. Dad's my problem, not yours." She stood up and left the room before Kyle could say another word.

"Oh, Lord, what have I gotten myself into?" he moaned.

Seven

O ver the next several weeks, some drastic changes were made at the Campbell house. Dad no longer spent his time playing matchmaker, which was a welcome relief for Wendy. She was sure it had taken a lot of energy for him to scheme and make those false 911 calls. Even though he'd done it out of love and concern for her, she was glad that whole scenario was behind them. Wendy still got goose bumps every time she heard a siren, but she felt a small sense of peace knowing that if the ambulance should ever go to her house again, it would be for a "real" emergency and not some trumped-up illness.

Another change, which was definitely for the better, was the fact that Dad had asked to go to church again. Wendy, wanting to please her father, was willing to accompany him. She hadn't completely dealt with her feelings of mistrust or self-doubt, but at least she was being exposed to the Word of God each week. That fact made her feel somewhat better about herself and her circumstances.

True to his word, Kyle Rogers had become a regular

visitor, both at the Campbell home as well as Wendy's barbershop. A few times, Kyle had taken her father out for a ride in his Bronco and had even made a commitment to see that he would go fishing in the spring—with or without Edna Stone.

"There's no reason your dad can't keep on doing some fun things," Kyle informed Wendy when he stopped by the barbershop one afternoon.

"I doubt that he could even bait his line, much less catch any fish."

"He doesn't have to," Kyle asserted. "I'll do everything for him, and all he will have to do is just sit in a folding chair and hold the pole."

If another customer hadn't come in, Wendy might have debated further. Instead she merely shrugged. "Spring is still a few months away. When the time comes, we'll talk about it."

Kyle flashed her a grin and sauntered out the door.

Wendy frowned. She found his warm smile and kind words unnerving—right along with the verses of Scripture he'd quoted on his last few visits. One verse in particular had really set her to thinking. It was Proverbs 29:35: "Fear of man will prove to be a snare, but whoever trusts in the LORD is kept safe." Wendy's trust hadn't been in the Lord for a long time. She wasn't sure she could ever trust again. After losing her mother, her father being diagnosed with crippling arthritis, then the episode with Dale, how could she have faith in anyone or anything?

There was also the matter of all the crude, rude men and boys who came into her barbershop. She wasn't a "perfect" Christian by any means, but it was difficult to look past all these men's bad habits and sometimes downright sinful ways. How could she ever believe that any man, except for Dad, could be kind and loving?

"Hey, Wendy, are ya gonna cut my hair or not?"

Jerking her thoughts back to the job at hand, Wendy turned toward the barber's chair. Gabe Hunter was eyeing her curiously. It had only been a few weeks, but the egotistic Romeo was back for another haircut.

He probably came in just to bug me, she grumbled silently. *Well, this time I refuse to let him ruffle my feathers. If he thinks he even has half a chance with me, he's in for a rude awakening!*

Kyle left Wendy's shop feeling more confused than he had in weeks. She seemed interested in the Scriptures he'd been sharing with her, and on one occasion had even told him that she and her dad were going to church again. That should have had him singing God's praises. It had been his desire to help both Wendy and Wayne find their way back to the Lord. In a roundabout way, he'd accomplished that, too.

"Then why am I feeling so down?" he vocalized, as he headed toward his Bronco.

You're lonely, Kyle, a little voice nudged. *You've convinced yourself that there is no room for love or romance in your heart. You're not trusting Me in all areas of your life, either.*

"What do you want me to do, Lord—ask Wendy on a date?"

No answer. That still, small voice seemed to have

vanished as quickly as it had come. Kyle scratched the back of his head and grimaced. He needed time to think. He needed time to pray about this. A drive up to Plumers Pond sure seemed to be in order.

"You've got a phone call," Dad announced, as he hobbled into the kitchen where Wendy was cooking.

"Who is it? Can you take a message? Supper's almost ready, and—"

"It's Kyle," her father said with a smirk.

Wendy turned the stove down, put a lid on the spaghetti sauce, and headed for the living room. "Hello, Kyle," she said into the phone. "What's up?"

"I—uh," Kyle stammered.

"You sound kind of nervous."

"Yeah, I guess I am."

"Well, you needn't be. I don't bite, you know." She chuckled. "Some of my customers might think I am pretty *cutting*, though."

Kyle laughed at her pun, which seemed to put him at ease. "Listen, the reason I'm calling is, I was up at Plumers Pond today, and it's still frozen solid."

"I'm not surprised," Wendy replied. "It's been a drawn-out, cold winter, and I'm beginning to wonder if spring will ever get here." There was a long pause, which left her wondering if maybe Kyle had hung up. "Are you still there, Kyle?"

"Yeah, I'm here," he said with a small laugh. "I was just trying to get up enough nerve to ask if you'd like to go ice-skating with me on Saturday night."

"Ice-skating?" she echoed.

"I just found out that the singles' group from my church is going out to the pond for a skating party. I thought it might be kind of fun, and I'd really like it if you went along."

Wendy's mind whirled. Was this a date he was asking her on? Not Kyle dropping by the barbershop for a short visit. Not Dad and her going to a Christian concert—but just the two of them, skating with a bunch of other people their own age. She did enjoy Kyle's company; there was no denying it. In all the times she'd seen him, he'd never once said an unkind thing, or done anything to make her think he was anything less than the Christian he professed to be. Still—

"Now it's my turn to ask. Are you there?" Kyle's deep voice cut into her troubling thoughts.

"Yes, I'm here," she said in a trembling voice. "I was just taken by surprise, that's all."

"Surprised that I ice-skate, or that I'm asking you out on a date?"

So it was a real date then. Kyle had just said as much. Now her only problem was deciding whether to accept or not. Wendy hadn't been on a date since she and Dale broke up, and that had been over four years ago. Could she really start dating after all this time? Could she trust Kyle not to break her heart the way Dale had? Of course, that could easily be avoided by simply not allowing herself to become romantically involved again.

"How about it, Wendy?" Kyle asked, invading her thoughts once more. "Can I pick you up around seven Saturday evening?"

Wendy licked her lips and swallowed hard. She

opened her mouth to decline, but to her surprise, she said, "Sure, why not?"

"Great!" Kyle said enthusiastically. "See you soon."

Wendy hung up the phone and dropped onto the couch with a groan. "Now why in the world did I say yes?"

Being with Kyle and the other young people turned out to be more fun than Wendy expected.

"You're a good skater," Kyle said, skidding to a stop in front of Wendy, nearly causing her to lose her balance.

"You're not so bad yourself," she shot back.

"Are you having fun?" He pivoted so he could skate beside her.

She nodded. "It's been years since I've been on skates. I wasn't sure I could even stand up on these skinny little blades, much less make it all the way around the frozen pond."

"How about taking a break?" Kyle suggested. "One of the guys has started a bonfire. We've got lots of hot-dogs and marshmallows to roast."

"I admit, I am kind of hungry. Guess all this cold, fresh air has given me an appetite."

"Yeah, me too. Of course, I could eat anytime. While I was growing up in northern California, Mom used to say all three of us boys could eat her out of house and home."

Wendy giggled. "So, is a voracious appetite your worst sin?"

He eyed her curiously. "You're kidding, right?"

She shook her head and reached up to slip her fuzzy,

blue earmuffs back in place. "You seem so nice—almost perfect. Dad thinks you're about the best thing to happen since the invention of homemade ice cream."

"Whoa!" Kyle raised one gloved hand. "I don't even come close to being perfect. I may strive to be more like Jesus; but like any other human being, perfectionism is something I'll sure never know."

Wendy shrugged. "Maybe I expect too much from people. Dad says I do anyway."

"Part of living the Christian life is being willing to accept others just as they are, Wendy."

Kyle reached for her hand.

Even though they both wore gloves, she could feel the warmth of his touch. It caused her heart to skip a few beats. Kyle's serious, dark eyes seemed to be challenging her to let go of the past and forgive those who had hurt her. She wanted so badly to believe Kyle was different from Dale or any of the guys who came into the barbershop, wanting more than she was willing to give. How good it would feel to accept folks for who they were and quit looking for perfection. Most importantly, Wendy would have to learn to trust again, and that frightened her. She might be able to trust the Lord, but trusting another man would put her in a vulnerable position. Wendy wasn't sure she could risk being hurt again.

The ride back to town was a quiet one. Both Wendy and Kyle seemed absorbed in their own private thoughts. Only the pleasant strain of Steve Green's mellow voice singing "My Soul Found Rest," filled the interior of

Kyle's Bronco. Wendy struggled with tears that threatened to spill over. She wondered if her soul would ever find rest amid the turmoil of life.

"This is my favorite CD," Kyle said, breaking the silence between them. "Steve Green has so many good songs. I always feel as though the Lord is speaking to my heart when I listen to contemporary Christian music."

Wendy could only nod. She didn't want to admit it to Kyle, but she rarely ever listened to any type of music. In fact, some music actually grated on her nerves, but the song that played now had a serene effect on her. She was beginning to think maybe she should start playing some Christian music in her shop. *That might even deter some of the crude lumberjacks from telling all their lewd jokes and wisecracks,* she mused.

"I'll bet someone could even get saved listening to Christian music like what's on this CD," Wendy said, hardly realizing she'd spoken her thoughts out loud.

"I think you're right," Kyle agreed. "In fact, some of the teens at my church found Christ at a Christian rock concert not so long ago."

Wendy frowned. "I've been a Christian since I was a child, but I strayed from God a few years ago." She had absolutely no idea why she was telling Kyle all this, but the words seemed to keep tumbling out. "After a bad relationship with a so-called 'Christian,' I was terribly hurt and started to get bitter about certain things." When Kyle remained quiet, she added solemnly, "God could have kept it from happening, you know."

"God doesn't always make things go away, just so

we will have it easy," Kyle put in. "Part of growing in our Christian walk is learning how to cope with life's problems and letting Christ carry our burdens when the load is too heavy for us."

"I don't do too well in the trusting department, either," Wendy admitted, leaning back in the seat and closing her eyes.

"Who don't you trust?" Kyle glanced over at her with a look of concern.

"Men," she announced. "I don't trust men."

Kyle's forehead wrinkled. "Not even your dad?"

She opened her eyes and shrugged. "Until he started making false 911 calls, I had always trusted Dad implicitly."

"But he really feels bad about all that and has promised it will never happen again," Kyle reminded. "Just last week, when I took him for a ride up to Plumers Creek, Wayne told me how guilty he felt for telling all those lies." He reached over to pat Wendy's hand. "Your dad's a Christian, but he's not perfect, either. Like I was telling you earlier tonight, we all make mistakes. It's what we do about our blunders that really counts."

"I think I can trust Dad again," Wendy said thoughtfully. "It's other men that give me a problem."

Kyle grew serious. "Other men, like me?"

She laughed nervously. "You get paid to be trustworthy."

"I'm not always working, though," he reminded. "I have to try and be a Christian example whether I'm administering first aid to an accident victim or teaching a sixth grade Sunday school class full of unruly boys."

"You teach Sunday school?" she asked in surprise.

He nodded. "Yep, every other week—on the Sundays when I'm not scheduled for duty. Sometimes those rowdy kids are enough to put anyone's Christianity to the test, too."

Wendy thought about the hyperactive, undisciplined kids who came into the barbershop. They needed to be shown the love of Jesus, too. There had to be a better way to deal with her customers than merely pretending to be friendly, or snapping back at guys like Gabe. At that moment, Wendy resolved in her heart to find out what it was.

Eight

Wendy brought her Bible to the shop to read during lulls. If she was going to find a better way to deal with the irritation she felt with some of her customers, she knew the answer would be found in the Scriptures. She also planned to buy a few Christian CDs, so she could play them at work—both for her own benefit as well as the clientele's.

Today was a cold, blustery Tuesday, and she'd only had two customers so far. She didn't really mind, though, because it was another opportunity to get into God's Word. She grabbed an apple from the fruit bowl on the counter, dropped into her barber's chair, and randomly opened the Bible to the Book of Matthew.

Chapter seven dealt with the subject of judging others. Wendy was reminded that instead of searching for sawdust in someone else's eyes, she should be examining her own life and looking for the plank which would no doubt be there, in the form of her own sin. She chewed thoughtfully on the Red Delicious apple and let the Holy Spirit speak to her heart. Instead of enjoying the unique variety of people who frequented her shop, she'd been judging them. Rather than allowing herself to get a kick out of the clean jokes and witnessing about the Lord to those who told off-color puns, she'd been telling herself that all men were bad. Even though Kyle Rogers had made an impression on her with his tenderness, patience, and kind words, Wendy had questioned his motives. This was judging. There was no getting around it, and according to God's Word, Wendy was no better than the worst of all sinners. If she didn't get herself right with the Lord, she, too, would be judged.

Without a moment's hesitation, she knew what she must do. Wendy bowed her head and prayed fervently, "Father, please forgive me for my negative, condemning attitude. Heal me of the hurt deep in my heart, and help me learn to love others, just as You do. Help me to trust You and become a witness of Your love and grace." A small sob escaped her lips. "And if Kyle Rogers is the man you want me to love and trust, then please give me some sign." When she finished her heartfelt prayer, Wendy opened her eyes. For the first time since her broken relationship with Dale Carlson, she felt a sense of peace flood her soul. She was released from all the pain of the past and knew that with God's help, she could finally be a witness for Him.

Wendy glanced out the front window and caught sight of Harvey, the mailman, slipping some mail into the box outside the shop. She stepped down from the chair. Taking one more bite of the crisp, juicy apple, she headed outside, not even bothering with a coat.

Kyle was just rounding the corner, heading up the street

toward Campbell's Barbershop, when he saw Wendy come out the front door. His mouth curved into a smile. He hadn't seen her since their date last Saturday night. He could only hope that she'd be as glad to see him as he was to see her now.

Kyle had spent most of the weekend thinking about Wendy and the way she made him feel. His resolve not to get romantically involved with any woman was quickly fading, and he seemed powerless to stop it. He'd read the Scriptures and prayed until there were no more words. He'd petitioned God to show him some sign that Wendy might be able to respond to his love. He didn't have a clue what it might be, but just the same, he'd made up his mind to come to the shop today and have a heart-to-heart talk with Wendy. If she would agree to at least give their relationship a chance, then he was going to trust God to work out all the details that seemed impossible to him. After all, if he was really trying to do the things Jesus would do, it wasn't his right to make decisions about the future. Fear that his job would get in the way of love or marriage could no longer be an issue.

Kyle watched in fascination as petite little Wendy, wearing only a pair of blue jeans and a long-sleeve blouse, covered with a green smock, reached into the mailbox. It was a cold day, and there was still snow on the ground. The sidewalk appeared slick, like the frozen pond, with ice glistening in the sun's golden rays. Kyle was about to call out for her to be careful when the unthinkable happened. Just like an ice skater who'd lost her balance, Wendy's body swayed first to one side, then the other. Her feet slipped and slid while she tried hopelessly to regain her balance. There seemed to be nothing Kyle could do but stand there and watch, as beautiful little Wendy went down, landing hard on her back and hitting her head against the icy, cold sidewalk.

Doing a fair share of slipping and sliding himself, Kyle raced down the sidewalk to Wendy's aid. When he discovered that she wasn't conscious, his paramedic skills kicked in. From the evidence of the apple core lying nearby, Kyle was quite sure Wendy not only had the wind knocked out of her, but was probably asphyxiating on a piece of that apple. He knew what he had to do, and it must be done quickly, or she would choke to death.

Kyle positioned her head and knelt closer. *Look, listen, feel for air. . .*his training ran through his mind.

Nothing!

He repositioned her jaw again, but to no avail. When he tried to give her mouth-to-mouth, it didn't work. Everything confirmed his worst suspicions: A small piece of the offending fruit must be stuck in her throat. He went into immediate action and was able to dislodge it, using the Heimlich maneuver. His initial burst of praise and elation faded at once when Wendy still didn't breathe on her own. Fearful for her life, yet relying on his faith, he began mouth-to-mouth resuscitation again.

Breathe, Wendy, Honey. . . God, please make her breathe. . . .

Though she started breathing, she still didn't regain consciousness. "Wake up, beautiful lady. I haven't told you what I came to say." Kyle quickly examined her to be sure nothing was injured. He prayed earnestly, "Oh, Lord, this is not the way I planned for things to be. I had a whole speech prepared for Wendy, and now I may never get the chance to say what's on my mind. Please, Lord—let her be all right."

Wendy's eyelids popped open. Someone's lips had been touching hers. They were soft and warm. She thought she'd heard a voice. Had someone called her *beautiful?* Kyle stared down at her with a look of love and concern etched on his handsome face. Where was she, and why was he leaning over her? She was sure that she must be dreaming.

"W–what happened?"

"I was coming to your shop so I could talk to you about something very important," Kyle explained, gently stroking the side of her face. He leaned closer and kissed her forehead, his tears falling to her cheeks. "I saw you slip and fall on the ice. You choked on that apple." He pointed to the small piece, just a few feet away. "Thank God you're alive!"

"I was just finishing the apple when I walked outside to get the mail. I–I—"

Kyle placed one finger against her lips. "Shh. . . don't try to talk right now." He probed the back of her head gently with his fingers. "As amazing as this may seem, there's not even a lump. Does your head hurt anywhere?"

She smiled up at him, tears gathering in her own eyes. "No, not really. I think I just had the wind knocked out of me."

"You looked so helpless and beautiful—just like Snow White, lying there beside that Red Delicious," Kyle said with a catch in his voice. "Only your apple wasn't poison, and I thank God you responded to the Heimlich maneuver, then mouth-to-mouth resuscitation so quickly."

"Mouth-to-mouth?" she echoed, bringing her fingers up to lightly touch her lips. "At first I thought I was dreaming. Then I opened my eyes and thought I'd been kissed by a very handsome man." A shiver ran up her spine, and she knew it was not from the cold. "And you must be Prince Charming, who came along and rescued me."

He nodded. "I know God sent me here today, but I sure didn't think I'd be playing the part of a paramedic on my day off."

She smiled up at him. "You've rescued me from a whole lot more than a fall to the ice and an apple stuck in my throat."

"Really? What else have I rescued you from?" Kyle asked, never taking his eyes off her smiling face.

She swallowed hard. "Your kindness, patience, and biblical counseling have all helped. I was reading my Bible right before I came outside, and God's Word confirmed everything you've been trying to tell me."

"I'm so glad," he said sincerely.

"Thanks for saving me," she whispered as she sat up. "I—I probably shouldn't be saying this, but I think I might be falling in love with you."

"You took the words right out of my mouth." He bent his head down to capture her mouth in a kiss so sweet it took her breath away.

"Oh, Kyle," she purred, when their lips finally separated, "if you keep that up, I might be forced to call 911."

He laughed heartily. "Guess I'd better get you inside to the phone then, because now that God has finally kicked some sense into my stubborn head, I'm liable to keep kissing you all day long."

Wendy drew in a deep breath and leaned her head against his strong shoulder. As they entered the barbershop a few moments later, she murmured, "Thank You, Lord. I think I can learn to trust both You and Kyle now." Her flushed cheeks dimpled as she smiled. "And thank you, Dad—our matchmaker 911."

WANDA E. BRUNSTETTER

Wanda was born in Leavenworth, Kansas, raised in Tacoma, Washington, and now lives in a small town in central Washington, where she enjoys four distinct seasons. Her hobbies include doll repairing, stamping, reading, and gardening.

Wanda began writing when she was a young adult and has had several hundred stories, articles, poems, puzzles, and puppet plays published with a variety of Christian publishers. She became a Christian at a young age and has served the Lord in some capacity ever since she was a teenager. She has two children, six grandchildren, and has been married for thirty-eight years to an out-going pastor. Together she and her husband, Richard, have a puppet ministry that they often share at other churches, Bible camps, and Bible schools. Wanda's first inspirational novel, *A Merry Heart*, was published with **Heartsong Presents**.

Wellspring of Love

by Pamela Griffin

Dedication

As always, I dedicate this story to my Savior,
who has rescued me in more ways than one.
Without His love and mercy,
I would not be here today.
With special thanks to my
"helpful critters" on this project—
Tracey B., Tamela H. M., and my mom, Arlene T.—
for their support and helpful suggestions.
I also wish to thank Sue from FCFI,
my mother-in-law, Mary, and my local police station
and fire station for their patience and aid in
answering my multitude of questions.

When you pass through the waters,
I will be with you. . .
when you walk through the fire,
you will not be burned.
Isaiah 43:2

One

S how me! Show me! Please?" Huge blue eyes shone wistfully from a face smudged with strawberry jam. "Pretty please with lotsa chocolate sprinkles, an' whipped cream, an' cherries on top?"

Cat McGregor eyed her five-year-old nephew with a mixture of love and frustration. "I haven't thrown one of those things in a long time, Sport. I'm not even sure I'd remember how. Besides, the ground is too muddy."

Trey lowered his head and kicked at a knothole on the wooden porch with the toe of his tan cowboy boot. "Aw, Aunt Cat. You always say that. All it ever does here is rain!"

Her heart twinged at his crestfallen look. Well, what was a little mud? Besides, didn't mud and boys go together? And it was such a nice day. . . .

Grinning, she tousled his mop of wavy blond hair. "All right then. Let's see *you* give it a try."

Uncertainty crossed his features, but he awkwardly raised the hand holding his new glow-in-the-dark Frisbee to his opposite shoulder, concentrated on the wide area off the back porch, and flung it hard. The disc shot at a downward angle and sliced through the new shoots of green grass.

"See," he moaned, "I don't know how. I need you to show me!" He clomped down the wooden stairs, retrieved the Frisbee, returned to Cat, and offered it to her.

She blew out an exasperated breath. Her gaze swept over the acreage of huge backyard—once her great-granny's farm—then back to Trey. The look in his eyes would have put a begging puppy dog to shame.

"Oh, all right." She pushed up the sleeves of her beige windbreaker. "Let's see what your old auntie can do."

"Aw, you're not old, Aunt Cat," Trey said with a smirk, exposing the gap of his missing front tooth. "Lonnie Miller says you're one of the purtiest gals in the whole county, an' that he's gonna marry you someday!"

Her cheeks burned. "You shouldn't tell tales, Trey. It's not nice."

Hurt furrowed his brow. "But I'm not telling tales! He really said it. Honest, he did! I heard him tell his friend at the gas station last week when you were pumping gas."

"Oh, he did, did he?" How dare the man! Having him for a fellow classmate in grade school and junior high had been bad enough. Cat continually had endured spitballs shot into her hair from behind—and the pencils and pens he borrowed were never returned—since alphabetical seating always placed her directly in front of the class clown.

"Well, let me tell you something, Trey Stockton," she fumed, anger at the absent culprit making her words come out with the speed of pelting BBs. "I am not now, nor ever, going to get married to anyone—nohow, noway. Is that clear? I don't need any man, and you can tell him I said so. Now, gimme that thing!"

She seized the plastic disc with one hand. Turning, she hurled the Frisbee with the force of a superhero. They watched as it sailed high and fast through the air in an upward arc, past the decorator well, to come to a sudden, rustling stop—high in the branches of a nearby oak.

Cat waited for it to fall. It didn't. Of all the crazy. . . how could it get stuck up there when there were no full-grown leaves—only buds—blocking it?

"Aunt Cat, how we gonna get it down?"

Her gaze swung to her nephew. His eyes were starting to tear and his mouth trembled. It wasn't often he received new toys—just the occasional used one from the thrift store. Since the fire at the day care center took Cat's job two months ago and their only income now came from her sister's job as a teller at the bank's drive-thru window—and the pretty jars of homemade preserves they sold to Brady's souvenir store—they'd needed to pinch pennies.

She looped an arm around Trey's bony shoulders, drawing him close. "Don't you worry, Sport," she said, her gaze lifting to the tree. "Aunt Cat has a plan. . . ."

Blaine Carson fiddled with the silver dial of the ancient radio, trying to find anything but country music and political talk shows. Too bad his CD player was broken. After sending the red marker clear across the numbered screen, he frowned and clicked off the radio. What else could he expect in this small, rural Texas town? Still, he was glad he'd moved to Loggin's Point. Big-city life had been exciting, and his job as a Dallas firefighter reward-ing—until last year had changed things, that is.

Giving a rueful shake of his head, he determined to forget the past. There was no going back and chang-ing it.

He glanced out the streaked window of his blue Ford pickup and smiled, waving to old Mrs. Celina Partridge sitting on the wooden porch of her cracker-box home. She continued swinging back and forth in her rocker, not acknowledging his greeting. He sighed and turned onto the street that would take him to the cramped apartment he shared with his old college roommate and fellow firefighter Mark Higgs. He looked forward to a steaming hot shower and some R and R. The guys who shared his shift had been noisy, sitting around the table in the kitchen, playing dominoes, while Blaine stretched out on a cot in the bunkroom. Blaine didn't know the game Forty-two, but it would've been nice if they'd at least asked him if he wanted to join in.

Three months at Loggin's Point hadn't gained him the people's trust or acceptance. Not one bit. Even most of the guys at the station treated Blaine as an out-sider, playing practical jokes on him, never considering him their equal. He wondered if it was because he was the youngest and newest of the bunch, or if it was because he'd seen a lot more action, coming from a big city, and they were jealous of his experience.

Staring out the windshield at the pasty gray sky

above the newly furrowed fields, Blaine pursed his lips in thought. Thankfully, the three days of rain had stopped, and the rest of the week promised sunshine. He looked forward to the singles' Bible study—since he'd been on duty and missed out the last time they'd met. At least that group didn't reject him.

The computerized sound of "Charge!" came from the passenger seat. He plucked up his cell phone—his good-bye present to himself before he'd left Dallas—and flicked it open and on.

"Carson here."

"This is Rogers. Tried to page you, but your pager must be off. Got an emergency. The engine is out responding to another call, and I need you to check it out."

Blaine sat up straighter, alert. Two calls at the same time? Having two calls within a twenty-four-hour weekday shift was rare enough in this sleepy little town. "I'm listening."

"You still got that slide ladder in the back of your pickup truck?"

"Yeah."

"Need you to head over to the McGregor place on 412 Mercer Lane—off the state highway, about four blocks from where you live. White frame house—green shingles—tall cedar trees out front. Cat's up a tree."

Blaine stared straight ahead, his hand tensing on the wheel. A cat? They were sending him out for a *cat*?

"You there?"

"Yeah, I'm here." There was no masking the disgust in his voice.

"Martha took the kid's call and dispatched a squad

car, but they probably don't have the equipment they need. Are you on it?"

"Yeah, I'm on it," Blaine growled and punched the cell phone off. This had to be another practical joke. He'd never thought Earl Rogers would gang up on him, too. He was a play-by-the-book professional who took his job seriously. . .come to think of it, so did all the firefighters at the station. Their pranks had only been played between calls and during off-duty hours—never during emergencies.

But a cat? That was considered an emergency?

Blaine shook his head and gunned the motor as he drove up the road leading to Mercer Lane. He didn't know much about small-town living. Maybe a cat up a tree was an emergency here in Loggin's Point. Still, he felt like ten kinds of a fool. He supposed he'd better get over his aversion to furry felines and fast, if he was to do this job.

Within minutes, Blaine found the location, pulled into the long, tree-lined gravel drive beside the patrol car, jumped out of his truck, and grabbed the slide ladder resting in the back among his other emergency supplies. As he approached the rear of the neat little farmhouse, two policemen hurried around the bend and toward him, one with a radio in his hand.

Good. Maybe they'd already taken care of the problem.

The stocky one acknowledged Blaine, a look of relief in his brown eyes as he tugged on the brim of his tan hat, his fast-paced gait never wavering. "Glad you're finally here. We just got another call—a robbery at the Food Mart. Takes priority over this, I'm afraid."

Blaine nodded, resigned.

"Don't think you'll have much of a problem," the policeman threw over his shoulder as he wrenched open the driver's door of the marked car.

"Wanna bet?" his younger partner said in a quick aside to Blaine as he hurried past. "She's spitting nails. Watch those claws!"

Blaine wistfully eyed the patrol car as it tore out of the drive, its red and blue lights flashing, its siren wailing. He wished he could go with them. Helping to apprehend a gunman would be preferable to the next few minutes, he was sure.

Sighing, he hefted the metal ladder under his arm to get a better grip and headed toward the back.

Cat straddled the thick limb, her legs dangling. Every time she tried to move, the sharp branch snaking up under the back of her windbreaker dug further into her shoulder blades. She should've known better than to climb this stupid tree! Any moron knew that muddy sneakers didn't provide good traction.

"Are you still mad at me, Aunt Cat?" a woeful voice asked from below.

She looked the ten or so feet down at Trey's upturned face and sighed. "No, Sport, I don't guess I'm mad at you at all. You only did what your mommy taught you."

She still wished he would have heard her when she had yelled after him *not* to call 911, but he had already slammed the screen door shut. Poor tyke had been pretty scared when Cat slid, lost her balance, and half-fell, half-groped her way several feet down through snapping twigs and boughs—until she'd come to a sudden and painful stop on the thick branch where she was now stuck.

Well, at least Officer Barnes and Officer Trask had left—and good riddance! She didn't need their help. She could get down fine on her own. If she could just think of a plan. . .

Footsteps squelching through the mud brought her head around, and she watched as a dark-haired stranger rounded the side yard. He came to a sudden stop, his mouth dropping open in surprise. One end of the long ladder he carried under a muscular arm thumped to the ground.

She eyed his attractive features, his trim, muscular build in slim-fitting jeans and T-shirt, and her heart hardened against him. Drawing herself up the best she could without spearing herself, she glared down. "Well, what do you want?"

She thought she saw his mouth twitch in amusement, but of course from this height it was impossible to tell.

"I got a call about a cat up a tree," he replied in a smooth voice, as rich as imported chocolate—and probably just as decadent. "But you don't look like any cat I've ever seen." From his tone, it was obvious he was mystified, yet amused, which only served to annoy her further.

Trey jumped in, his head tilting back to look at the stranger. "I called 911 all by myself," he declared proudly. "Just like Mommy told me to do if anyone gets in

trouble. Aunt Cat tried to get my Frisbee, but fell
down and got stuck. Are you gonna rescue her?"

"Aunt Cat, huh?" the stranger repeated, no longer
trying to hide his smile as it stretched wide across his
disgustingly handsome face. "Well, well. I'll see what I
can do, Partner. Looks like you're a hero. You were
right to call 911."

He ruffled Trey's hair, then repositioned his ladder
under his arm and headed in her direction, his laughing gaze moving upward to her.

Cat flung one hand out, palm facing him, while
holding tightly onto the branch above with her other
hand. "Just hold it right there," she snapped. "As I told
the two policemen that were just here, I don't need any
help. I can get down perfectly fine on my own."

One dark brow lifted. "Hmmm. Yeah. I can see
you're handling it quite well." He continued to walk
toward her, never breaking stride.

"I mean it," she reiterated. "I don't want your help.
I have a plan." Desperate, she lifted her sneaker, placed
the sole on the limb, and again tried to gain leverage
while hoisting herself up, both hands clutching the
branch above her. Her foot slid, and she landed with a
jarring thud on her bottom, shaking the limb. Pain
screamed along her inner thigh. Even through the
thick denim material she could feel the scrape. The
ache in her leg rivaled the pain stabbing her back.

"Tell you what," he said as he pushed the short,
wooden ladder she'd used aside with his foot and
positioned his tall, metal ladder firmly against the
trunk. "I'll set this here, just in case. How's that?" He

moved to stand under her, his hiking boots planted about a foot apart, lean fingers casually splayed against his hips, face tilted upward.

Craning her neck, Cat leaned front and sideways to see him better, trying to figure out what he was up to, ignoring the tension this produced at the back of her windbreaker. Her hands moved to grip the branch she straddled, to steady her. "I told you, I don't need any help. I can figure this out by myself. Just go away."

"Well, Ma'am," his voice changed to a slow drawl, "I'm afraid I can't do that. You see, this is part of my job, and it wouldn't be right for me to just walk off, now would it?"

"Stop patronizing me! I'm not a child!"

"Yes, Ma'am. I can certainly see that."

Heat flushed her face as she leaned further over. "Oh, you are the most irritating ma—"

Her words broke off as she heard the unmistakable sound of the branch up her jacket cracking. Her hands flailed in surprise as the sudden lack of restraint unbalanced her. Falling forward, she made a quick grab for a handhold. One hand caught air. A sharp twig slapped against her other open palm, and she caught its thicker branch. She yelped, somehow managing to keep her legs looped around the limb while she swung sideways. Her shirt had come loose from her waistband, and the rough bark grated against her tender midriff. She hugged the now-bowing limb like a child cuddling a teddy bear.

"Don't panic," the steady voice beneath her commanded as she clung in her tenuous position. "Let go of the branch. I'll catch you."

"Not on your life," she gasped, her nails digging into the wood.

"Listen to me. That limb looks like it could give way any second. It doesn't look strong enough to support you. I've caught people before—this is not a first for me—and there are only about thirteen feet separating us."

Thirteen? That sounded a lot worse than ten.

A creaking sound from directly beneath her emphasized his urgent words. "Can't you use the ladder?" she said, biting the inside of her lower lip, half in resignation, half in fear.

"It's not a stepladder, and there's not enough time for me to climb the tree. Now, let go. Come on, Kitten. I've done this kind of thing for years. Trust me. It's going to be all right."

His cajoling words shattered any softening she might have felt toward him. She tightened her hands around the branch and slowly inched her body upright, her trembling arms the only evidence of her fear. "I said. . .I can do it. . .by myself."

A bee whizzed by her ear. Without thinking, she swatted at it with a quick flap of her hand. The motion set her off balance again. She pitched sideways—and down.

Air rushed by, a branch thwacked her shoulder, and the next thing she knew, a grunt sounded as she hit something solid and warm. Strong arms immediately wrapped around her. Their bodies flew backwards, tumbling to the muddy ground.

Winded, she lay against her rescuer for a moment,

her ear against his chest, able to hear the rapid and strong thud of his heartbeat through the soft, blue, cotton fabric. She lifted her head and looked close into magnetic, ebony eyes.

"Well, I gotta admit," he drawled after several pulse-racing seconds had elapsed, "you've got to be the prettiest and bravest cat I've ever come across in the whole state of Texas." A grin turned up one corner of his mouth. A laugh line, much like a dimple, winked at her. "And definitely the orneriest."

Two

Pink tinged her scratched cheeks, and her blue green eyes sparked. Her mouth opened, but before she could speak, an incredulous and amused female voice sailed to them from the porch. "Ahem! Am I interrupting something?"

Cat's entire face flooded with color. She pushed away from Blaine, and he reluctantly dropped his arms from around her, allowing her to stand.

"Of course not, Shelby, don't be ridiculous," Cat snapped.

Blaine watched her pluck a few twigs from her red gold cap of springy curls, then wipe vainly at her muddy jeans, before he, too, struggled to get up. She looked as though she weighed no more than one hundred pounds, but she sure knocked the breath out of him when she'd fallen into his arms. Literally and figuratively. He'd never been much attracted to redheads, but there was something about the slight figure he'd held that had made him never want to let go.

"I'm a hero, Mommy!" the little boy squealed as he ran to the woman. "I called 911, just like you told me, and the man came and rescued Aunt Cat."

"What?" The woman, whose red hair was a few shades darker than Cat's, caught the boy to her. Her confused gaze lifted from her son to Blaine, and then to Cat. Alarm registered across her face, her eyes widening. "What happened to you?"

"I'm all right. I was trying to get Trey's Frisbee out of the tree," Cat said, self-consciously putting a hand to her scratched cheek to wipe away a spatter of mud. "I got stuck."

"Stuck?"

"I'll explain later." Cat's eyes flicked Blaine's way. "I guess I owe you my thanks."

Her reluctance amused him. "All in a day's work, Ma'am," he said with a grin. She quickly broke eye contact.

The other woman walked down the steps and toward him. "Well, I have no idea what's going on here, but from what I gather, you helped Cat in some way. I'm Shelby, Cat's sister. Would you like some coffee. . .or maybe the use of a shower?" Her dark blue eyes sparkled with mirth. "I have some of my husband's old clothes packaged for Goodwill inside. You're about his size, I think."

Blaine cast a curious glance down at his muddy clothes and could just imagine what the back of him looked like. The aroma of fresh-brewed coffee wafted through the screen. The offer was tempting—yet Cat's horrified gasp at hearing her sister's words helped him make his decision.

"If you've got an old sheet I can use to put over the

seat of my truck, that should do fine. Name's Blaine Carson, by the way." Finding a clean part of his jeans, he wiped off his hand and held it out to Shelby. "I'm new to your community. Only been here about three months."

Recognition lit her eyes as she shook his hand. "You go to Spring of Life Church, don't you? I think I've seen you there a couple of times."

"I do when I'm off duty. I spend my time at the fire station when I'm not."

"Oh! Then you're the new firefighter Ginny told me about." Shelby looked from Blaine to Cat, then back to Blaine again, her smile widening. "I've heard a lot of nice things about you."

Blaine could imagine the wheels spinning in the woman's head and believed Shelby might be considering playing the role of matchmaker. Strangely, the thought didn't bother him, though he'd always shied away from such things in the past.

Cat's eyes narrowed. "The man asked for a sheet, Shelby. Shall I go find him one?"

"No," Shelby said, the grin still on her face. "I'll be back in a flash."

Trey ran in after her and the screen door slammed, leaving Blaine and Cat alone. Instantly, she shifted her gaze sideways to a decorator well made of gray rocks and covered with potted plants. Ivy looped around the wooden crossbar, and a platform covered with an outdoor green carpet lay over what would have been the opening. Whoever had designed the thing had done a good job, as it closely resembled an old-time well.

Blaine cleared his throat to break the silence, hoping she would look at him. She didn't.

What was there about this little wildcat that intrigued him? He studied her profile, her pert nose and stubborn chin. Scratches covered a good deal of her face, but he could see that normally the skin was creamy and without blemish. A few freckles peppered her nose and cheeks. He wouldn't call her beautiful, but she was pretty—and she wore no wedding ring.

Her blue green eyes flicked his way, and she lifted one reddish brown brow. Realizing he was openly staring, he looked back out over the yard. "Nice well."

"It came with the house." Her words were reluctant, but at least she was talking. "Well, thanks again. . ." She started to move toward the porch stairs.

Suddenly Blaine realized he didn't want her to go. "Do you go to Spring of Life Church, too?"

She hesitated. "Yes."

He wondered why he'd never seen her there. He doubted he would have forgotten her. "There's a singles' Bible study tomorrow. I was wondering if you might like to go with me?"

"No." Her reply came fast.

Blaine pushed a hand through his hair and grimaced when his fingers came into contact with slimy mud. He could hardly blame her for her refusal, with the way he knew he must look. Probably close to resembling the Swamp Thing. Still he decided to give it another shot. "Maybe after church some Sunday you might like to go and grab a bite to eat?"

She turned on him, her eyes frosty. "Listen, Mr.

Carson, I appreciate your help earlier, but I'm not interested."

"Blaine."

"All right, Blaine, then," she gritted through her teeth, then calmed some. "Look, I know you're new to these parts, so you obviously don't know how things are."

"And how's that?" he asked with a puzzled frown.

"I don't date. I don't need a man to ruin my life, and I'm perfectly happy with being single." With that, she marched up the stairs and into the house, shutting the flimsy door firmly behind her.

Blaine stared at the screen in bewilderment. A siren wailed at the front, probably the ambulance. He shook himself out of his stupor, then strode toward the gravel drive to tell the paramedics their services were obviously not needed here today.

※

"Ouch! What are you doing back there?" Cat craned her neck to look over her shoulder, trying to see what torture her sister was inflicting upon her bruised and cut body.

"Oh, hush up," Shelby said, dabbing between Cat's shoulder blades with the wet cotton ball again. "This stuff is guaranteed not to sting, or Trey would've never insisted I buy it."

"Well then, you better get your money back, because it sure does." Cat winced as the icy cold cotton traveled along the cut. She turned face front again, her eyes fastening on the pine dresser in her lemon yellow bedroom. "How big is it? Is it pretty deep? It feels like my whole back is split open. My legs don't feel too good, either."

"You're lucky your head isn't split open with that stunt you pulled today, Catherine Inez McGregor," Shelby muttered, ruthlessly wielding the cotton again. "And then after Blaine rescued you and was so nice to you—you left him standing on the porch, without so much as a good-bye!"

Cat winced both at the detested name and the cotton coming down hard on the back of her thigh. "Hey, easy with that thing! Maybe I should have accepted the paramedic's help, after all."

Shelby's touch gentled. "Sorry, Kiddo. But sometimes you get me so riled. I just can't figure you out."

"What can't you figure out?"

"Why you didn't say yes when he asked you to that Bible study. He's such a nice guy, and you could use a good man."

Cat shot upward, clutching the thick towel to her breast, and turned on the bed to face her sister. "You were eavesdropping," she said incredulously.

Shelby had the grace to blush. "The window in the bathroom was open and is right next to the porch, remember. I couldn't help but overhear."

Cat wasn't going to let her off that easy. She narrowed her eyes. "I thought the sheets were in the linen closet."

"I had to get the poor man a towel, too. He was dripping with mud from head to foot." Shelby's expression relaxed, and she sank next to Cat on the flowered bedspread. "He's such a nice guy, Honey. You really should give him a chance. Besides being drop-dead gorgeous, he has a personality that would charm the birds from the trees."

Cat ignored the unwanted way her stomach dipped at the reference to him and grimaced. "Don't mention trees. Anyway, you said the same thing about Tanner."

A stricken look covered Shelby's face, and Cat felt instant remorse.

"Shel—I'm sorry. I shouldn't have said that."

Her sister ignored her. "Blaine is nothing like Tanner," she stressed, her voice strained. "Tanner wasn't a Christian. I knew that and married him anyway, despite what the Bible had to say about it. I was bowled over by his good looks and charm, and now I'm paying the price."

"You can't go on blaming yourself forever," Cat said, putting a gentle hand on her sister's arm. "It's not your fault that he ditched his responsibilities to you and Trey and ran off."

At mention of her son, Shelby's eyes misted. "Do you realize Trey's never even seen his father?"

The question was unnecessary, spoken in an ago-nized tone, a memory relived. The night Tanner walked out on Shelby, she had come to Cat's apartment in tears, four months pregnant. Cat assured her then that he would come back, but he never did. No one had even heard word of him in all this time. It was as if he'd just vanished off the face of the earth.

Tanner's desertion had been the final brick Cat laid in her heart as a wall of distrust to keep out men. The first one had been laid due to her father.

She held the towel over her chest with one hand and the other she hooked around her sister's shoulders.

Hugging her tight, Cat wished she could take all of Shelby's pain away.

Blaine walked down the cluttered aisle of Piggly Wiggly, searching for his brand of bread. He preferred to do his shopping after dark when there were fewer shoppers. Cardboard cartons sat piled on the floor, one open to display packages of sticky buns. A blond stocker, with the physique of a linebacker, knelt on the floor with his price sticker gun, slapping each item with it as he took it out. Hearing the wheels of Blaine's cart squeak by, he glanced up. His hazel eyes took on a measuring look. "Carson." He gave a curt nod. "Off duty tonight?"

"Yeah. Thought I'd stock the pantry. How's it going, Miller?"

"Can't complain," Lonnie Miller said, the clicks of his price gun coming slower until they stopped altogether. "Heard about the episode with Cat last week."

Blaine's hand stopped in mid-reach for a package of cinnamon-raisin bagels. He hadn't told anyone about the rescue; didn't think Cat would appreciate public interest. "How'd you find out?"

"Haven't you heard? News travels fast in Loggin's Point. It's common knowledge now. Besides, Jake and I are good friends," Lonnie muttered, mentioning the fire captain on Blaine's shift. His eyes narrowed. "Before the city decided the town was growing and they needed to hire you paid professionals, I was a volunteer firefighter for Loggin's Point, ya know."

Blaine set the bagels on the red plastic seat of the cart. He had a strong suspicion Lonnie had helped the news of Cat's rescue along. What Blaine knew of the man from when he'd seen him at his cousin's gas station, Lonnie was a braggart and a big mouth. Blaine never felt comfortable around him.

"Cat and I go back a long way," Lonnie continued, his drawl growing louder, emitting a warning. "I've had an interest in that gal for a long time. Plan to marry her someday."

Blaine's jaw clenched. "Oh?" he said, feigning disinterest, though the thought of Lonnie and Cat together made him feel sick.

The sound of a rattling cart, its wheels squeaking and bumping with great speed over the tile, got both of the men's attention. They watched as it rounded the corner and made a beeline straight for them, a frowning Cat pushing it. Her pixie-like face flamed red, and Lonnie paled, jumping to his feet. She completely ignored Blaine, her blue green eyes snapping in Lonnie's direction as she unleashed the full fire of her fury.

"How dare you, Lonnie Miller!" she fumed in a low voice, her knuckles white on the cart's red bar. "How dare you spread your lies all over town and make it sound like there's something between us? I've just about had it with you!"

Lonnie's mouth dropped open as though he would say something, but he only stared.

"I am so mad right now I could easily ram you with this cart, but since that probably wouldn't be the Christian thing to do, I'd better get out of here—fast."

After impaling the wide-eyed giant with one more vicious glare, the tiny woman spun away and sailed down the aisle with her full load, her tennis shoes slapping the white tile.

Forgetting about the bread, Blaine considered, then took off after her, following her to the checkout. She set a gallon of milk on the black conveyor belt, then turned to glimpse over her shoulder.

Blaine smiled. "Hey there!"

A frown marred her forehead. High spots of color still reddened her cheeks.

"You okay?" he asked.

She gave a brusque nod, and her glance fell to his cart. Her brows sailed upward as she looked back up at him. "Only a package of bagels? You should use the express lane for that."

He looked over at the next lane. The cashier handed a teenage boy his change. No one stood behind him.

"Thanks," Blaine said, smiling. "I think I'll just do that very thing."

Deciding he would continue the rest of his shopping later, Blaine moved his cart with the small package to the express lane, ignoring the cashier's raised brow as she stared from his massive cart to the red handheld carry baskets piled on the floor, shook her head, and scanned the price of the bagels.

Blaine looked forward to the next few minutes. He only hoped his strategy would work.

Cat was still fuming as she wrote the check and made a conscious effort to steady her hand so her signature was at least legible. She handed it to the young cashier, said a stiff "No, thank you" to the bag boy when he made a move to wheel her cart of bagged groceries outside, and hurried through the automatic doors into the night. She came to an abrupt stop.

In the outside fluorescent lights, Cat noticed Blaine standing next to a newspaper machine, studying the headlines through the glass. His velvety dark eyes lifted, and a smile turned up the corners of his mouth.

"Thought I'd check and see what today's top story was."

His deep voice sent a strange warmth through her. Irritated that her heart had skipped a beat upon seeing him outside, Cat gave a brisk nod and continued toward her compact car.

Blaine hurried her way and fell into step beside her. "Missed you at church Sunday."

"I had a headache." Cat quickened her pace, causing the cart to rattle noisily along the pavement.

Blaine's long legs easily kept up. "Sorry to hear that. Oh, by the way, there's a singles' dinner at the church Friday after next, in the cafeteria—"

She came to a dead stop, her head whipping his way. "Look, like I told you before, I don't date. And I would appreciate it if you'd stop bothering me about it."

His hands flew up, as though in surrender, and he gave an innocent shake of his head. "I'm just passing along the information, like our group leader told us to do."

"Uh-huh." Cat gave him a skeptical look, then pushed the cart to her maroon Omni parked next to a tall parking lamp. She wished he'd just go, but apparently he had no intention of doing such a thing.

"This your car?" he asked unnecessarily as she moved to slide the key into the lock. She shot him a look as the hatchback popped open. To her dismay, she watched him lift the groceries from the cart.

"Thanks, but I can handle it." She tried to take the sack from him.

He shook his head with a grin, his hold on the bag tightening. "Nope. My mama raised me to be a gentleman."

"Really, I don't need—"

A look of mock horror covered his face. "You wouldn't want to offend my mama, now would you? She wouldn't like it if I strayed from what she taught me. Not at all."

Cat opened her mouth to protest his silly words, then closed it. Oh, why not? If she let him have his way, she could leave that much sooner.

She watched as he piled the bags into her car, the muscles under his black shirt and in his arms rippling with the motion. His longish, dark hair lifted in the cool breeze, the lamp's white glow bringing out silvery blue highlights. After he'd deposited the last bag onto the carpeted shelf, he turned her way.

Embarrassed to be caught staring at him, she averted her gaze to the laughing pig on the neon store sign. "Thanks," she muttered, putting her hand out for her key ring once he'd slammed the hatchback shut and removed the key from the lock.

When he didn't move, she looked at him curiously.

His dark eyes had gone serious. "I really wish you'd reconsider going with me to the singles' dinner."

"I thought you said you weren't asking for a date." She eyed him with exasperation.

"No, what I said is that I was passing along the info. Now I'm asking."

"Why?"

"What?"

Cat tilted her head, her chin lifting a fraction. "Why? Why are you so interested in seeing me? You don't know me. Never even saw me before last week."

Blaine shrugged, clearly puzzled. "So?"

"So," she said, moving forward to jab his chest with her forefinger, "I'll tell you what I think, Blaine Carson. I think you're out for the chase—just like Lonnie and every other man out there. You see a woman, decide you want her, and do everything you can to catch her. Only problem is, once she's caught, your interest soon dies and you dump her, then move on to the next likely prospect—which isn't me, for your information." Her chin rose higher. "*So*, how do you like them apples?"

His eyes hardened and his hand shot up and wrapped around her finger still pointing to his chest. Warmth sizzled through her at his touch. She retreated a small step, now flustered.

"I'll tell you what I think," he said in a low voice, his words coming fast. "First of all, you don't know anything about me and have no right to lump me into some category. If you did know me, you'd know my social life has been pretty much nil these past three years. I don't know where you got your ideas about men, but you're wrong if you think we're all like that. I would never hurt a woman for my own selfish desires, for any reason."

His eyes softened, drawing her in like dark whirl-pools, and his expression relaxed. His thumb moved to caress her finger. She shivered.

"You asked why I want to see you," he said, his voice low, warm. "Well, I'll tell you why. I happen to think you're cute, funny, and interesting. And I want to be your friend."

His other hand moved to tap below her collarbone with his fingertip, enunciating his words. "I also think you're brave, loyal, and a little reckless. You have an independent streak a mile wide, and until you let down that wall you've built around yourself and let others inside, you won't be happy. It must get awful lonely in there, huh, Cat?"

Shaken by his assessment, not wanting to admit how close he was to the truth, she struggled to display an outward composure. "You came to that conclusion after only a ten-minute meeting, huh?" she said flippantly, trying to keep her voice from trembling. "Now who's assuming too much?"

His dark brows shot up. "So tell me. Am I wrong?"

Her mouth opened to speak, then closed. She dropped her gaze. "I don't want to discuss this anymore. I have to go now. May I have my keys?"

He released her finger, turned her hand over, and placed the key ring in her palm. "Think about the dinner," he coaxed softly, then turned and walked away.

Numb, Cat stared at his broad back and watched as he reentered the well-lit store. She opened the driver's door, slid behind the wheel, and stared at the car parked in front of hers for a minute before starting up her Omni and backing out.

Cat wanted to escape, get home and close herself up in her room. She felt invaded, vulnerable; as if he'd discovered some long-ago locked box that had been hidden, containing the painful events of her life. And, Cat knew if she wanted to keep things the way she wanted them—the way they were—she couldn't risk letting him get near enough to find out what was inside.

That was one key Blaine Carson could never have.

Three

Hands in his jacket pockets, Blaine stood under the church roof on the outside landing above the curved stone stairs and watched the sudden downpour. All around him, those churchgoers who also hadn't thought to bring their umbrellas converged in small groups, visiting and waiting for the rain to diminish so they could run to their cars. Murmuring voices, laughter, and the constant loud spatter of rain on cement filled the air.

Blaine felt a tug on his jacket and looked behind him.

"Hey there, Mr. Fireman," Trey said, a big smile on his face. "Guess you won't need to put out no fires today, since God's doing it with the rain, huh?"

An answering smile tilted Blaine's mouth. "Guess you're right about that, Partner. How's it been going? Learn to throw that Frisbee yet?"

Trey's face went solemn. "Naw, I gave up."

"Well, maybe I can teach you. I used to be a pretty good Frisbee thrower in my day—" Blaine stopped, mentally shaking his head. What was he doing? It sounded as if he were trying to invite himself over.

Though he would like to see Cat again, he wasn't the manipulative sort to use a child for that purpose. He quickly backpedaled, changing the subject. "So how's school going? What grade are you in now—first?"

Trey shook his head. "I was with Aunt Cat at the day care before it burnded down. Now she stays with me at home while Mommy goes to work. But I'm going to kindergarten next year," he added proudly.

"Your aunt worked at the day care?"

Blaine had been on duty that night and helped to put out the fire. All the while, he'd silently thanked God no one was in the old building at the time. A post-examination pointed to worn electrical wiring as the culprit. There were a lot of older buildings in town— some over fifty years. Maybe it was time for the department to send someone on a routine check.

"Trey? Honey, your mommy wants you."

At the sound of the uncertain, husky voice coming from behind, the chill in the air evaporated and warmth surged through Blaine. He turned as the boy darted back into the church with a resounding, "Bye!"

Cat looked terrific in a bone-colored dress spattered with bluish flowers that intensified the color of her eyes and brightened her hair even more.

"Hello, Cat."

"Hi." Her smile was lukewarm at best, but her attitude wasn't dismissive. Rather, she seemed anxious. Why? Her gaze zipped away from his to watch the curtain of rain.

"I didn't see you in church."

She readjusted the strap of her beige handbag over

her shoulder in a nervous gesture. "I worked in children's church today. Several of us take turns. Today was mine."

No wonder he'd missed her before. "I'll bet you're good with kids."

Her face softened and she smiled at him, a real one this time. "I love children. Love to teach them, play with them—just be with them. They're such fun."

Blaine returned her smile. Again, her gaze sped away from his. She acted like someone in a dentist's waiting room, in line for a root canal—fidgety, dreading the ordeal, yet unable to leave.

"That dress looks nice on you," Blaine said when the quiet intensified between them.

Bright pink heightened her cheekbones. "Thanks. . . Well, I guess I should go find Shelby."

"Cat?"

She hesitated, then turned back to face him.

"Have you given any more thought to this Friday night?"

Her face sobered. "I told you; I don't date."

"I understand, but that doesn't mean you can't come by yourself—just to join in and take part in the fun. Maybe your sister might like to come with you?"

"Shelby doesn't go to singles' events, and I'm really not interested in that kind of thing, either."

" 'That kind of thing?' " Blaine hesitated, wondering what he could say to change her mind. He felt it would help her to mix with other adults and be a part of something worthwhile. Maybe even take that little-girl-lost look out of her eyes he'd glimpsed from time to time.

"The singles' group isn't some kind of lonely hearts club for people looking to find a mate, Cat. We spend time learning how to best use our 'singleness' to grow in God and become servants for Him."

"Oh." She still didn't look too thrilled with the idea.

Shelby emerged from the open church door, Trey leading her by one hand. "Well, hi," she said, smiling at Blaine. "What are you two talking about?"

"I was telling Cat about the singles' dinner this Friday," Blaine said, hoping to enlist Shelby's aid. He ignored Cat's exasperated sigh.

"Really?" A glimmer of interest lit Shelby's eyes. "I heard about that from Ginny. Proceeds are going toward a foreign missions trip to Mexico this summer, right?"

He nodded. "They're planning quite a shebang to draw interest, from what I hear. They made flyers and spread them all over town. The dinner will have a Mexican theme."

"Appropriate." Shelby grew thoughtful. "Maybe I'll contribute my famous tortilla pie casserole. It's a winner at our house."

"Hey, that would be great! I'm sure Sandy would really appreciate that. She's looking for all the help she can get."

"Excuse me," Cat inserted, "I forgot I need to talk to the children's church director."

"Can I come with you?" Trey asked eagerly.

"Sure, Sport."

Blaine watched her hurry back into church, the hope in him deflating like a punctured tire.

"You really like her, don't you?"

Blaine jerked his head around at Shelby's low, inquisitive words. He thought about ignoring her remark, but the knowing look in her eyes changed his mind. He heaved a sigh. "Is it that obvious?"

She grinned. "Only to me—and maybe to Cat. She told me about your meeting in the store parking lot last week." Her expression sobered. "Mind if I ask a question?"

"Shoot."

"What are your interests in Cat? Just friendly? Or more of a serious nature?"

Momentarily taken aback, he shrugged. "It's too early to tell, but I can guarantee you, I would never do anything to harm your sister. You have my word on that. I can tell she's hurting from something, and I don't like to see her block herself off. I want to help if I can."

Shelby's eyebrows lifted in surprise. "Yeah, you're right. She has been hurt, and you're very perceptive to see it. Most men she's snubbed usually think that Cat feels she's too good for them, and they lose interest." She cocked her head in curiosity. "So what makes you so different?"

"I have six older sisters and I'm the only boy—a surprise that came to my parents in their middle age. Guess I was spoiled quite a bit with not just one mama, but seven to take care of me." He grinned. "Coming from a nurturing family like that, I learned how to be sensitive to other people's needs."

"Yeah, I'm sure you did," Shelby said thoughtfully.

A smile beamed across her face. "I like you, Blaine, but what's more, I trust you. I'm going to do everything I can to help you with your plan. I think you're just what my sister needs."

Cat stitched the leg of the trousers she was making for Trey's Easter suit before easing up on the pedal of the sewing machine and snatching up the ringing phone. "Hello," she said distractedly.

"Cat? This is Stephanie Kramer. Do you have a moment? I'd like to talk to you about something."

Cat's eyes widened at hearing her former employer's voice. "Stephanie, good to hear from you. Is something wrong?"

"No. Actually, I was wondering if you'd be interested in working for me again in the fall? I've decided to open another day care and rent a newer building this time. A space is available in that shopping center strip—in between the secondhand clothing store and the Laundromat—where the deli used to be. I would increase your salary and give you, say—a two-dollar raise?"

Cat tightened her hand around the receiver in anticipation. She missed her young charges, and more money was icing on the cake—icing they could really use at this time. "I'd love to work for you again."

Stephanie let out a sigh of relief. "Great! To be honest, you were one of my best workers and a favorite with the little ones. I'll fill you in later on the details. I still have papers to sign and renovations to make. . . ."

After talking with Stephanie a few more minutes,

Cat said good-bye and hung up the phone. She let loose with a squeal that brought Shelby running from the kitchen into the cramped sewing room.

"What happened? What is it?"

"Stephanie is opening another day care in the fall—and she offered me a job and a raise!"

"Oh, Sweetie, that's wonderful!"

"You bet it is! Now I don't have to feel so guilty that I'm not pulling my weight around here."

The smile faded from Shelby's face. "I never thought that. You've been a big help taking care of Trey while I'm at work, and shopping for groceries, and making his clothes."

"But I haven't felt right about not helping out with the finances."

Shelby sank onto a nearby chair, idly wrapping the wet dishcloth she still held around one finger. "You know, Cat, actually I think you do too much around here, if you want the truth. You should take time off for some fun."

"I love being with Trey. That's fun to me."

"Yes, I know. But I'm talking about adult companionship. Getting out, having a good time. Going somewhere where people your own age are. . ."

Cat narrowed her eyes in suspicion. "Such as?"

Shelby cleared her throat. "Well, actually that singles' dinner does sound nice."

"You're beginning to sound like Blaine! Well, I'll tell you what I told him: I'm not interested." Cat turned back to her sewing machine, lifted the needle, and cut the thread. Repositioning the pale blue material under the presser foot, she brought the needle down again.

"It might be fun, and it is for a good cause. I've decided to donate my tortilla casserole and a pie and to help with the cleanup afterwards."

"Fine, then. You go." Cat turned, a smirk on her face. "Besides, that clinches it. If you're going, who will watch Trey?"

"Well, actually, that's the night of Alex's birthday party. I've already talked to Ginny, and we think it might be fun for Trey to spend the night there."

Cat raised a brow. "Isn't he a little young for sleepovers?"

"He'll be six at the end of May. Besides, he and Alex are best buddies."

"Fine. Do whatever you want," Cat said, turning back to her task. "Just don't get me involved."

"You might enjoy it—"

The whir of the sewing machine cut off Shelby's words.

Two days later, Cat went around to the back of her sister's dark green van and opened the rear door. "Sure you can handle it?" Shelby asked, hesitating.

"No problem. Go take care of the paperwork."

Shelby and Trey headed for the black door of the quaint red-and-white building of the souvenir shop set off the U.S. highway. A painted steer looked down at them from the timbered wall, with the words "Brady's Texas Souvenirs" underneath in yellow. The hot sun beamed down, bathing the countryside with its blinding glare.

Cat straightened, swiped the back of her hand across her forehead to remove the errant curls from her eyes, and reached for the large cardboard carton. Carefully, she tugged it across the carpeted shelf.

The sound of tires slowly crunching on pebbles and coming to a stop in front of the store didn't deter Cat from her task. A door slammed shut and footsteps crunched her way. Probably a tourist looking around.

She pulled the box so that it teetered on the edge of the shelf against her stomach as the jars rattled inside, then slid her arms underneath and gave a mighty heave.

"Need some help?"

Blaine's voice at her elbow startled her. She tightened her hold just in time to keep from dropping the box. The clatters and clinks of glass were alarming. His large hands shot out and underneath the carton, steadying it. To her chagrin, she abruptly felt the weight shift from her arms to his.

"Sorry, didn't realize you didn't know I was here," he said.

"Blaine, I can handle it."

"I'm sure you can." Dark glasses shielded his eyes, however, his expression was grave as he assessed her. "But this thing must weigh close to fifty pounds. As long as I'm here, why not let me carry it for you?"

She opened her mouth to protest.

"Is it so hard to accept help, Cat? Sometimes people need people. There's nothing wrong with that."

I don't need any man's *help,* Cat thought bitterly. But she said nothing, instead averting her gaze to the colorful masses of bluebonnets growing wild along the grassy slopes bordering the highway.

Blaine exhaled deeply. "If you'll just show me where to put this, I'll be on my way. I'm on duty tonight."

Cat gave a stiff nod and moved toward the door, Blaine behind her. The tinkling bell announced their presence, and Shelby turned from the counter.

"Blaine! How nice to see you. Just set that down right here." She patted the smooth wooden counter in front of her and looked at the white-haired man wearing silver wire-rimmed glasses. "Fifty jars—all accounted for, Mr. Brady."

The man smiled as he opened the carton's flap and pulled out a small jar etched with the shape of Texas. A red piece of calico material covered the top, tied in place with a gold cord. "Ain't nothin' like Shelby and Cat's homemade strawberry preserves. Tourists love 'em. Peach and plum ones, too."

"Shelby and Cat made these?" Blaine asked in surprise, lifting out a jar to inspect. He pulled off his sunglasses to get a better look. His admiring gaze lit on both women, before he turned to the store owner. "How much?"

"Four dollars each—but I guarantee you've never tasted anything so good in your life."

"I'll take ten of them."

Cat gasped, and Blaine turned to her with a smile. "My sisters and mother love this kind of stuff. So do I."

Check written, purchases made, Blaine replaced his dark glasses, grabbed the two white plastic sacks in which Mr. Brady had put the carefully wrapped jars, and gave the girls a nod. "Well, Ladies, I'd better be on my way. Afternoon."

Shelby turned to Cat after Blaine walked out. "I'll be right back." Before Cat could respond, Shelby was out the door.

"Blaine—wait up a sec!"

He turned, sacks in hand, and waited for Shelby to run up to him.

"That was really sweet, what you did. I just wanted to say thanks."

He grinned. "I don't get to visit my family often since they live over a day's drive away. When I do go home, I don't like to show up empty-handed."

She tilted her head, smiling. "You know, Blaine, you're a nice guy. I hope my obstinate sister figures that out soon."

"Speaking of Cat—have you changed her mind about the dinner? Is she going?"

Shelby shook her head, the smile leaving her face. "She's being as stubborn as a mule. She won't even listen to me when I try to talk to her about it, and I have tried—several times." A twinkle lit her eye. "But don't worry. I have a plan."

A plan? Blaine sobered. "Your sister used those same words when she tried to get down from that oak tree. Almost broke her neck with that 'plan' of hers."

Shelby laughed. "Believe me, Blaine. My plans are guaranteed not to fail."

Four

C at set her shoulder bag on the overstuffed plaid chair in the cozy, paneled den and looked at her sister skeptically. "You don't look sick to me."

"Well, I felt fine before you left to take Trey to the party—" Shelby reached for another tissue from the box on the coffee table and sneezed. "I think it must be hay fever. It's that time of the year, you know."

"I've never known you to have allergies. Interesting how such a thing would develop—and on the night of the dinner, as well." Cat crossed her arms against her chest, giving her sister a long, level look. "Too bad you won't be able to go—and after you worked so hard in the kitchen last night, preparing all that food. What a shame."

"I know," Shelby sighed, her expression miserable, "and I promised Sandy I would help with the cleanup afterwards."

Cat's sober gaze never wavered from her sister's face, which suddenly grew brighter, and Cat waited for what she knew was coming.

"Hey, I've got a great idea!"

Cat raised one eyebrow. "Oh?"

"Why don't you take the things for me?"

"Wow. Why didn't I think of that?" Cat replied in a derisive tone. She uncrossed her arms. "Shelby, I wasn't born yesterday. I know your tricks, and if you think you can wheedle me into going tonight. . ."

Shelby squinted and her mouth fell open. Repeated rapid breaths huffed from between her lips until it ended in one loud sneeze.

"Congratulations. That one sounded much more real."

"Just what have you got against the singles' group?" Shelby asked with a frown, as she wiped her nose with another tissue.

"Nothing. In fact, the mission trip they've planned sounds interesting. It's your trying to hook me up with Blaine that I'm opposed to."

"Who said I was trying to hook you up with him?" At Cat's raised eyebrows, Shelby relented. "Oh, okay, so what if I am? He's a nice guy, Cat. I'll bet half the girls in the county would love for him to ask them out."

"Tell him, not me. You might even compose a list of names and phone numbers to make his job a little easier."

Shelby's mouth narrowed. "Why are you so pig-headed? Can't you see what a catch he is? Take a good look at him sometime."

"Forgive me if I choose not to allow my heart to be trodden upon," Cat shot back sarcastically. "But I'm not letting any man near enough to do that. I'd think, after what you went through, you'd understand—even if you don't agree."

"Cat, I told you; Tanner wasn't a Christian. Blaine

is worlds different than he was."

"Maybe Tanner wasn't a Christian, but Daddy was—wasn't he?" Unwanted tears filled her eyes, and she angrily swiped at them with one hand. "He went to church every Sunday. He told me how much he cared about his 'kitten' and would never leave me." She laughed bitterly. "Guess he must've suffered from acute memory loss, huh?"

Shelby sobered, her eyes intently searching Cat's face. "Just because someone goes to church doesn't make him a Christian, Cat. Christianity is about a relationship with Jesus—a decision to accept and follow Him." She bit her lip, searching for words. "I think Daddy went to church because he knew it would please Mama, not because he really wanted to go."

"Oh, yeah, he sure wanted to please our mama, didn't he?" Cat's voice wavered, though her expression was fierce and her words biting. "That must be why he walked out on her and took up with his secretary—because he wanted to make Mama so happy."

Shelby shook her head. "You were too young to know what went on back then—"

"I was seven—and I heard every word!"

"What? What did you hear?"

Cat shut her eyes, trying to get past the staggering pain of that night, to form the difficult words she'd never uttered. Slowly she sank to the chair, almost sitting on her purse.

"I woke up and heard Mama and Daddy fighting, so I went to my door and opened it," she began, her words stilted. "I heard Daddy say, 'Fine! I'm outta here, and you'll never have to see my face again!' He picked up his suitcase and stormed down the hall and past my room. I cried out his name and put my hand on his sleeve, trying to stop him. He completely ignored me and slammed out the front door."

Tears trailed down her cheeks as she opened her eyes and looked at Shelby. "And *that* is why I will never trust a man. First Daddy lied to me and made me believe he'd always be there for me, but I never saw him again. He never even visited us! Then Tanner lied to you and disappeared—just like Daddy."

Shelby slid off the couch, knelt on the carpet, and hugged Cat close. "Oh, Honey—if only I would have known! You don't have the whole story. No wonder you've been so bitter."

"What story?" Cat studied Shelby's serious gaze, as teary as her own.

Shelby settled back on her legs and licked her lips, her brow furrowed, as though uncertain how to begin. "I was working really late on a book report that night at the kitchen table when they started fighting. It's like they forgot I was even in the next room. Mama accused Daddy of sleeping with his secretary, and he kept telling her it wasn't true. I really don't think it was— then. He tried to get her to listen to him, but she kept yelling, and then she ran to their room and threw a bunch of his clothes in a suitcase. She told him to get out, that she never wanted to see him again."

"Mama threw Daddy out?" Cat whispered, stunned. She shook her head slowly, feeling as if everything was crashing down around her and she was dangerously close to getting buried in the rubble. What was real, and what was a lie? Cat wasn't sure anymore.

"But he never came to visit us," she insisted faintly.

"Mama got complete custody. I don't know why Daddy didn't come—he must have had visitation rights, but I really don't know. Once he left, you know Mama never brought up his name. Whenever I'd ask about him, she'd get mad, so I learned not to ask."

Shelby paused and looked down at her hands tucked between her legs. "I just want you to know, Cat, it wasn't all Daddy's fault. As for Tanner, I'm just as much to blame as he is. I constantly preached to him and nagged him, trying to get him to go to church with me. I thought once we were married, I could change him and make him a Christian. All I ended up doing was driving him away. Even the Bible says that a wife should win her unbelieving husband by her actions, not her words."

Confused, Cat stood on shaky legs and seized her purse. "I can't talk about this anymore. I'm going for a drive." This was too much to absorb at one sitting. She had to escape, had to find some semblance of reality.

Shelby's eyes met hers in understanding. "Please take a walk first or do something else to calm down before you get behind the wheel. Okay?"

Cat grabbed the covered casserole and pie off the table, unwilling to argue anymore. "Yeah, okay. I'll drop your stuff off at the church while I'm at it, but I'm not staying."

"Thanks." Shelby's voice sounded meek, and Cat nodded. She just had to get out of the house before she came unglued.

"Cat McGregor! Why, hello." The blond standing at the outside door of the church kitchen smiled. "It's been ages since I've seen you! Come in, come in."

"Hello, Sandy." Cat forced an answering smile, holding up the dish. "I brought Shelby's casserole, and the pie is in the car."

"Oh, wonderful!" Sandy wiped her hands on the apron tied around her colorful dirndl skirt before taking the dish and sticking it in the oven where two dishes were already warming. Three women hustled around the efficiency kitchen, arranging platters, cutting vegetables, and stirring something over the stove. The aroma of spiced meat, cheeses, corn, and tomatoes hit Cat's senses, making her mouth water.

"Well, I can see you're pretty busy," Cat said. "I'll just get that pie for you and be out of your way."

Sandy's brow furrowed with disappointment. "Oh, but you're staying, aren't you? Shelby said you might."

"No, I—"

Cat's words were interrupted as a short, dark-haired woman hurried through the doorway that led to the cafeteria. A panicked look covered her elfin face.

"We're out of glue," she said with a moan, waving a photograph in her hand. "And I was almost finished."

"I'll see if I can find some tape." Sandy started opening drawers.

Curiosity got the better of Cat. "Are you making a poster?"

The young woman nodded, offering the picture for Cat to see. An adorable little Mexican girl with long, black hair and shimmering ebony eyes stared back. A clown missionary with a painted face gave her a one-armed hug as they both smiled into the camera.

Cat's heart turned over with compassion.

"I'm making a poster of our mission trip from last year. Care to see it?"

Cat hesitated only a second. "Sure. Let me get the pie first."

"Okay. Well, it's out there on a table. By the way, I'm Marie. You must be Cat. I've heard Sandy talk about you—all good, so don't worry." She grinned. "You sound like you're really something else with kids."

"I love being with them."

Sandy located the tape, and Cat fetched the pie, then followed Marie to one of the long tables covered with red cloth. The room was transformed into a flare of Old Mexico by the wide sombreros hanging on the wall, the festive outfits the servers wore, the silk carnations, and netted red glass candleholders all along the tables. Someone had donated a colorful wall tapestry of a sleepy Mexican town at siesta. Whoever was in charge of the decorating had done a good job.

Cat turned her attention to the large poster on the table and studied the collage of snapshots with interest. Soon she became engrossed, forgetting all about her problems.

Loud metal clanking broke Cat's concentration. Startled, she looked up.

Blaine and two other men brought in brown metal folding chairs from the back room, setting them alongside the tables. He caught her eye and hesitated, then raised a hand in acknowledgment, an uncertain smile on his face.

She returned the wave, swallowing over the lump in her throat, and hurriedly broke eye contact. He looked fantastic in a black shirt, the long sleeves rolled partway up, and matching jeans and boots. The sight literally robbed her of her breath.

Relief warred with a strange sense of disappointment when he didn't walk her way, but instead continued to set out the chairs. *They must be expecting a big crowd,* Cat thought as she studied Blaine from beneath her lashes. Except for his lack of olive skin, he could fit the part of a dashing Mexican conquistador any day.

"Cat?"

She jumped and turned to look at Sandy.

"We have tamales, tortillas, fajitas, and lots of other good stuff to eat. We'll start serving in five minutes; that's when we expect people to start arriving. Why don't you go ahead and find yourself a spot?"

Cat's gaze snapped with disbelief to the round face of the clock above the serving bar. Almost seven o'clock already? Where had the time gone? She'd been here a full thirty-five minutes!

"I should go." She rose to leave, but Sandy's hand on her shoulder stopped her.

"Why not stay? Don't worry about the five dollars, since Shelby donated that food."

"Oh, I can pay. It's not that. . ."

"There's going to be a talk afterwards about the mission trip," Sandy cajoled. "You might be interested in their presentation."

Cat hesitated. The tantalizing aroma filling the cafeteria was enough to make any man—or woman—beg. She inhaled deeply, then nodded. "Okay. It might be fun."

"Great! I'll bring you out a plate with a little of everything. Iced tea okay?"

Cat nodded and moved away from the poster to find a seat in the corner at the far side of the room. Sandy brought her a heavily laden plate, and after a silent prayer, Cat dug into the delicious food. Soon the cafeteria was buzzing with talk as people arrived and found seats. When the chair across from hers skidded away from the table, Cat wasn't surprised to look up and see Blaine.

"Hi," he said as he balanced a Styrofoam plate in one hand. It was piled high with beef tamales, cheese enchiladas, and other treats. He set his tea down. "Glad you could make it."

Cat's gaze sailed to her plate. "Shelby couldn't come, so I brought the food. I was looking at that poster over there and lost track of time."

Blaine's touch on her hand, which held the fork, caused her head to snap up. "No matter what your reasons for being here, I'm glad you are." His words came softly, his dark eyes intense.

Flustered, Cat looked away, pretending sudden interest in the wall hanging. "Pretty, isn't it?"

"Yeah. Pretty." Blaine's gaze never wavered from her face.

She was relieved when the chairs around them filled up. Conversation flew along both sides of the table. Blaine's good-natured personality shone through. A middle-aged widow expressed her need to relocate to a smaller apartment on Saturday, and Blaine volunteered to help with the move.

During the meeting, Cat listened with interest as the leader outlined the mission trip and the fund-raising needed to sponsor it. She wasn't all that surprised when Blaine volunteered to help at a car wash the group planned for June. He told them his job prevented him from taking two weeks off to go to Mexico, but he wanted to help in whatever way possible.

When the meeting ended, Cat found herself offering to help with the cleanup. She told herself that she was simply taking Shelby's place, and there was no other reason for her decision to stay.

After the men stacked the chairs and tables, Blaine came into the kitchen, mop in hand, wheeling a large metal vat of sudsy, steaming water. He smiled at Cat, and her heart did a crazy flip-flop as she returned to her task of putting the serving plates into the dishwasher. While they worked, Blaine whistled a popular contemporary Christian tune. His presence seemed to make the time fly by. Before she knew it, they were finished, and it was almost ten.

Blaine stopped her as she headed out the door. "Don't you have a jacket? It's gotten chilly."

She glanced down at her short-sleeved, aqua T-shirt, decorated with a heart-shaped wreath of spring flowers, and shook her head. "I hadn't planned to stay."

He slid off his windbreaker and, before she could protest, wrapped it around her shoulders. The body warmth from his jacket felt comforting yet unsettling at the same time.

"I'll follow you home. I only live a few blocks from your house."

Cat bit her lip. She wouldn't argue with him. She knew better by now.

Cat made a conscious effort to drive cautiously, going slower than usual, aware of his truck headlights behind her following her every move. After they pulled up the long, tree-lined gravel drive in front of the house, Blaine jumped from his vehicle and came over to hers.

She thought about rolling down her window several inches and handing him his jacket through the crack, then told herself she was being silly. Her fingers went to the handle, but he opened the door before she could and held out his hand. Swallowing hard, she took it and wished he didn't have to be such a gentleman. It would be easier to dislike him if he were rude, or cruel—or belligerent, like Lonnie.

He walked with her, their steps crunching over the rocks, and stopped at the foot of the three stairs leading to the porch. Turning to her, he smiled, his face tender in the glow of the incandescent porch light. "I'm really glad you came tonight, Cat."

His soft-spoken words made her shiver, though she had no idea why she reacted so strangely. She moved to shrug out of his jacket, but he pulled the edges of it firmly together, stopping her.

"Keep it," he insisted. "You still look cold. I can get it another time."

It was on the tip of her tongue to argue that she was only a few feet away from her house; but she was unable to think clearly when he looked at her like that with his liquid dark eyes framed with those impossibly thick lashes. And she knew, without a doubt, he would kiss her.

The thought was both frightening and exciting. She'd never been kissed, though several had tried. She wanted to run up the steps and charge through the front door.

At the same time, she wanted to stay.

He reached out and tucked a mass of springy curls behind her ear. His fingers were warm, sending that odd little shiver through her again. He searched her eyes, as though trying to find something there. She stood statue-still, unable to move, unable to breathe. His head inched lower.

His lips had barely brushed hers when the creak of the front door hinges made Cat jerk her head back in surprise. She retreated a few steps. Her gaze met Blaine's, then swung to the porch, as if she'd been caught doing something wrong.

And she had. She'd temporarily forgotten her grudge and allowed a man to kiss her.

"There you are," Shelby said, then promptly sneezed into a tissue. Her eyes and nose bloomed red, and her voice sounded clogged, making her words come out funny. "Sandy called to led me know you stayed. Thanks for following her home, Blaine. I don'd like her driving alone at nide."

Still flustered, Cat rubbed her upper arms. "You really sound sick."

Shelby grimaced. "It started after you lefd."

"Maybe your little lie caught up with you?"

Shelby ignored Cat's mocking words and looked at

Blaine. "I was going to invide you over to eat dinner with us Sunday abder church, but I'm not sure how I'm going to feel by den. Hab you made plans to visid your family on Easter?"

Disappointment clouded his features. "Can't. I'm on duty that night. I have to be at the station at five."

"Den I insis' you spend the abdernoon wid us. I'm making baked ham ad cradberries." She tried to sound tempting, but only succeeded in sounding more nasal.

"Sounds like a winner to me," Blaine said, grinning, then looked at Cat, his eyes going soft. "I'd love to come and be a part of your day."

"Gread. See you den." Shelby began to close the door.

Not certain how she felt about Shelby's invitation to Blaine, Cat averted her gaze and fled up the porch stairs before her sister could disappear. "Thanks, Blaine. Good night," she tossed over her shoulder.

She was confused, uncertain, afraid to be alone with him. Shelby's earlier revelation about their father had rocked her world, and Cat knew she would have to question her long-standing views and think things out sometime in the future.

But the electrifying moment Blaine's lips had touched hers shook her beyond belief. It had felt so right.

And that could be nothing but wrong.

Five

After a mediocre meal of franks and beans in the cheerless station kitchen, Blaine sat on the edge of his bunk, picked up a monthly newsletter he received from an international Christian firefighters ministry, and scanned the helpful words. This installment dealt with being quick to hold your tongue and not react during problems.

Well, he'd sure done that, though it hadn't been easy.

Shaving cream in his jacket pockets. The act was so juvenile it reeked of something Lonnie Miller might do. He'd visited Jake at the fire station earlier and left shortly after Blaine arrived for duty. The smug look in Lonnie's eyes should have warned Blaine something was coming, but he'd been without a clue.

Sighing, he settled back, propped his feet up, and leaned his head against the white plaster wall.

Mark, his round face florid and his gray T-shirt and dark hair wet with perspiration, sauntered in, a towel draped around his neck. Obviously he'd just come from the weight room. It wasn't often that Blaine and his roommate shared a shift, but this holiday weekend, they did.

"Hey, Buddy, whatcha readin'?" Mark pulled a few things out of his locker in preparation for a shower.

Blaine held the bulletin up, wishing he could interest his friend in going to church with him sometime. Mark's dark brows lifted, but the expression in his hazel eyes looked bored. "Heard about the joke the guys pulled on you earlier."

"Yeah," Blaine muttered. "I'm beginning to think they'll never accept me. I've been here four months now."

Mark slammed the locker shut. "It's tough, I know, but they gotta admire you for never fightin' back and always takin' it on the chin. I know Reggie was commentin' on it the other day." His sober gaze swung to Blaine. "Lonnie was behind today's prank. He's upset cause you stole the woman he thinks is his girl."

Blaine slapped the newsletter down on the cot. "Well, she's *not* his girl." The brief spurt of anger died when he remembered last weekend after the singles' dinner, how Cat had escaped into the house before he could say a word. He should have never tried to kiss her. "And unfortunately, it doesn't look as if she'll ever be mine."

"You've got it bad, don't you?" Mark regarded him with sympathy.

Blaine stared at the neat row of made bunks along the wall. "I can't explain it. It's like I want to be with her all the time, and all I can do is think about her when I'm not."

"Well, good luck to you, bro. As far as I know, Cat

has never dated—not even in high school. You've heard of prom queens and homecoming queens? Well, she was known as the Ice Queen of Buckley High. It'd take a miracle to thaw her out."

Blaine inwardly groaned at Mark's decree. Yes, he was finding that out for himself.

The shrill sound of the alarm pierced the air. Shoving his personal woes aside, Blaine shot up from his cot, grabbed his bunker pants, Nomex waterproof jacket, and the rest of his gear, then headed for the waiting fire engine, Mark hot on his heels.

Cat slammed the door of her Omni and rushed to the house to join her sister. They'd taken separate cars to church this morning, since the children's church director called Cat in as an extra worker. Easter services meant overflow, as well as extra time for preparation and cleanup. Acting out the Resurrection story with puppets had been rewarding, and Cat wasn't all that sorry she'd missed the main service. Besides, she would receive the pastor's taped message Wednesday night.

She entered the small olive-and-cream-colored kitchen with its mustard accents. Shelby was at the stove, busily preparing dinner. She turned from stirring the corn, a strange look in her eyes—as if she was about to say something Cat might not want to know. "Did you hear about the fire in town Friday night?"

"What fire?" Once Cat left church, most everyone had gone. Except for the children in her class, she'd barely spoken to anyone today.

"Ginny told me about it. Sounds as if it was pretty

bad. That shopping center strip on Robyn Avenue. Five of the stores in the complex were gutted before they could put it out."

Cat let her purse slide off her shoulder and to the floor. "Oh, no! That's where the new day care was going to be!"

Shelby nodded, looking troubled, seeming distracted. "Yeah, I know. . , . Cat, Blaine was on duty that night. And I didn't see him at church today."

The soft words rattled Cat to her very marrow. "Maybe he had to work," she said, willing her voice not to tremble.

"I don't think so. He said he had a late shift, remember?"

Cat didn't want to remember. What Shelby was suggesting was too horrible to consider. Surely they would have heard if something had happened. . . .

The front screen squeaked open and Trey shouted through the house, "He's here!"

The relief that gushed over Cat was enormous, and she didn't even question her actions as she whirled and ran from the kitchen, through the den, and out onto the sunny porch.

Package in hand, Blaine took the three steps, looking tired but marvelous—and definitely in one superb piece. "I overslept," he explained with a rueful grin. "Happy Easter."

Without thinking, Cat threw her arms around his neck in a welcoming hug, startling them both. She pulled back and stared at him, the shock on her face mirrored in his. A slow grin tilted his mouth.

"It's nice to know I've been missed."

Embarrassed, Cat made an elaborate show of smoothing the skirt of her buttery yellow gabardine dress. "I—Shelby was just telling me about the fire. . . and I–I'm glad to see you didn't get hurt."

His expression sobered, and Cat noticed for the first time how bloodshot his eyes were. "It was bad, though thankfully no lives were lost. I'm afraid it was arson this time. A bunch of teenagers with a grudge. Police caught them later. The leader was the same one who held up the Food Mart about a month ago."

"Arson?" Cat's eyes widened in shock. "In Loggin's Point?"

Trey grabbed Blaine's arm in barely contained excitement. "What's in the sack, Blaine? Didja bring me somethin'?"

"Trey," Cat gently reprimanded.

Blaine winked at her in amusement, sending shock waves through her heart. He turned to Trey. "As a matter of fact, Partner, I did bring you something." He pulled a shiny red fire truck, still in its boxed package, from the sack.

"Oh, boy!" Trey grabbed the gift, his blue eyes shining.

Cat ruffled his hair. "Tell Blaine thank you, then you may go play with your fire truck."

"Thanks, Blaine!" Trey gave him a one-armed hug then shot down the stairs and around the back of the house with his new toy.

"I know it's not very Eastery, but I wasn't sure how Shelby felt about chocolate bunnies and that sort of thing," Blaine explained, sounding uncertain. "One of my sisters is a health nut and doesn't let her kids touch the stuff."

"It's perfect," Cat said, smiling. "Ever since Trey met you, he's said he wants to be a fireman when he grows up."

Blaine exhaled deeply and looked away. "Sometimes the job is really hard. Like Friday night. And other times."

Cat bit her inside lower lip, wondering at his pained expression. Again she thought how tired he looked. "Let's sit on the glider and talk. Okay with you?"

Blaine nodded. He followed her to the cushioned swing and sank onto the narrow seat about a foot away from her. Pulse rate increasing at his close proximity, she clasped suddenly clammy hands together in her lap. He seemed unaware of her tension as he stared off into space.

"I thought when my friend Mark contacted me in Dallas about a position here, I'd get away from the crime of the big city; but it's everywhere, isn't it?" He turned anguished eyes her way. "Dallas. . .Fort Worth. . .Loggin's Point. . .doesn't really matter how large or small the town is. There are always people with a grudge. People wanting to make others pay."

Cat wasn't sure what he was leading up to and remained silent, waiting.

"Last year in Dallas, we got a call—a six-alarm blaze—really bad. We worked rescue, my buddy Grant and I." He paused, rubbing his closed eyelids with two fingers. "It was an old apartment building, and Grant worked alongside me, sweeping the building to make sure everyone was out. The bell on his SCBA mask started jingling—a sign he wasn't getting fresh air from his tank. The nearest exit was blocked, and I couldn't reach him. He tried to get out another way, but the section of roof over him collapsed."

Cat's heart twisted at his pain. Without thought, she laid her hand over his to comfort. He turned his hand over until their palms met and clutched her hand hard.

"We found out later a gang leader lived in one of the lower apartments. A rival gang thought they'd do him in. They didn't care who else died as long as they stuck to their agenda." Blaine shut his eyes, expelling a strained breath. "It took me a long time to forgive and let go, but eventually I did. Friday night brought it all back again. The grief of knowing I failed Grant, the loss of a good buddy. . ."

"You didn't fail him, Blaine," Cat said, tears swimming in her eyes as she shared his pain. "You're not the type; being close like you two were, I'm sure he knew that, too."

His eyes flew open and he looked at her, as if he'd never thought of it that way. Slowly, he lifted her hand to his lips and kissed it. "Thank you for that, Cat. It helps."

Heart pounding, she could think of nothing more to say, and they sat on the porch swing in companionable silence.

Over the next several weeks, Blaine became a fixture at

their house during his off hours, thanks to Shelby's invitation. Cat didn't argue, yet she wasn't sure how she felt about it. A shift had occurred between them since he'd bared his heart, and Cat had learned to marginally relax in his presence. Still, she couldn't let go of her bitterness that acted as a locked gate to the past, keeping Blaine securely on the outside. Where she wanted him. Yet, why had it become so hard to convince herself of that lately?

One unusually hot day, Blaine and Cat sat in the shade of the infamous oak tree where they'd first met, drinking lemonade and talking about inconsequential things. Trey sat on the platform's edge of the well, playing with his fire truck. Shelby had long since moved her potted plants inside, away from the scorching sun, but the ivy hanging from the crossbar looked in danger of being mangled by Trey's enthusiastic play.

"Trey, come down from there," Cat yelled. "Your mama won't be too happy if she comes home from work and finds you tore her pretty ivy."

Grudgingly, Trey obeyed.

"He's a good kid," Blaine said. "You must be proud."

"We are." A half-smile formed on her lips. "Since Shelby and I moved here, he's come to mean a whole lot to me. I sometimes think of him as my own."

Blaine watched the warm breeze ruffle Cat's curls and noted the tender expression on her face. She would make a good mother. Aware his thoughts were taking him into territory he wasn't yet ready to explore, he cleared his throat. "I got the impression you'd lived in Loggin's Point all your life."

"I have. I meant when we moved to this house. It used to be my great-granny's home, though I never visited when I was little. She died before I was born." A flicker of something passed across Cat's eyes. "When the house was left to my grandma, she didn't want it. She was happy where she was. Her two younger sisters lived up north and weren't interested in the house either, so Grandma decided to sell. Years later, after Tanner left Shelby, she discovered the place was on the market again, and we took everything we had out of savings and grabbed it up. We were able to legally divide the property in order to get great-granny's house back in the family again. Our neighbor, Mr. McNichols, bought the adjoining farmland."

Blaine listened with interest, watching Cat's eyes as they sparkled. The subject was obviously dear to her heart.

"Tell me about your family, Cat," he said, after he took a long swig of lemonade.

She fidgeted, averting her gaze to her drink. With her finger, she traced the condensation on the glass. "Mom is living in California with her new husband. Shelby and Trey are really the only family I have now."

"What about your father?"

A shutter seemed to slam across her face. "I haven't the faintest idea where he is, and I really don't care to know." The clipped, abrupt words didn't mesh with the dismal expression now in her eyes.

Blaine reached out and touched the forearm she'd rested on the metal arm of the lawn chair. "Hey, I'm here, if you need to unload."

"No. I really don't want to talk about it. Thanks anyway." She quickly stood. "Hey, Sport," she called, a false brightness in her voice, "lunchtime!"

As Trey ran their way, Blaine reluctantly rose from his chair. "Guess I should be going. I've got some things to do around the apartment." He wished Cat felt comfortable enough to confide in him, but obviously she still considered him an intruder. Then again, so did most of the people in town. He was an outsider in their eyes, and he wondered if that would ever change.

"Hey, Blaine—you comin' to my birthday party?" Trey asked eagerly.

"Well, I don't know. . ." He shot a glance Cat's way.

She hesitated, then offered a faint smile. By the frosty look in her eyes, she'd definitely frozen him out once again. "Of course, you're welcome to come," she said stiffly. "Noon on Saturday, two weeks from now."

"I'll have to check my schedule, but I'll be here if I can." Summoning a grin, he handed her his glass. "Well, I'll be moving on. Have a good one."

Cat watched Blaine tousle Trey's hair, then go. A flurry of disturbing emotions wreaked havoc inside her. To be around the man was disquieting. Yet she found that somewhere along the line she'd started looking forward to seeing his smiling face when she opened the front door to his knock. She now more than tolerated his pleasant company, the way he bonded to Trey, the tender look sometimes in his eyes when he caught her gaze. However, his unexpected question concerning her father had unsettled her.

Next time he came over, she should pull back, refuse

to see him, offer any excuse before he got too close and she lost her heart to him. . .

Cat had a sneaking suspicion it was already too late.

Six

S helby placed the final plate on the picnic table. The cheery party plates showed a little boy driving a red fire truck with a Dalmatian by his side. "Oh, no."

"What's wrong?" Cat straightened from tying red-and-white helium balloons to the birthday boy's chair.

"I forgot the Rocky Road ice cream. I was going to pick it up when I got off work yesterday." Shelby sighed. "Think you can hold down the fort while I make a quick run to the store?"

"Sure." Cat's gaze went to the seven kids playing in the backyard. Trey was showing Alex and another boy his fire truck. Two boys pitched a half-deflated ball back and forth. One little girl, no more than five, gyrated with a dusty hula hoop, trying to get it to spin. Alex's three-year-old sister, Amy, had an inflated swim float around her middle, though there was no pool. Amazing what kids could dig up from the shed to entertain themselves.

"But I'd rush if I were you," Cat warned. "If Trey gets a peek at his birthday cake, there'll be no holding him back."

Shelby laughed and hurried toward the house. "I

promise, you won't even miss me."

Cat settled back against the lawn chair to watch her temporary charges. She hadn't seen Blaine in two weeks and wondered if he was scheduled to work or would come to the party. Though she was loath to admit it, she missed his easygoing personality and his wacky sense of humor. She missed *him*.

Uncomfortable with her train of thought, Cat looked out over the sunny yard to the trees laden with ripening peaches and plums, right at the edge of their property line. Soon it would be time to pick their fruit and make preserves again. . . .

"Miss Cat," a small voice piped near her ear, breaking her out of her lazy reverie. "I gotta go potty."

Cat looked sideways into Amy's very serious plump baby face. "Can't it wait until Miss Shelby gets back, Sweetie?"

"Uh-uh. Right now."

Cat exhaled a resigned breath. Quickly she rose from her chair, pulled the swim float from the child's middle, and took her tiny hand. She didn't like leaving the kids unsupervised, but she'd learned from past mistakes when she worked with Amy in the day care that when the little girl said she had to go "right now," she wasn't kidding. Besides, what could happen in the few minutes she would be gone?

Cat helped Amy wash her hands. From the open window she heard the sounds of children playing and laughing. Trey's angry yelling rose above the rest, and Cat grimaced, sensing trouble. Suddenly a horrendous cracking sound rent the air, like a branch breaking from a tree, followed by a terrified scream.

Several of the children cried, "Miss Cat! Miss Cat!" but she was already out the bathroom door and heading toward the porch. Her gaze whipped over the backyard in quick assessment.

Three children stared at her, their eyes wide with shock, their mouths partway open. Two others stared at the well. The little girl, Tracy, was crying.

"What's wrong? Where's Trey—" Cat stopped and stared. The platform of the well had a jagged hole in the middle where it had caved in. She felt sick and dizzy as horrible realization flooded her. "Alex, quick— go call 911. Tell them Trey fell into the well," she rasped, running toward the structure. Putting her hands on its stone rim, she looked down into its black depths, tears blinding her eyes.

She could hear no sound from within.

"Hurry!"

Alex ran for the house. Seeing the swim float Amy had used lying nearby, Cat grabbed it on impulse and forced it through the small opening of the well. "Trey! Can you hear me? Grab the float!"

Trey had learned to swim as a toddler, but Cat had no idea how deep the well was, or if there was even water inside. Was he seriously hurt? *Please, dear God, don't let us lose him,* she cried silently over and over again. *Please, protect him!*

Frantic, she tore away the ivy that hung in her way then tried to pull up the splintered, rotting boards to make the hole bigger, but she only succeeded in slicing her hands. "Trey! Trey, can you hear me!"

"Cat, what's wrong?" Blaine jogged from the side of the house. "What happened?"

Her head shot up in relief that he was there. "It's the well! Trey fell inside, and I can't see him! I have to get him out before it's too late!"

At her panicked words, Blaine became the calm professional, trying not to show his concern. He tossed the birthday present he'd brought to the ground and rushed to look down the well, but he couldn't see a thing. "Trey!"

No child's voice piped back. Not even a groan or a whimper.

He moved away, hurrying to the front as he spoke. "I have some rope in my truck. I'll get it." He was back in less than a minute, tying two of the three thick ropes together with sturdy knots. "I worked rescue in Dallas, and I'm certified in EMS. Trust me, Cat. Did you call 911?"

She vaguely nodded, her face pale with shock, her hands bleeding as she continued to vainly pull at the jagged boards.

Blaine gently moved her aside, then began ripping up the carpeting and rotten boards himself. "More help should be here soon. You keep watch out front and show them where to go when they get here. Take the other children with you." He hoped giving her that minor job might enable her to get her bearings and help her feel as if she was contributing something to the rescue. Even as he spoke, sirens wailed in the distance, growing steadily louder.

The shell-shocked look in Cat's eyes remained. She stood stiff, as if she hadn't heard him. Blaine wished he could hold and reassure her, but there wasn't time.

"You'd better call someone to pick up the kids, too," he said, tying the thick rope around the tree trunk. "And pray, Kitten. Just pray."

Cat gave a stiff nod and sped to the front, immediately returning with the two policemen Blaine had seen the day of the tree rescue. Cat looked awful. He sent her a reassuring smile, wishing there was someone somewhere that could soothe her. And where was Shelby?

"What's up?" the older officer asked after Cat hurried back to the children.

Blaine briefly filled them in as he took the long line of rope and anchored it under his arms. "Any idea how deep the well is? I can't see bottom."

"I thought all these old wells were sealed long ago," the policeman said, shaking his head. "My guess is it must go down at least thirty—forty feet, but that's just a guess."

Blaine nodded as he made the final knot. "I've got over sixty feet of rope here. Hopefully, it's enough. I worked rescue in Dallas and have experience getting people out of tight spots. You two hold the rope and lower me inside. I'll need one of your portable radios for communication and a flashlight."

The younger policeman handed Blaine the requested items. Blaine tucked the radio and flashlight in his belt, turned the light on, then went to the rim of the well and lowered himself down the narrow hole. With both hands, he gripped the rope above him while the two policemen held tightly to the cable. Jagged pieces of board scraped his side, but he ignored the sting.

As Blaine felt himself being lowered deeper inside the bowels of the earth, he again heard sirens blaring. Good. The more help they had the better. *Please God, let me find him alive.*

"Trey?" he called down again, his voice echoing into the inky darkness below and bouncing off the clammy round wall of stone. "You okay, Partner? I'm coming to get you out now."

Silence.

❦

Crossing her arms and rubbing them in her anxiety, unmindful of the blood that smeared her skin, Cat stared at the ambulance as it sped up the gravel drive. Though the day was hot, gooseflesh covered her, and she felt as if she might throw up. The children were quiet, awed by all the noise and action. No more than five minutes had passed since Blaine had come; yet it felt like an eternity.

"In the back," Cat said in a trembling voice to two EMTs who ran her way with medical equipment. She wanted to follow but knew she had to wait for their neighbor to arrive and take charge of the children until their parents could be notified.

A rusty blue Mustang shot into the driveway between the ambulance and fire truck that had come less than a minute earlier. Cat stared in disbelief as Lonnie exited the car. It was the first time she'd seen him since their encounter at the store. His expression was sheepish, though concerned. "I heard the news on my scanner. I want to help if I can."

Unable to form words, Cat motioned over her shoulder and watched as Lonnie ran toward the back of the house.

She felt so useless, so incompetent! She should have known better than to leave six small kids in the backyard unsupervised. It was all her fault. All of it. Shelby would hate her—but no more than Cat already hated herself. If something should happen to Trey. . . No. She couldn't allow herself to think that way. Blaine had told her to trust him. He didn't realize how difficult it was for her to trust any man, yet she had no choice in the matter now. Trey's life was in Blaine's hands—and God's.

"Dear Lord in heaven," she whispered yet again, "please let Trey be all right. Please let your angels encamp about him and protect him. Please. . ."

She could think of nothing more to say as she watched Shelby's dark green van pull into the drive.

While an EMT bandaged Cat's hands a few minutes later, she observed her sister from several feet away with a mixture of awed pride and empathy.

"On the way home, I felt as if God was telling me to remain in peace and just trust Him," Shelby told a reporter from a local news station, who, like the rescuers, had arrived on the scene within minutes, along with his cameraman. "I didn't know what He was talking about, but I prayed the whole drive back."

She looked toward the well. Fear clouded her eyes, but her voice was calm, assured. "Now I know, and I choose to trust God and have faith that He can bring my little boy back to me. I won't believe anything less."

The cameraman shook his head at Shelby's statement. From his sober expression it was evident he thought her sister in denial. Cat lifted her chin and stared him down. "You're right, Shelby. Nothing is impossible for God."

The anchorman made his closing remarks as he faced the camera, promising to keep the TV audience updated.

"You really should get stitches on that hand," the EMT said to Cat as he fastened the last bandage.

Cat gave a distant nod, her gaze focusing on the well and Officer Trask speaking into the walkie-talkie. For her, life had stopped at that well and would only continue when Blaine and Trey appeared. Everything else was trivial.

Cynthia Little, a pastor's wife who lived down the lane, strode their way. Putting an arm around each woman, she herded Cat and Shelby toward the house. "Why don't we go inside now? I'm sure they'll have Trey out soon."

"I want to stay," Shelby insisted.

Suddenly Officer Trask turned his face toward them. "He's alive!" he yelled over the distance. His remark was met with loud cheers and smiles from the onlookers.

"Alive!" Cat breathed, tears of release rushing to her eyes. She felt like laughing and crying at the same time.

"Thank You, dear Jesus." Shelby's words came low. She let out a sound between a strangled gasp and moan, and Cat moved to hug her sister.

"Is he hurt?" Shelby called to the policeman when she could talk again.

"Don't know, Ma'am." He shook his head. "There's been some static and other problems. I haven't been able to get a clear message till now."

I just thank You, Lord, that he's alive. Cat's gaze flicked over the men aiding in the rescue. She could tell by the expressions on their faces that this had become personal to them, not just another job. They really cared about Trey and his safety.

A bee had stung Lonnie earlier, and though his face had turned beet red, he'd only brushed it away with one hand, never letting go of the rope or moving from his position at the back of the line of men. Perhaps Cat had misjudged him. She had definitely misjudged Blaine.

Shelby was right. There was no man like him.

"That's the signal," Officer Barnes said. "Pull!"

Gritting their teeth, the trio pulled the thick rope hand over hand. Sweat poured down their faces. The reporter came to life, and the camera started rolling again. Shelby and Cat drew closer to the well, arms tight around one another. Cat was barely aware of the stabbing pain this produced on her bandaged palm as she focused on the opening of the well.

An EMT tapped Shelby's shoulder. Cat and Shelby both turned.

"Ma'am, it'd be better if you wait in the ambulance. Once we get that boy in our hands, we'll head there as fast as possible." He glanced at Cat, then at the blood seeping through her bandaged hands. "You, too, Miss.

You need further medical care."

Shelby opened her mouth to argue, but Cynthia looked her way, her eyes gentle. "He's right, Shelby. Once they get Trey out, they'll need to head to the hospital without delay."

Cat cast one more glance toward the well, watching the rope as it slowly slid upward, inch by inch, with each strong pull. Then, grudgingly, she hurried after Shelby and Cynthia to the front of the house and the waiting ambulance.

Seven

C at sat alone on a vinyl bench in the back of the ambulance and stared at the bottles, syringes, strange machines, and hoses in the glass-fronted cabinet. Shelby sat up front with the driver, since she wasn't injured and Cat was. And they waited. To keep out nosy reporters, the doors had been shut— protecting them from harassment, yet barring any outside communication.

Had something gone wrong? How much time had elapsed?

These thoughts no more than flitted through Cat's head when the back doors swung open. Trey lay blanketed and buckled up on a gurney, an oxygen mask covering his nose and mouth. He was pale, shaky, and wet—but gloriously alive! Cat sent a silent thank you to heaven as the two EMTs lifted the stretcher into the ambulance.

"Trey, I'm right here, Honey. So is your mommy." Moisture sprung to Cat's eyes, and she glanced at Shelby, whose face was pressed against the glass partition. Tears streamed down her cheeks, and the widest smile Cat had seen in a long time beamed across her face.

For a second, Cat thought the wiry, dark-headed EMT would order her out. Then he looked at the red-spotted bandages on her hands and gave a curt nod. She scooted as far to the edge as she could, trying to stay out of the way in the crowded confines while the two men fastened the stretcher against the wall. The doors slammed shut, and the ambulance took off, its siren wailing.

"Mommy?" The thin word came muffled through the mask, but it was the sweetest music Cat had ever heard.

At the EMT's nod, Cat moved closer so she could hear better, yet far enough away so as to not interfere with the two men working over Trey. "She's here. She's sitting up front and is very happy you're all right."

"I losted my new fire truck," he said sadly. "It falled down the well. Can I have another one?"

The redheaded EMT took time to throw a grin her way. Cat held back the laugh that wanted to spring forth, and let the tears drip down her cheeks. Trey sounded oh, so normal. He would be all right.

"Don't worry, Sport. Of course I'll buy you another. I promise. I'm just thankful you took swimming lessons when you were a baby."

"I didn't swim. My legs hurted too much when I landed in the water. My foot still hurts."

Cat stiffened. A full minute must have elapsed before she tossed the float down to him. "Sure you did, Trey. Before I threw you the swim float—remember?"

Trey winced as the ambulance hit a pothole in the

road, jostling his leg. "The man catched me and held me."

"Blaine?" Cat asked, furrowing her brow in puzzlement. "No, Honey, Blaine didn't get there till later."

"Not Blaine. The man in the well. He told me I'd be okay." Trey yawned. "I'm sleepy."

Cat exchanged a stunned look with the two EMTs while shivers raced down her spine. "What did this man look like, Trey?"

"Couldn't see him. Too dark. His voice was soft and pretty, though." He closed his eyes, his words coming fainter. "He held me, even after I had the float."

"Trey. . ."

The dark-headed EMT shook his head. "He's in shock. Obviously doesn't know what he's talking about." His expression grew puzzled.

"What?" Cat insisted.

He hesitated, then his gaze swung her way. "His ankle looks fractured. X-rays will determine that for sure. Falling as far as he did, and with such an injury. . . well, frankly, I don't see how he could have stayed afloat. This boy is lucky to be alive."

The redhead caught Cat's gaze, a knowing look in his eyes. "Maybe luck isn't the right word here, Juan," he said quietly. "I think miracle fits better, don't you?"

An overwhelming sense of peace and God's strong love flowed through Cat. She turned to stare at Trey's small face beneath the mask while the men continued working over him. Fresh tears blurred her vision.

Yes, definitely a miracle.

In the Emergency Room, Cat sat on a stark white

gurney, screened in by pale green curtains. The strong smells of rubbing alcohol and cleaning products hit her senses—the smells of a hospital. A doctor had put five stitches in her hand earlier, and now Cat waited for someone to come to her small, U-shaped cubicle to tell her she could go. She wanted to see Trey and get a report on his condition.

A sudden commotion alerted Cat. She slid off the gurney and peeked through the curtains. From her vantage point, she could see the open door that led into the hallway. Blaine stood next to the entrance, surrounded by a group of men and women with microphones and cameras. Cat's heart plummeted when she saw that his hands were also bandaged. She hadn't known he'd been hurt!

She hesitated, then stepped out of the curtains and closer to the questioning throng in time to hear Blaine's words.

"I'm no hero. If you want to give credit where credit is due, then look up. It's because of God that boy is alive today. I was just an instrument He used."

Wonder filled Cat, and a smile tilted her lips. No, Blaine was like no other man.

A reporter caught sight of her and quickly strode her way. "Lane Simmons from WCJS news. You're Cat MacGregor, Trey Stockton's aunt, aren't you? Tell me, Ma'am, why wasn't that old well sealed? Were you not aware of the danger?"

Cat blinked as the microphone was shoved at her face and the camera zoomed in on her. "I. . .uh. . .no, I didn't know. We had no reason to believe it hadn't already been taken care of—"

"What are you people doing here? Where's security?" The curt questions came from a heavyset head nurse in white uniform, who came barreling through the doorway. "This is an emergency room, not a newsroom. Outside—all of you."

After the nurse shooed them from the room, Cat caught Blaine's concerned gaze studying her from the hallway. He covered the distance between them. "You okay?"

Still shaken by the sudden onslaught, she nodded and glanced down at his hands, then back at his face. "Are you?"

A young nurse came up to Cat. "You can go now." She handed her some papers along with a prescription the doctor had filled out.

After the nurse left, Blaine nodded toward the doorway. "Let's go sit down somewhere."

"I'd like to check on Trey."

"I'd wait if I were you. He's sleeping. I checked earlier. Shelby's with him."

Deciding she would take Blaine's advice and go later, Cat followed him to the pastel yellow-and-cantaloupe-colored waiting room on the floor of the children's ward. Framed prints of brown teddy bears with blue bows hung on the wall. Blaine sat next to Cat on a slick, nylon-covered couch.

"What happened to your hands?" she asked.

A rueful grin lifted the corners of his mouth. "Rope burns. I didn't have my gloves. It's not serious—looks worse than it really is."

An overwhelming sense of tenderness and respect flooded Cat, and tears came to her eyes. She gingerly lifted his closest hand with both of hers and placed a kiss on the curved fingers sticking outside the white bandage.

Blaine inhaled sharply in surprise. "What was that for?"

"Because I'm grateful. Because I've come to realize just how wonderful you really are. And because. . .because I think I'm ready to start letting that wall down now."

Blaine studied her, his countenance serious. "I don't just want your gratitude, Cat. . .but I guess it's a starting point." He grinned.

Feeling suddenly shy, she averted her gaze but didn't let go of his hand. "I still can't believe that old well wasn't properly sealed. All this time we've lived there and to think it was like that the whole time. . ." Her words trailed off, and she shivered.

"I'll see to it arrangements are made to locate a well contractor and seal up the well," Blaine assured. "The previous owners obviously thought bolting a wooden cover over the opening would do. It's not your fault, Cat. You didn't know."

She looked at him, grateful for his comforting words.

His expression grew thoughtful. "Did Trey tell you about his experience while he was down there?"

Tiny hairs stood erect at the back of her neck. "You mean the man in the well?"

He nodded. "I didn't see anything. What do you think?"

"I think. . .I think we teach children that God sends His angels to help us, and we read about ministering angels in the Bible all the time; but when it actually happens to us, it's hard to grasp, isn't it?" Tingles coursed through her. "It gives me a warm feeling though—kind of unreal, but closer to God. Does that make sense?"

"Perfect sense. When I worked in Dallas, a fire destroyed a pastor's home. There were only two of us in that part of the building, checking for occupants. We found a little boy. His room was in flames. Later the boy told his parents that three men saved him. The man carrying him out, me, and the tall man who walked behind us."

Cat shivered again, feeling tears come to her eyes.

Blaine looked at her in concern. "Cold? Hospitals always are like ice boxes."

"I'm all right. Just in awe of our Creator."

"Yeah, I know what you mean," he said quietly.

He glanced down at his bandaged hand between her two bandaged ones. "We're quite a pair, aren't we? Guess we won't be doing any tree-climbing or Frisbee-throwing for a while." He winked at her, the creases by his mouth deepening as his grin widened.

Cat laughed. "Well, I sure won't miss that!" Her smile faded. "Blaine, about that day—I'm sorry. I wasn't very nice, and I guess I haven't been very nice for a long time. I–I think I'd like to tell you a little about myself now. If you still want to hear it, that is."

"I want to know everything there is to know about you," he assured, his voice gentle.

Head close to his, keeping a light hold on his bandaged hand, she swallowed hard and finally allowed the painful words she'd kept locked up to spill out.

❧

"I can't do this. I feel silly!" Cat turned to Blaine, the wind whipping her curls into her face. They stood atop a grassy slope at the highest point in town, the place for which Loggin's Point was named.

He grinned. "What's it going to hurt? And just maybe it'll help."

Cat raised a brow. "Mr. Fulton might not agree—since it will end up on his land."

"Let me worry about Mr. Fulton," Blaine said, lifting his fingers to stroke her cheek. "Now, come on. No more excuses."

Warmth zinged through Cat at his touch, as it always did when he held or kissed her. In the one and a half months since Trey's rescue, all the townspeople had come to accept Blaine with open arms. Even Lonnie made peace with him. Blaine had told her that the practical jokes at the fire station had ceased. He was considered "one of the guys" now and treated with friendliness and respect.

For days after the rescue, newspaper headlines blazed with "The Miracle at Loggin's Point," and Trey was cited as "the miracle boy." Yet soon another story took its place, and Trey's rescue faded into the background. His cast had come off last week, and now he was just a normal boy, playing with his brand-new fire truck—and over a dozen other toys sent to him while he was in the hospital. The story made national news, and numerous gifts had arrived from all over the country. Shelby donated most of them to a nearby orphanage. The donations of money went toward paying the high hospital bill and sealing the well.

Another miracle took place—one that only Cat, Shelby, and Blaine knew about. Cat had finally allowed the Lord to change the bitter waters in her life and make them sweet. She now drank from the spring of living water the Lord promises to those who ask Him, experiencing His love. And she'd forgiven her father.

Yet Blaine didn't think that was enough. He cocked his head and looked at her now. "Well?"

"Oh, all right," she said halfheartedly, and was thrilled when he rewarded her with a tender kiss on the lips. "Tell me. Are you always this bossy?"

"I'll give you a lifetime to find out."

The breath snagged in Cat's throat, and her eyes widened. "Blaine Carson, did you just propose?"

"I was going to wait until you got back from the mission trip, but I'm an impatient man when it comes to some things." His expression grew serious. "Kitten, will you marry me and make my life here at Loggin's Point complete?"

"Really?"

He nodded.

"Yippee!" Cat sang out as she turned and hurled the Frisbee over the cliff.

Tears of happiness filled her eyes while she watched the wind carry the orange disk through the pale blue, cloudless sky and over the grove of trees. As she let go, she released all the pain and bad memories concerning her father's abandonment. Blaine had told her that forgiving meant forgetting and letting go. She had to admit, the action of hurling the Frisbee did make the letting go seem more real, as Blaine had said it would. She knew this was just a small beginning of her healing, but it was a step in the right direction. The Lord would lead her the rest of the way.

Laughing, Blaine grabbed her wrist, swinging her back to face him. She went willingly into his arms.

"Does that mean yes?"

"Most definitely."

He kissed her deeply, then whirled her around.

Cat had never felt so loved or so free.

But whoever drinks the water I give him
will never thirst.
Indeed, the water I give him will become in him
a spring of water welling up to eternal life.
JOHN 4:14

PAMELA GRIFFIN

Pamela lives in Texas and divides her time between family, church activities, and writing. She fully gave her life to the Lord Jesus Christ in 1988, after a rebellious young adulthood, and owes the fact that she's still alive today to an all-loving and forgiving God and to a mother who steadfastly prayed and had faith that God could bring her wayward daughter "home." Pamela's main goal in writing Christian romance is to help and encourage those who *do* know the Lord and to plant a seed of hope in them who don't. Pamela invites you to check out her website: http://home.att.net/~words_of_honey/Pamela.htm.

Man of Distinction

by Tamela Hancock Murray

One

I wish you wouldn't go to that awful place."

Veronica Van Slyke paused in front of the heavy double doors that served as the gateway between the security of her childhood home and the larger world. Though she wasn't eager for a confrontation about her new mission, Veronica knew her mother's objections displayed her concern and love. She kept one hand on the brass lever and tightened her grip on the Bible with the other. "I'll be fine, Mother."

"How do you know that?" From her perch on the antique divan in the formal living room, Tess set her fashion magazine aside. "Just because A Place of Our Own is run by the church, that doesn't mean there won't be trouble." She shook her head and muttered, "I wish our congregation wouldn't try to take on the impossible. Why can't we just send money to Africa like everybody else?"

"We do designate money to foreign missions."

"That is neither here nor there." Her mother's gaze pierced her. "You're much too beautiful for such a ministry, Veronica. Who knows what undesirables will make a pass at you?"

"Thanks for the compliment, Mother, but I'm sure no one will bother me." Letting go of the lever, she placed her hand on a slim, jean-clad hip. "I know you and Father don't understand why I want to lead the Bible study at the shelter, but it's something I have to do."

"You're right. We don't understand. You don't have any idea what it's like to live in poverty, but we do."

"I know." Realizing she was in for the familiar lecture her mother never tired of delivering, Veronica leaned against the doorway that led to the living room.

"I know your generation is used to people making millions overnight on the Internet with an idea and a shoestring, so your father and I don't expect you to understand how truly difficult it is for most people to earn a living, much less to afford luxuries. But we built up our wealth the old-fashioned way." She pointed her forefinger at Veronica for emphasis. "Through hard, hard work. We lived and breathed consulting for years before the company got off the ground. Even now, you see how many hours a week your father puts in at the office."

"I know."

Tess shook her head at her daughter. "Why do you want to throw it all away? Why do you want to go to a place where you don't belong, where you'll be shoulder to shoulder with a bunch of lowlifes too lazy to work for a living?"

"Haven't you been reading the church newsletter or listening to anything anyone has said about our shelter?" Veronica didn't wait for a reply before she explained,

"Most of the residents are there because of a temporary setback, and they are all either working or looking for work. It's just difficult for many of them because they don't have the skills or education to get high-paying jobs. Scraping together enough money for the first month's rent and security deposit on an apartment isn't easy on minimum wage."

"Your father and I started with nothing, and we managed because we made the effort."

"And I do appreciate what you and Father have done." She looked into her mother's eyes, willing her to understand. "But I've been praying about this, and I really believe God wants me at the shelter. Otherwise, Pastor Juan never would have mentioned it to me."

"Pastor Juan!" Blue eyes, that mirrored Veronica's narrowed. "How long has he been out of seminary? Two days?"

"Try two years."

"As your generation likes to say, 'Whatever.' " Tess waved a manicured hand. "What does that babe in the woods know about life? It's a shame Reverend Evans retired. He would have never dreamed of such a crazy idea, at least not for you. Certainly you're not the only person who can teach a Bible lesson."

"No, but he knows I teach Sunday school."

"Three year olds are a far cry from adults."

"Maybe adults will actually be easier to teach," Veronica speculated. "That's why Pastor Juan is so popular with the young Singles, Mother. He encourages us to serve."

"So he does—but he might not be so popular with

the finance committee when they find out why our pledge will be greatly reduced next year."

"You don't mean that."

Tess allowed silence to permeate the room for several long seconds, a technique she had refined for effect over the years. "No, I suppose I don't," she finally answered. "Though the thought is tempting."

"Tempting or not, there's nothing anyone can do to change my plans for tonight. I promised Pastor Juan I'd be there, and I will."

"Will he be there?"

Veronica shook her head. "He has another meeting."

Tess's mouth tightened into a thin line. "I wish he would be there to protect you, if for no other reason."

Veronica smiled in spite of herself. "I know I'll always be your baby, but I can take care of myself."

"That's what you think, until some crazy loon makes up his mind to stalk you." Tess raised an eyebrow. "As I told you before, you have no idea how attractive you are. Do you know how many women pay good money to dye their hair blue-black, the way yours is naturally?" She patted her pageboy bob, colored at a salon to mimic the black sheen hers had held in decades past. "Or how many others pay a hundred and fifty dollars for a spiral perm?"

"I guess I can thank Nana's genes for saving me so much money, even though she never liked her curls, either." Grimacing, Veronica ran a hand through several smooth ringlets. "I'd gladly trade these curls for straight hair like yours." Extending her arms, she examined hands the color of porcelain. "And while I'm at it,

I wouldn't mind skin that would tan."

Her mother's look conveyed no sympathy. "If only your father didn't need to prepare for his big presentation tomorrow, he could drive you to the shelter."

"You know you're welcome to come along, Mother." Knowing her mother would never consider venturing near the homeless, Veronica suppressed a smile.

"You know my bridge club is due to arrive in less than an hour." Exhaling in obvious exasperation, she renewed her admonitions. "Do be sure to park in a space that's well lit. And lock your doors. I worry that someone will try to steal such a flashy car," she added, referring to the red Mustang that had been their gift upon Veronica's college graduation.

"That's why I have good insurance," Veronica quipped. Then, seeing her mother's expression of genuine worry, she added, "I know the shelter's not in the best part of town. I'll be careful."

"Just come straight home after the study. Please?"

"All right." Closing the door behind her, Veronica had no qualms about making the promise. Though she looked forward to the study, she could think of no reason why she would linger once she presented her lesson on the parable of the prodigal son.

On the road, Veronica suddenly felt nervous. Yet her fear was not for her personal safety, but that she would fail in doing the Lord's will. She turned off the Christian music radio station though The Newsboys were singing one of her favorite tunes. "Lord, guide me as I teach tonight. Help me to inspire, edify, and convict those You want Your word to touch. Help my family to understand why I want to serve You. In Jesus' name, amen."

Veronica remembered the verses in the Book of Matthew that had inspired her when she first attended Pastor Juan's adult Sunday school class. *And Jesus came and spake unto them, saying, "All power is given unto me in heaven and in earth. Go ye therefore, and teach all nations, baptizing them in the name of the Father, and of the Son, and of the Holy Ghost: Teaching them to observe all things whatsoever I have commanded you: and, lo, I am with you alway, even unto the end of the world." Amen.*

"The Great Commission. Oh, how I pray You will bless my puny efforts, Lord!" she pled as she turned into the parking lot.

Cracked and rutted pavement reminded her that there was still much work to do, even though she agreed with the decision to open the shelter sooner, rather than waiting for the funds to make all of the needed improvements. Searching for a parking space, she was forced to park at the end of the row, in front of room eleven.

"Lucky number eleven," she mumbled. "This place isn't even big enough to have thirteen rooms." Light from a bare bulb on the left side of the door lit the immediate area as well as could be expected. "At least I can tell Mother I did the best I could to park near a light."

The old motor inn contrasted with the sprawling home she'd left on the other side of town. Before her church purchased the property, the lodge had been vacant for over a decade. Only after much labor by Veronica and other church members did the old inn become habitable.

A few days had been devoted to clearing debris and eliminating bugs and rodents. Then came cosmetic changes. Fresh white paint concealed an exterior that had once been hot pink. Broken and missing turquoise shutters had been replaced in a more modern and tasteful royal blue. She had helped the Young Singles raise funds for new carpeting. The dark green indoor-outdoor fabric had been selected for its durability rather than eye appeal. Even with these marked improvements, the shelter was far from ideal. She was all too aware that homeless families had to jam into small, sparsely furnished rooms.

Still, A Place of Our Own offered rooms that were clean and warm. Volunteers took turns providing a light breakfast, bag lunches for those who worked, and an evening meal. No doubt, the shelter offered a better alternative to living in a car.

As she passed several rooms, a train rumbled by, blaring its horn as it sped over tracks located a few feet behind the property. *Guess there are some things you just can't fix,* she thought. *Hope there aren't too many trains passing this way in the middle of the night.*

Suddenly nervous as she ventured to the largest part of the building, Veronica clutched her Bible and stack of note cards, scribbled with insights, to her chest. Though darkness had settled, some of the shelter residents sat outdoors in a small courtyard, wearing coats as a precaution against the Virginia winter. Smokers conversed, their friendships forged by a shared habit. A small group of men stood away from the smoke as they talked among themselves. Some children played on an old, flimsy swing set. Veronica made a mental note to mention replacing it at the next Young Singles' meeting.

She walked through the courtyard and tensed when she noticed her presence garnered furtive looks. Trying not to appear self-conscious, Veronica became aware that her simple but expensive clothing made her appear alien in her present surroundings. She was grateful she had left her pricey jewelry at home, choosing to wear a small pair of gold hoop earrings and a gold cross that swung from the end of a matching chain.

Determined to overcome her uneasiness, she flashed a smile in the group's direction. "Hello."

A few shy murmurs and nods were her answer.

Scanning the group of nonsmokers, her eyes locked with another pair of eyes so vivid an emerald that genuine brilliant cut stones couldn't compare either in richness or sparkle. In an instant, she discerned their owner wasn't much older than she. She wondered why he hadn't bothered to run a comb through his disheveled, blond-streaked, brown hair. The rest of him was hidden underneath a short cloth coat and baggy jeans.

Turning to enter what was once the motel office, she found herself wondering about his story, yet there was no time to linger on wayward thoughts as she made her way into the small room where she was to give her lesson. A couple of older women were already seated, chatting as they waited for her to arrive. Upon greeting them, she was pleased to discover they were eager to participate in the study and had brought their well-worn Bibles.

Her voice carried into the lobby as she spoke the

opening prayer, drawing a few more people into the study. Most of her students were women of various ages. A couple of men sat near the back of the room. Veronica noted with a slight bit of disappointment that neither was Mr. Emerald Eyes. Since none of the newcomers carried a Bible, Veronica wondered if they were motivated to come to class out of boredom or simple curiosity. Regardless of their reasons, she was glad they had joined the group.

"It looks like I'll have to ask that you share Bibles this week," she announced. "But next week, I'll try to bring Bibles for those who don't already have them. They'll be yours to keep."

"No strings attached?" a young woman asked, heavy doubt coloring her voice.

"Well," Veronica answered, "I'd be pleased if you'd attend the study every week as long as you're here. You can bring your new Bible with you."

Her inquisitor rolled her brown eyes upward. "I knew there would be a catch."

"There's no catch. If you don't want to continue the study or if you leave A Place of Our Own, the Bible is still yours to keep."

The woman's expression changed from hardened to amused. "Did you know you sound just like one of those ads on TV?"

Good-natured laughter filled the room.

Even though she felt heat rise to her cheeks, Veronica grinned. "I guess I do sound like an advertisement, don't I? But if you had made the greatest discovery of all time, wouldn't you want everyone else to know about it, too?"

Since the lesson had taken an unexpected turn, Veronica decided to abandon her notes on the prodigal son and let the class talk about what it means to be a Christian. As the discussion progressed, the group became more animated, and everyone wanted a chance to speak. Before Veronica realized it, hours had passed and she needed to wrap up the lesson. Upon dismissing the class, she prayed aloud that the Lord would bless them and protect them in the following week.

Most of her new students were smiling as the class ended. Veronica felt the Holy Spirit had touched the group, resulting in a much better introduction than the one she had planned. Flushed with success, she waved a cheerful good-bye to Max, the shelter operator, on her way out.

"I guess I don't have to ask you how it went," he observed.

"It's that obvious, huh?"

"You look like the cat who swallowed a canary." He gave her a warm smile. "See you next week, then?"

"See you next week."

Whistling as she left the building, she noticed that the light in front of Room Eleven had been broken in her absence.

That's strange. At that moment, she noticed how the night sky seemed darker than when she'd first arrived. A bone-numbing chill coursed through her as a feeling of fear gripped her gut. *I'd better go back and tell Max there's been some vandalism.*

She whirled around in the direction of the lobby. Without warning, a body pressed against her from behind. She felt a strong arm grab her waist. Realizing she was in danger, Veronica opened her mouth to scream. Before a cry could escape, a hand clapped over her mouth.

Two

A male voice growled in her ear. "Do what I say and you won't get hurt. I have a gun."

The instructions came as no surprise, but the pitch of the voice was a shock. Veronica had expected threats to be delivered in a deep, commanding tone. Instead, the utterance seemed youthful.

The sharp jab at her waist showed Veronica he meant business, no matter what his age. Nodding her assent, she prayed robbery was his sole intent.

Apparently convinced he had frightened her into submission, he took the gun out of her side and searched her jacket pockets for valuables. A wave of nausea hit her as he retrieved a red wallet. Though she carried only a few dollars in cash, she knew he could wreak havoc with her credit cards.

"Is that it?"

She nodded, sending a silent plea to the Lord that the robber wouldn't do something foolish now that he had what he wanted. In a flash, everything she had heard about self-defense ran through her mind.

Scream to get someone's attention. Don't yell, "Help!"

because no one will respond. Scream, "Fire!" instead. But the hand still clasped over her mouth assured her that trying to shout, or even to whisper, would be to no avail. She looked from side to side, searching for someone, anyone, who might come to her assistance. There was no one.

New words of caution echoed in her mind. *Struggle and run. A gunman seldom hits a moving target.*

For an instant, she thought about wriggling out of the strong hold and fleeing as fast as she could; but so far, the robber hadn't seemed eager to use his gun. *If I make a break for it, he might panic. No. Better to submit to robbery than to risk real injury.*

"Keys," he muttered. "Where are they?" Anticipating her answer, he slid his hand from her mouth to her chin.

"My inside pocket."

His hand returned to her mouth. "Get 'em. Now."

Mumbling unintelligible words, she motioned for him to release his grip so she could move.

"Okay, but you better not scream."

Heart beating so frantically she could hear it pulsing in her ears, Veronica fumbled as she tried to unzip her jacket.

"Hurry up! What's the matter with you? Don't you know you should have your keys out before you get to the car?"

Just what I need. Safety advice from a robber. Aloud she quipped, "Sorry to inconvenience you."

"You'll have more than that to worry about if you don't watch it."

Her fingers finally touched the tip of the key ring a

friend had given her in a show of humor. The pewter medallion was engraved with an image of an angel and inscribed with the slogan, "Drive no faster than your guardian angel can fly."

My car. I wish he wouldn't take my car. Veronica swallowed as she remembered something else she had heard. *Don't ever get in a car with a criminal. If you do, you're dead.*

"Here." She turned and faced him. The robber who had kept her in fear these past few minutes looked to be no more than a boy, barely a high school sophomore. A dingy knit hat covered his hair, although she guessed it to be light brown, judging from the peach fuzz on his tender face that mocked a goatee. "You can have the car." Though her words were acquiescent, she clung to her keys. "If you're even old enough to drive."

He had opened his mouth to answer when his dark eyes caught sight of the necklace resting on her white turtleneck sweater, exposed by her open jacket. Crooking his fingers, he motioned her to surrender that as well.

"My cross?" Her chest tightened at the thought of relinquishing her most precious memento. She would have preferred that he take the car. Shaking her head, she clutched the necklace. "No. Not my cross. It was a gift from my grandmother."

"Then she can buy you another one, pretty lady. She must be rich enough to buy you a thousand crosses."

"No, she can't—"

Without another word, the boy yanked the cross from Veronica's neck. The gold filigree chain broke. Tears betrayed her fear and upset. She was so distraught, she barely heard a shout.

"Hey!"

Veronica gasped as she spotted a tall man racing toward them from a few doors down. Following her lead, the robber's head snapped in the same direction. A look of panic crossed his face when he realized he'd been caught.

Remembering the gun, Veronica became fearful for her would-be hero. *Please, don't let him shoot!*

Her prayers were answered. After one last glimpse at her car keys, then quick glances in every direction, the boy decided to take off running across the parking lot. Veronica's rescuer stopped rushing toward her and changed directions in a flash to pursue the thief. Within a few seconds, he easily overtook the boy before he reached the other end of the lot. Jumping on top of the robber, her rescuer wrestled him to the pavement and pinned him down with his hands and knees.

Overcoming her fright and caution, Veronica rushed to their side. The man who had stopped the robbery was talking to the boy.

"Josh, what are you doing? You know this means you can't stay at the shelter anymore."

The robber looked remorseful for the first time. "I'm sorry, Caspar. I wasn't going to hurt her. I mean it. It's just that I owe Rock money."

Speechless upon discovering they knew each other, Veronica stood aghast.

"For drugs?" Caspar asked.

Josh's sullen expression was all the answer he needed.

Caspar grabbed Josh by the collar with both hands.

"If you weren't on that stuff, you could have outrun me."

"Is that a good thing?" was the sarcastic reply.

"Yes. Because then you wouldn't be pulling such a stunt to start with. You'd be back on the track team at school, in the physical and mental form a senior should be." Caspar rose to his feet, bringing Josh up with him as he maintained a firm clamp on the boy's thin arm.

"Aw, who needs the track team? I'll never amount to nothin', anyway. Just like my daddy always said." Josh's shoulders hunched in defeat.

Feeling an unexpected surge of sympathy, Veronica blurted, "Of course you'll amount to something. Don't listen to anyone who tells you otherwise."

Both Caspar and Josh turned to her, surprise evident on their faces. As soon as she saw Caspar's emerald green eyes, she realized he was the man she had exchanged looks with in the courtyard. An undeniable spark of interest flashed on his handsome, clean-shaven face. Without warning, a mixture of pleasure and embarrassment filled her. She looked down at her boots.

"It will be hard for him to amount to much in prison," Caspar said.

The thought caused Veronica to return her gaze to Josh.

A fearful light shone in his hazel eyes. "You're not gonna press charges, are you, Lady? I wasn't going to hurt you. And look," he added, handing her back the items he stole. "Here's your wallet. And your necklace."

Veronica accepted her possessions, yet she wanted to remind Josh how serious his actions had been. "You wouldn't be giving them back now if you hadn't been caught. Not to mention, you were planning to take my car, too."

"I'm sorry." He averted his eyes.

Sorry you robbed me or sorry you got caught? She looked at Caspar. "I didn't bring much money with me tonight, but I'd like to reward you for your courage." Becoming conscious of the pearl set in silver that Josh had missed on her right ring finger, she pulled it off and handed it to Caspar. "Here. This isn't expensive, but keep it as a token until I can reward you properly."

Pushing a palm toward her, he shook his head. "No, thanks. I don't want the ring."

Ignoring his protest, she continued to hold the ring in her outstretched hand. "You can give it back when I give you the money."

"I don't want that, either."

She looked at Caspar and wondered how he could turn down her offer. He seemed to own little in the world. He could have used a new coat to replace the one he was wearing, with its frayed corners and one pocket threatening to come loose. Though oil stains on faded jeans identified him as a mechanic, she guessed he didn't even own a car—yet he helped her keep her new one. She longed to reach out to him, to do something for him in return.

"Please. Let me reward you."

As Caspar shook his head, Josh became angry. "What's the big deal? I said I wasn't planning to hurt you. Seems to me you have plenty of money. If you weren't rich, you wouldn't be able to offer him a big reward."

His churlish attitude brought a frown to Veronica's

face. "But I thought you were going to hurt me. You threatened me with a gun."

With a sheepish look, he took his weapon out of his jeans pocket. "This? It was just a toy."

Veronica would have felt foolish had the toy not looked—and felt—so realistic.

"This may seem like fun and games to you," Caspar pointed out, "but can't you see you really scared her?"

"I'm sorry."

"Maybe, but you'll be eighteen in a couple of months. That's old enough to be tried as an adult in a court of law." Caspar paused. "That is, if they don't decide to try you as an adult this time."

The sound of a car pulling into a lot broke into their discussion. As soon as Veronica saw the silver Lincoln with the license WIN 4 WEN, she groaned.

"You know them?" Caspar asked.

"It's my father."

A man whose youthful physique and lithe step defied his silver hair jumped out of the car. As he approached, Veronica noticed his costly suit made him appear out of place. "Veronica! What are you still doing here? Do you have any idea how worried your mother is?"

"I'm sorry." Feeling her cheeks grow warm, she felt like a miscreant child instead of the woman she was.

"I'm just glad you're all right." Tilting his head upward, he looked down his nose at Josh and Caspar. The hard glint in his eyes was a sure sign his assessment was unfavorable. "Are you friends of my daughter?" His tone indicated he was hoping against hope that they weren't.

"We just met," Veronica rushed to respond.

"That's right," Caspar agreed. "Although I'm afraid Josh here isn't exactly a friend. He tried to rob your daughter."

"Caspar!" Josh wailed.

"Rob her?" Her father's eyes widened in shock as he put his arm around her shoulders. "Baby, are you all right?"

"I'm fine, thanks to Caspar." She nodded toward him.

Wen Van Slyke extended his hand to Veronica's rescuer. "Thank you. I'll see to it that you're properly rewarded as soon as we settle matters with the police. I take it they'll be here soon?"

"No one's called them," Veronica said.

"What?" Obviously distressed, Wen instructed Caspar not to let Josh get away as he headed toward the car to place the call on his cell phone.

Eyeing the vise grip Caspar had on Josh's arm, Veronica knew he wouldn't be going anywhere anytime soon.

Moments later, after all was recounted to the police amidst a few curious onlookers who had gathered, Veronica felt a pang of compassion for Josh as he was escorted into the police car.

"Sorry to see him go like that?" Caspar asked.

"Is it that obvious?"

"It's all over your face. You do-gooders are all alike."

Veronica would have been insulted had she not seen the teasing glint in his eyes. "What do you think will happen to him?"

"Unfortunately, he's got a record. I imagine he's

looking at jail time." Caspar sighed. "I've been trying to encourage him to do something more with his life, but as you can see, I haven't been too successful."

"Don't blame yourself. He has to make that decision."

Veronica's father interrupted. "Let's go home, Honey."

"I'll be right there."

He gave Veronica a hesitant glance. "All right. I'll be waiting in the car. I think I'd better follow you home."

Veronica normally would have objected, but she was still too shaken to dispute her father's orders. In fact, she welcomed the security, but there was a more urgent matter at hand. "About that reward—"

"No, I won't take it."

"But if you hadn't shown up when you did, I'd be out of a car—and I certainly wouldn't have gotten back my wallet or necklace." She held up the tiny cross for him to see. "My grandmother gave me this. I wear it every day as a memento of her."

"I'm surprised Josh bothered with a cross. It's not exactly his favorite symbol. Guess he thought it was valuable."

"Hardly more valuable than my car, at least not in monetary terms." She paused. "You know, it's funny. He was just about to take my car keys when he saw the cross and argued with me about that, instead. If he hadn't seen it, he would have been out of here with my car, long gone before anyone could have helped."

"Guess that's not the first time the cross saved you, huh?"

"That's just what I was thinking." She smiled. "You must be a born-again Christian."

"I know how they think."

"Oh." His avoidance of a direct answer was a disappointment, something she knew he would discern by her flat tone of voice. Deliberately she tried to soften it. "I take it you must know someone who's born again."

"Do I?" He looked into her eyes. "Since you're so eager to reward me, I think I've finally figured out how you can do it."

"How?"

"First of all, keep teaching your Bible studies."

Veronica raised an eyebrow. She wondered why someone so reluctant to say he was a Christian would be eager for her to continue teaching the Bible. "You really want me to?"

"Yes. I think a lot of people might benefit from knowing more about the Bible." He sighed. "Maybe if Josh had gone to the study instead of looking for drugs, he wouldn't be in police lockup tonight."

"Perhaps." She fell silent for a moment, thinking about how God might use her study. "And second of all?"

"Second of all, after each of your Bible studies, you can share a cup of coffee with me at the diner a few blocks from here." He flashed her a smile, revealing surprisingly white teeth. "I'll even let you treat."

Veronica hesitated. Though she felt a burden to teach the homeless, she hadn't considered spending one-on-one time with a homeless man—not even one who seemed as nice as Caspar. *Lord, is this what You want me to do?*

"Although I guess I should find out your name."

"Veronica. Veronica Van Slyke." Feeling heat rise to

her cheeks, she was eager to avert attention from herself. "And you're Caspar. . ."

"Just Caspar." His warm smile poured over her like sunshine, bringing light to the black night. "So is that arrangement agreeable?"

She hesitated for a second.

"Look," Caspar's voice was soft, but the disappointment in his eyes was evident, "it was just an idea. If you're uncomfortable, you don't have to go with me anywhere."

"No. I'm not," she declared. "I'll be glad to share coffee with you at the diner," she said, just as her father tooted his car horn. "I'd better go. See you next week."

Three

I don't like it. I don't like it one bit." Sitting at the table in their breakfast nook, Tess picked at the bowl of high-fiber cereal that was her breakfast staple.

Veronica wished she hadn't mentioned the arrangement she had made with Caspar to her parents. "I know. But I promised Caspar—"

"Caspar, Caspar, Caspar! He's all you've talked about this week. Isn't there anybody else at that shelter?"

"Yes, but he's the only one who saved me from being robbed, and he's the only one I'm supposed to have coffee with at the diner."

"I agree with your mother," Wen added, having just downed a second cup of Viennese cinnamon-flavored coffee. "I think this man is taking advantage of you."

"How can that be, Father? He doesn't even know me."

"A con man can smell money a mile away. It's his business to know who has wealth so he can choose his next victim. That's how he makes his living." Her father gave Veronica a direct look. "Your mother and I have protected you all your life. Now that you're a grown woman and ready to strike out on your own, you've got to understand something. When you've got money, you're a target for all sorts of people who'd like you to part with it."

"Don't I already know that?" Veronica rolled her eyes, then took her own cup of coffee in both hands. She concentrated on the pool of dark liquid to keep from facing her father's gaze.

"You mean the robbery?"

"Of course."

"That's only one example of victimization. The most Neanderthal type, using force to take your possessions."

Though she didn't answer, Veronica shivered as she remembered how frightened and helpless she'd felt. She sipped her coffee, as though consuming hot brew would warm her soul.

Her father wasn't finished. "But most con artists, especially men looking to woo a young woman, are more subtle." He sat back in his chair at the head of the breakfast table. "I'd hate for you to find that out the hard way."

Seeing a hole in his otherwise airtight argument, she leapt at the chance to show her father she wasn't as naive as he assumed. "But aren't con men glib and well-dressed? You know—the type that you'd never suspect were really broke and looking to clean out your bank account? You saw Caspar for yourself. Even you must agree, he hardly fits that description. Besides, he'd be pretty silly to think he'd find a lot of rich women hanging out at a homeless shelter."

"If he's smart, he knows rich women help the homeless."

"But if money were his only motive for helping me,

wouldn't he have jumped at the reward you offered him?"

"I wish he had. Then I could just pay him and not give him another thought." He furrowed his brow. "It worries me that he wants more contact with you."

"I admit, I hadn't set out to become entangled in this mission beyond teaching the study, either. But I've been praying about this. I've come to believe that the robbery and the way Caspar rescued me are God's ways of saying I must become involved with the homeless as people, not just as objects of pity to throw money at and then forget."

"We're proud of you for wanting to obey the Lord as your heart tells you," Tess intervened. "But as your father said, this is a dangerous world. You don't know the first thing about this Caspar person."

"I know he was courageous enough to stop a robbery in progress. He didn't have to do that."

"That's nice." Tess's tone indicated she thought the gesture was anything but. She shook her head disbelievingly. "Caspar! Really! What kind of mother names her child after a cartoon ghost in the comic books?"

"At least Caspar's a friendly ghost," Wen quipped.

As Veronica giggled, Tess shot her husband a withering look before returning her attention to her daughter. "And what about his last name? Does he have one of those?"

Feeling foolish, Veronica chose that moment to butter a piece of cold toast she had no intention of eating.

"You don't know his last name. I thought as much." Setting down her coffee cup, Tess looked at her husband. "Do something, Wen."

Swallowing the last bit of sausage made from ground turkey meat, Wen thought for a moment. Looking from his wife to his daughter, and back to his wife, he finally said, "Tess, she's a grown woman. If being robbed wasn't enough to scare her out of going back, I don't know what I can do."

"Thanks, Father."

"Not so fast. I do want you to realize you are going back over our most ardent objections."

"I know. I understand why you object, but I promised I'd teach the lesson."

"I suppose that's for Caspar's sake, as well?" Tess wondered aloud, swirling her orange juice with such a violent motion that Veronica thought it might spill out of the glass.

"No, Caspar doesn't even come to hear me speak."

"Then don't go. He'll think you're not teaching anymore." Her father's expression was triumphant. "Problem solved."

"But I promised him I'd keep teaching. That was part of the deal. Besides, what about the rest of the people in the study? They had nothing to do with the robbery or the rescue. Would it be fair to them if I canceled out now?"

"Well—"

She threw out her trump card. "Would breaking my commitment be the Van Slyke way?"

Hearing her parrot one of the business tenets he had taught her, Wen swallowed. "Oh, all right. I suppose you do have a point. Go ahead and teach the class, but I don't want you going anywhere with that man."

Caspar popped open a can of soda. Feeling sorry for himself as he always did when he had to leave work and go to the shelter, he studied his uninspired surroundings. Buff-colored walls displayed cheap pictures of idyllic oceanside scenes. The nearest beach was a three-hour drive away whether one fought the traffic on I-95 going north or south. With summer months away, even despite Virginia's temperate weather, the pictures left Caspar feeling more depressed than cheered.

The rugged carpeting covering the floor felt scratchy to his feet, so he only removed his shoes for bed. The furnishings, though in good condition, could have been described as "Twentieth-Century Cheap Motel," causing him to wonder if it had been salvaged from the original owners. At least the small color television was in working order, and it even had a remote control.

Caspar sat on the edge of the bed. He wished the church hadn't skimped on mattresses. The one on his single bed was so hard that at times, he fantasized about sleeping on the floor. . .as if a person could get a good night's sleep in the shelter in any event. Trains reverberated along tracks just behind the building off and on all night. To make the noise worse, the engineers always blew ear-splitting horns when approaching a nearby railroad crossing.

At least it was Wednesday night. That meant Veronica Van Slyke would be arriving to teach her Bible study. A pleasant image of the black-haired beauty came to mind. He would have never imagined such a flower would appear in the midst of such gloom. Sighing, he dreamed about what she might be like when she wasn't scared out of her mind. He was looking forward to finding out.

Caspar was certain of one fact. Veronica was as wealthy as she appeared. Wen Van Slyke was well-known in the consulting business. His formidable wit and sound judgment had earned him a fortune over the years. Caspar would have bet his bottom dollar that Wen's daughter had never rested her pretty curls on anything less than a down pillow. In fact, he was betting on Veronica Van Slyke. She just didn't know how much.

Hearing the clicking sound of a key being inserted into the doorknob, Caspar watched as the door opened and his new roommate entered. After the robbery, the shelter lost no time in filling the bed vacated by Josh. Over the past week, Caspar had found Eric, a day laborer struggling to pay child support, pleasant enough.

"I see you got some work today," Caspar greeted him.

"I sure did. Landscaping at the shopping strip." As he tilted his head southward in the direction of several strip malls, a wide smile flashed white underneath several layers of dirt that clung to his face. "Made it back in time for supper, too. Max says it's spaghetti tonight."

"Again?" Clutching his stomach, Caspar tried not to sound disagreeable.

"That's my favorite!" Closing the bathroom door behind him, Eric ran the water for a much-needed shower.

Never having been a pasta fan, Caspar couldn't have cared less if he never saw another spaghetti noodle, but

Eric seemed to need a friend. He'd be disappointed if Caspar didn't accompany him to the table. Finishing his soda, he pressed the buttons on the remote, changing channels aimlessly until he found a sportscaster reporting on the latest football game.

"So," Eric interrupted all too soon as he emerged from the shower, "are you going to that study tonight?"

"The Bible study?"

"There isn't anything else happening here, is there?" Eric joked.

"I suppose there isn't." Caspar grinned, trying to keep his voice casual as he responded. "I think I'll go."

"Good." Sitting on his bed and facing Caspar, Eric flipped through the pages of the Bible he had retrieved from the top of his nightstand. "You don't know what we're supposed to read for the lesson, do you?"

Caspar shook his head. "Sure don't." He didn't care to find out, either. There would be plenty of time to listen to Veronica teach.

"I think Jan said something about the parable of the lost son."

"Oh." Caspar searched his memory, trying to recall the story. He was certain he'd heard it long ago at Sunday school. Over the years, the details had become blurred.

"Since we don't have anything to do until suppertime anyway, why don't you and I go over that passage together?"

"Uh, I guess we could." At that moment, the newscaster's face on the television screen was replaced by the words NASDAQ and S & P 500, along with several arrows heading both up and down. "But don't you think we ought to watch the news first?"

Looking at the television, Eric laughed. "Like either one of us has any stocks. If I did, I wouldn't understand half of what they were talking about, anyway. Do you?"

"I know enough to get by."

"Our situation isn't the greatest, but at least the stock market going up and down all the time is one worry we don't have, huh?"

"Uh, yeah." Caspar observed his roommate. Eric was young enough that most of his future lay before him. "But don't you ever dream?"

After seeming to contemplate Caspar's question, Eric shrugged. "I'd just like to have enough money to get out of here and keep my kids fed. Even if it means my ex-wife squanders half of it on booze for her new boyfriend—not that she wants to, mind you. I don't think she has much choice."

"Maybe you should consider putting a stop to that."

"How can I? If I cause trouble, the court might decide I can't see my kids at all." Caspar caught the sadness that filled Eric's brown eyes before he bowed his head. Caspar was about to say something sympathetic when Eric lifted his head. The cheerful expression on his face seemed deliberate. "Besides, what's important today will be as dust tomorrow." Holding up his Bible, he tapped it with his forefinger. "What's in this book is important forever."

"Yeah. Like you said, who cares about the stock market, anyway?" Though he pressed the "off" button on the remote, causing the television to go black, Caspar made no effort to find a Bible.

"You do have a Bible, don't you?" Eric's stare bored into Caspar.

Caspar squirmed, though he hoped his uneasiness wasn't visible. "I think I might have one at home, I mean, I think I used to have one. Somewhere."

Eric shook his head, but his expression was non-judgmental. Pulling out the drawer of the nightstand, he extracted a Bible and extended it toward Caspar. Reluctantly, Caspar accepted the volume, bound in cheap, imitation red leather. "It's in the Book of Luke, chapter 15."

Nodding, Caspar opened the Bible and began leafing through the pages. He remembered that Luke was one of the Gospels, but wasn't sure where to find it. Seeing Eric turn to the passage without hesitation, Caspar suddenly felt inferior.

It was a feeling he didn't like. . .one he was determined to shed.

Four

Veronica gathered her Bible study materials as her students filed out of the makeshift classroom. A nervous smile touched her lips at the sight of Caspar, who remained seated in a folding chair. She almost wished he'd forgotten their agreement or would let her out of it somehow, but he hadn't.

"Ready for that cup of coffee?"

"Ready." Her tone of voice exuded more conviction than she felt.

He held the door for her as they exited into the night.

At least he's a gentleman. A breeze that would have been welcome in July bit her cheeks on the frigid winter night. Veronica was thankful that her faithful leather jacket kept her shielded from the cold.

Few pedestrians were out on the sidewalk that ran parallel to a busy highway. Cars sped by in a continuous flood, pausing only when commanded by red stoplights. Veronica was grateful that Caspar's pace wasn't so quick. Exhaling, she watched a burst of steam form as her heated breath hit the crisp air.

Usually driving among the rushing vehicles, Veronica hadn't made the effort to give the neighborhood more than a passing glance. Her first foray as a pedestrian allowed her to study the businesses dotting the landscape. Most of the older structures had long since been torn down to make way for strip malls and big, boxy stores. Only a few with slanted windows, zigzagged rooftops, and the circular shapes that identified them as creations of the 1960s remained.

Storefront signs boasted attention-grabbing colors and remained lit even though most of the shops had long since closed for the evening. Not proficient in Spanish, Veronica could nevertheless make a guess at what some of the merchants sold. At least one store specialized in groceries appealing to Latin cooks. Another rented Spanish videos.

"Do you speak Spanish, Veronica?" Caspar wondered aloud, interrupting her thoughts.

He looked surprised when she shook her head. "Why do you ask?"

"You were so intent on those signs." He smiled.

"Just trying to decipher them." She twisted her mouth. "If I plan to continue to work with the homeless in this area, maybe I should become more proficient. Foreign languages were never my strong suit, though."

"Mine, either." He flashed her a sheepish grin that managed to be charming.

Staring back at more storefronts, Veronica noticed most of the signs were written in English and supplemented with pictures. Dollar signs usually meant those without bank accounts could cash checks. Signs with depictions of diamonds, cash, and valuables marked the pawnbrokers. At closing time, they had taken their merchandise out of the windows, yet still shielded them with bars. The irony didn't escape Veronica. "Look at those bars."

Caspar peered into that direction. "What about them?"

"They're meant to keep the criminals out, but if anyone's caught stealing, they'll be behind bars that will keep them in." Turning toward him, she noticed he was still facing forward. Viewing his profile, Veronica discovered she liked Caspar's straight nose and defined jaw. "Ironic, isn't it?"

"I suppose. Unfortunately, the merchants have reason to keep their goods behind bars in this area."

Veronica shivered at the thought of becoming a victim of yet another crime. "I'd never be out tonight like this without you."

A pleased smiled lit his handsome features. "You think I can protect you, huh?"

"As if you have to ask." His confident stride and fearless demeanor were enough to ward off most would-be attackers. By his quick thinking and action during the robbery, Caspar had already proven she could feel safe with him.

His appearance at the study that night had confirmed her first impression. Caspar's sharp answers and insightful comments had displayed an impressive intellect. "I must say, Caspar, I was wowed by the answers you gave tonight."

He flashed her a smile. "All that cramming beforehand

must have paid off."

Certain he couldn't have been serious, Veronica giggled. She expected him to join in her mirth, but a chagrined look crossed his face instead. She decided to pretend she hadn't noticed as they approached an intersection and were forced to wait for traffic before they could cross.

"Have you been a Christian all your life?" she ventured.

"I guess you could say that. I went to Sunday school every week until I was eight. I stopped going to church after Mom died."

Despite the fact that his mother's death was long past, Caspar's pain was palpable. Veronica fought the urge to put a consoling arm around his shoulders, settling for words that would surely prove inadequate but demanded to be expressed. "I'm so sorry. How terrible to lose your mother at such a young age."

"Yes, it was." He searched her face. "Are you close to your mother?"

A twinge of guilt surged through her. Tess was so different from Veronica, and not a woman who let anyone, even her own daughter, get too close. Yet Veronica couldn't imagine life without her. Yes, she did love her, and she knew her mother loved her more than anything else.

"I'm sure Mother knows I love her," she finally answered.

"Are you?" His voice was kind. "Are you really sure?"

"You've inspired me to remind her tonight. Just in case."

"You do that. Because she might not be there tomorrow. That's what I learned from Mom's death." Caspar's voice was bitter. "You can't depend on anyone or anything."

"You can depend on God."

"Right." He didn't look convinced.

Veronica wished she hadn't blurted a cliché to someone suffering from such obvious pain. She sent up a quick prayer for guidance before she spoke. "Look, I know that expression sounds trite, but it's so true. The twelfth chapter of Luke says, 'Are not five sparrows sold for two farthings, and not one of them is forgotten before God.' "

Caspar's eyes narrowed. "The Bible's right about one thing: Money talks."

Wondering how he could have perceived that from the verse she cited, she shook her head in puzzlement.

Caspar seemed only too glad to answer her unspoken query. "Even Jesus compares the worth of the birds to money—and why not? The dollar bill is the only thing you can count on."

"No, Caspar. I know money must be on your mind a lot since you don't have a lot of it right now, but Jesus' comparison was only an illustration. There are many more passages all throughout the Bible that caution us to avoid love of money."

Rather than answering, he set his gaze on the diner that was now within sight. Not wishing him to be in a sour mood when they entered, she tried to lighten the course of their conversation. "Maybe I'll teach on that subject next week."

"I'm sure you'll have a standing-room-only crowd." A hint of a smile offered hope.

"You know, I'm glad you encouraged me to continue teaching the Bible study."

"Really?" The hint blossomed into a grin. "Why?"

"Because God's already started to use it to reach more people. I counted three more students than last week. . .not including you."

"Not bad for your second class," he noted. "Especially at such a small shelter. I think they really related to the lesson."

Veronica nodded. "I almost didn't teach that lesson. I thought since it's one of Jesus' most well-known and popular parables, it might be old hat, but they seemed to enjoy it. I was pleased when we had such a good discussion."

"Oh, they, I mean, we, are all on such a rough part of our life's journey, that the thought of going home again is very appealing," he said as they reached the diner's entrance. Extending his arm, he opened the door and allowed her to enter before him.

"Maybe. Although sometimes, the thought of leaving home for good is pretty tempting to me."

Eyeing a vacant booth beside the front window, she tilted her head in its direction. Nodding, he followed her to the table, where they scooted into position on faded red vinyl, facing each other.

She hadn't planned to order more than a cup of coffee, but once she was seated, Veronica yearned for a serving of chocolate. She grabbed a menu propped between silver metal spokes beside the salt and pepper shakers.

Flipping it over to the back cover, she spotted a list of enticing treats.

"Are you planning to order dessert?" Caspar asked, interrupting Veronica in the midst of deciding between the chocolate meringue pie and the hot fudge brownie sundae.

"I'm thinking about it," she confessed. "Why don't you order dessert, too?"

"I just might." He gave her a lopsided grin. "Guess I had you pegged wrong."

"How's that?"

"I thought a woman as thin as you wouldn't think of eating dessert, especially this late at night."

Certain that Caspar meant to compliment her but too shy to acknowledge his observation, she opted for levity. "Would it make you feel better if I said if I eat a slice of pie, I'll feel really, really guilty?"

His gaze flickered over her in way of appraisal. She couldn't help but feel flattered by the approval in his eyes.

"I'm sure you'll feel guilty, no matter what I say," he observed. "I've never known a thin woman who didn't have a love/hate relationship with food."

Placing the menu flat on the table, Veronica leaned toward him. "So you're telling me you know many such women?"

For the first time since she met him, Caspar seemed at a loss for a response. Her curiosity piqued, she rested her elbow on the table and propped her chin on her palm, waiting to see what he would say. Her reward was to watch him bumble. "Not really. Not any. None at all.

At least, none that matter."

"Really?"

"Yes, really." He seemed a bit annoyed.

I'm glad to hear that. Surprised by the thought that was as unwelcome as it had been unexpected, she wondered what could have caused such an idea to pop into her head.

"Veronica?" Caspar's voice brought her back to the present. "Care to order?"

"Oh. Yes." Suddenly realizing she no longer craved chocolate, she asked for a bottle of springwater.

"Sorry. We don't have anything like that here." The waitress placed one hand on an ample hip to show her disgust.

"You're not going to watch me make a pig of myself eating apple pie a la mode while you sip on water, are you?" Caspar pleaded.

"Oh, all right. I'll have the chocolate meringue pie and a cup of decaf coffee."

"That's more like it."

As a grin illuminated his handsome features, Veronica studied his emerald green eyes. They were what had first caught her attention. *What would have happened if we had met in another time, under better circumstances? Where did you come from, Caspar? How did you end up in the shelter? Where will you go when you decide to leave?*

She was trying to think of a way to ask him in a tactful manner when he presented his own observation. "I find it interesting someone like you would want to teach the homeless."

"Rather than staying safely tucked away at church, teaching Sunday school?"

A roll of his eyes revealed she'd read his mind. "I should think someone in your position would be living the life most of the shelter residents only dream of."

"Money does solve a lot of problems, but it brings its own set of different dilemmas." She sighed. "I guess I do sound ungrateful, when there are others less fortunate; but in a way, I actually envy the freedom you have."

"Is that how you see life in a homeless shelter? As freedom?"

"Well, I admit, the situation can't be ideal. But you are free. You don't have to answer to anyone."

Caspar's twisted lips revealed he disagreed. "I still go to work every day, so I have to answer to my boss."

"True."

They uttered the next sentence together. "So, where do you work?"

Realizing they'd expressed the same thought in the same words, both of them broke out into snickers. Caspar's laugh had a pleasant, musical quality. Veronica found herself wanting to hear it again. "You first," she said. "Where do you work?"

"Oh, I seem to do something different every day."

His answer didn't surprise her, since many of the shelter residents worked as day laborers.

He added, "I work in construction."

Her eyes involuntarily focused on his hands. Though unmistakably masculine, they seemed well kept for someone who worked at manual labor.

A look from Caspar told her she'd been caught staring. "What were you expecting? Permanent dirt under my fingernails?"

"Maybe I was," she quipped.

"Not every aspect of the construction industry involves direct contact with dirt."

As she considered indoor work such as plumbing, fixtures, and electrical wiring, Veronica had to agree. "Too bad you don't get to play in the mud all day."

"That would be fun, wouldn't it?" He grinned. "I'm sure whatever you do all day is far more interesting."

"I work in the Guthrie Museum of the Fine Arts," she explained as their desserts were set before them. She was just about to attack the frothy pie when Caspar stopped her.

"No blessing?" he chided. "Or are you afraid to say grace in public?"

"As a matter of fact, I usually do say a blessing, whether I'm alone, at home with the family, or eating out." Her tone was more defensive than she meant, so she made sure her next comment was spoken softly. "If I'm in public, I say it silently. I didn't suggest we say grace together here because I didn't want you to be uncomfortable."

"Go ahead. You won't bother me."

Pleased, she complied with a brief prayer that could only be heard by the two of them.

"Thank you," he said afterwards. He cut into his hot apple pie with a generous scoop of vanilla ice cream already melting on top and placed a bite into his mouth. "Ummmm. Tastes better since it's been blessed."

Unsure as to whether or not he was being sarcastic, she was contemplating a smart retort as she bit into her chocolate when he changed the subject. "So, what do you do at the museum?"

"Oh, I seem to do something different every day."

Her imitation of his earlier explanation was rewarded by a gentle laugh. "I happen to be interested in art, myself. I'm particularly fond of the Pre-Raphaelites."

"Really?" She didn't bother to conceal her surprise. "Art History was my major in college. I specialized in the Pre-Raphaelites."

As he leaned toward her, Caspar's voice revealed his fascination. "Then you must be familiar with *The Long Engagement* by Arthur Hughes."

"It shows a couple standing next to a tree." She nodded. "I've seen it."

"At the Smithsonian? During their special exhibit?"

"As a matter of fact, I did." A thought occurred to her as she sipped hot coffee. "I wonder if we passed each other."

"No. I never would have forgotten you."

His compliment causing a sudden attack of shyness, Veronica averted her eyes. She lifted them in time to see a chagrined look cross his face.

"Anyway, that painting has been my all-time favorite ever since I saw it." He looked beyond her, as if summoning an image of the painting to his mind. "It was so realistic; I could almost feel the purple velvet cloak she wore. The ivy on the tree seemed three-dimensional, too."

Astounded, Veronica marveled at his knowledge.

Most people with a passing interest in nineteenth-century art might drop a few illustrious names such as William Morris, but to describe a less famous artist of the period and to describe a work in such detail was beyond elementary knowledge. She wondered how well versed he was on other subjects near to her heart and mind. She was more curious than ever as to where he'd learned about art and how someone like him had ended up at the shelter.

Could his mother's death have been a factor? What about his father? Did he have any brothers and sisters? What happened to his family, the network of people who should have been his support system?

Before she could decide what to ask next, the waitress had presented the check. Veronica resolved to keep her promise to meet with Caspar each week. Only now, rather than harboring fear and doubt, she looked forward to their visits with great anticipation.

Five

With a confident motion, Caspar slipped the long end of his red necktie into the open ring fashioned from the shorter portion. He pulled the loop toward the top button of his white shirt, gradually tightening it to form a perfect Windsor knot. As he tugged around the shirt collar to be sure any trace of red was concealed, Caspar caught a glimpse of the gold cuff links decorating his wrists. Whirling toward his bed, he grabbed the coat of his favorite black suit that lay in wait on top of the blue spread. He tossed on the coat and fastened the top button, bringing the fashionable lapels together in a manicured *V*.

I hope this is the right suit to wear to an evening service at a church. Surely it must be a formal occasion.

Checking his watch, Caspar noted that twenty minutes remained before Veronica was due to arrive. He wasn't comfortable with the idea of a woman picking *him* up, but his present circumstances forbade him to observe old-fashioned traditions.

"Who am I kidding?" he muttered. "This isn't a

date. She sees me as some poor soul she wants to help, that's all."

He became conscious of his beating heart as he visualized her deep blue eyes gazing into his. He marveled at ringlets so black, they reflected blue in the light, framed by exquisite alabaster skin and mesmerizing features. Such a contrast might have appeared garish on a woman using artifice to achieve the effect, but the perfect balance of color revealed that she was every bit God's own creation.

No wonder she loves Him so much. He gave her such beauty, inside and out.

Plopping on the bed, he thought about the evening he'd anticipated ever since last Wednesday night. Veronica's invitation to her church had been a welcome opportunity to enjoy her company beyond the confines of the bustling diner. He wasn't familiar with either musical group scheduled to perform contemporary Christian music. Even the term "contemporary Christian music" was alien to him. What he did observe was how her face lit up with excitement when she talked about her favorite tunes.

He thought about how easily Veronica committed to any mission that furthered God's kingdom. Her passion was contagious. Caspar had fallen away from his faith in the years between his mother's death and meeting Veronica. Her enthusiasm and genuine commitment made him hunger to know more about her God. Veronica's Jesus wasn't the God of Caspar's childhood, the One who began each sentence with, "Thou Shalt Not." That God took his mother before she celebrated her thirtieth birthday. Caspar found loving Him to be difficult.

Veronica's Jesus was different. He was a God of, "Thou Shalt," and though Veronica made clear that God allowed Christians to be tested through suffering, she reminded her students that His love sustained.

I wish my dad had known the Lord when Mom died. Maybe then he wouldn't have become so bitter, so disillusioned, so dependent on the fleeting rewards of his business. Unwilling to remain focused on such pain, Caspar remembered the lesson in Galatians of the previous week: *But the fruit of the Spirit is love, joy, peace, long-suffering, gentleness, goodness, faith, meekness, temperance.*

He'd witnessed Veronica's display of these qualities as she taught the Bible. Most of the students participating in the study wanted to learn and enjoy fellowship with others. Occasionally, some attended to challenge her, offering up belligerent questions and comments, yet she always provided a Scripture-based answer in a sweet voice accompanied by a kind expression. As a result, her detractors at the shelter were fast disappearing.

Just thinking about the peace Veronica exuded made Caspar want to be around her. "If only I could have what she has. Maybe it would fill the hole in my heart."

Eric's arrival from work interrupted his musings. His roommate's eyes widened in apparent shock when he saw Caspar's suit. "If the clothes closet has stuff that good, I'd better get myself down there today!"

Cringing, Caspar fought a combination of embarrassment and pity for Eric. "This didn't come from the clothes closet. It—it's from—my other life."

Eric's eyes filled with understanding. "Say no more. I hate to talk about the way things used to be, too." He smiled. "But I can see from the looks of you, I'll be watching TV by my lonesome tonight." Eric hesitated before asking the next question. "So where are you off to?"

"Church."

"Oh. So that explains the monkey suit." Extending a hand, he patted Caspar on the shoulder. "I'm really sorry, Man. Was it anyone close?"

Caspar was baffled. "Anyone close?"

Eric looked puzzled. "You are going to a funeral, aren't you?"

"A funeral?" Caspar laughed in spite of himself. "No. There's a concert, followed by a worship service. I thought I'd try to look my best."

Shaking his head, Eric cast him an amused look. "How long has it been since you've been to church, especially in the evening?"

Caspar clenched his teeth in embarrassment. "It's been awhile."

"I reckon that getup's fine to see some hoity-toity orchestra at the Kennedy Center, but it's way too dressed up for a Sunday night worship service." He tilted his head. "Which church is it, anyhow?"

"The one that runs this shelter."

"Then you're definitely too dressed up. You'll be way out of place if you wear that. Just put on a pair of blue jeans and any old shirt."

Caspar hesitated, but decided to take Eric at his word. As he retrieved a clean, but worn, pair of jeans from the tiny closet, Eric asked, "So, how are you goin' to get there?"

"Veronica Van Slyke will be here to pick me up in a few minutes."

"The teacher? You're one lucky dude." Eric let out a whistle of appreciation.

The gesture instigated unexpected ire. "She's not like that." Even Caspar was surprised by the menacing tone of his voice.

"Okay!" Waving his hands in surrender, Eric's eyes flashed with fear. "I just meant she's—pretty. That's all."

They were interrupted by a soft tapping on the door. Pretty Veronica Van Slyke had arrived.

⚮

Later, surrounded by a large, denim-clad congregation, Caspar was glad he'd taken Eric's advice. Both groups, comprised of local musicians, played soft rock music. Rather than searching for answers to angst or promoting casual love and drugs, the lyrics praised and worshiped Jesus Christ.

He watched Veronica sing with almost every song without benefit of a lyric sheet. Her amazing memory was surpassed only by her melodious soprano. She hit high notes with no effort, her voice vibrating smoothly to the end of each line.

After the last encore, a man in his twenties introduced himself as Pastor Juan and led the crowd into an informal worship service. Unlike the formal services Caspar remembered, people swayed and clapped to the music. They lifted their hands in praise and surrender to Jesus, and even responded to the questions Pastor Juan asked during the sermon. At first, their enthusiasm seemed strange, but soon, Caspar came to enjoy it. He wanted what everyone else in the congregation seemed to possess.

"Who has accepted Jesus Christ as their personal Savior?" the pastor asked.

Before he finished the question, a roar of applause and shouts of joy filled the sanctuary. Cutting his glance to her, Caspar wished he could clap and shout along with Veronica. He noticed she was making a point not to look at him.

"I see not all of you applauded." The pastor's voice was not condemning. "But you can. If you want to make a public proclamation of accepting Jesus Christ as your personal Savior right here, tonight, just come up to the altar."

"Is that all there is to it?" Caspar asked over a new burst of applause.

"That's the first step," Veronica shouted.

Feeling a nudge from the Holy Spirit, Caspar knew the time was right. "I'll do it."

"You'll do it? You'll accept Jesus?" Her blue eyes grew wide. "Caspar, I had no idea you were ready to make a commitment."

"I am."

"Are you sure?"

He nodded.

She placed a soft hand on his. Her warmth was consoling, though her expression became serious. "Don't do it because I brought you here. Not unless you're ready."

"I know my decision seems sudden to you, but I've

been thinking about my spiritual life ever since I first went to your Bible lessons. This is what I feel called to do."

Her face brightened with joy. "Then go ahead. I'll be watching."

Eyeing the crowd, Caspar suddenly felt shy. "Will you go with me?"

Veronica seemed surprised. "Why, sure."

He took her hand in his. Her touch revealed a woman of strength, but one of gentleness. With her by his side, making his public declaration to the Lord didn't seem so daunting.

The altar was so crowded, Caspar had to squeeze in to find a spot to kneel. Veronica remained behind him, keeping one hand on each of his shoulders as he confirmed to the pastor his acceptance of Christ. At that moment, an unexplained feeling of peace entered him. Finally, he was closer to possessing the joy Veronica exuded.

Turning to her, he saw tears in her eyes. Obviously unashamed, she let them flow down her cheeks unchecked. "Happy Birthday!"

In a spontaneous motion, they embraced. Rather than being conscious of Veronica's physical form, he felt as though he had touched her soul.

"You did what?" Tess's fork clinked against the china plate.

Veronica consumed a bite of beef Stroganoff. "I invited Caspar here for dinner."

"For what night?"

"I didn't make a definite date. I wanted to plan the dinner for a night when you'd both be home. Maybe in the next couple of weeks." She glanced at both of her parents, each sitting at either end of the dining room table. Pouting her lips, she hoped her expression was pleading enough to elicit sympathy. "I really want both of you to meet him."

"I've already met him." Moving pieces of chopped lettuce on his salad plate aside, Wen speared a cherry tomato.

"I hope this isn't your way of asking us to take him in." Leaning far over, Tess placed a hand on her daughter's. "I know you want to help this man, Veronica, but you can't save the world."

"I don't have to save Caspar. He's already been saved." Veronica's voice was saturated with joy. "He accepted Christ as his personal Savior at the concert."

Tess's mouth dropped open. "He goes to our church?"

"No, he goes to the Sunday afternoon services at the shelter. Actually, I invited him to the concert."

"You invited him?" Wen's face was stern. "You've made yourself entirely too vulnerable to this man."

"But I've known him for weeks now. I wouldn't have believed this when we first started going out for coffee, but we talk for hours. The waitress practically has to run us out." She couldn't resist a self-satisfied smile.

"Don't think I haven't noticed," Tess remarked. "You're always late getting home on Wednesday nights."

Wen furrowed his brow. "What could you two possibly have to talk about?"

"Everything that matters. . .and a few things that don't."

Going over their conversations, Veronica relived how they had shared their hopes and dreams. They both wanted to hike along the Swiss Alps. Take an Alaskan cruise. Visit all the great landmarks of Europe. Make a pilgrimage to Jerusalem. Sighing, Veronica visualized the way Caspar's handsome features changed when the subject of conversation turned to Christ. The spark in his eyes showed more than polite interest. He hungered for the Lord.

Wen's voice cut into her musings. "Veronica, we agreed that you could gallivant to this little hole-in-the-wall diner every week with this man we don't know, even though it was against our better judgment, but you had us convinced this was part of your so-called ministry at the shelter. We never dreamed for a moment you'd consider letting him into your life like this. I think your relationship has gone far beyond a ministry."

Veronica averted her eyes. She didn't want to admit how much she anticipated her Wednesday night meetings with Caspar. Reticence had vanished, replaced with a comfort level she only felt with her closest friends. She couldn't deny she loved him as a dear friend, which was more than she thought possible when he first suggested they share coffee at the diner. But beyond that? She dared not think about it.

"If I didn't know better, I'd think you actually harbored romantic feelings for this man." The fright in Tess's blue eyes showed.

"That's preposterous," Veronica answered more quickly than she intended. "Besides, he's hardly in a situation where he should be looking for romance. He only wants a friendship."

"If that's so, then why did he accept your invitation for an evening out?" Wen queried.

"It wasn't a date."

"I know young people claim they don't date anymore," Tess said, "but what you're talking about is pretty close." She let out a labored sigh. "I wish he had accepted your offer of a reward, Wen."

"I think I know why he didn't accept," Wen said. "He didn't want to be bought off so easily. He knows our daughter comes from wealth, so he's holding out for more."

"He doesn't want money."

"How do you know?" Wen asked, his voice rising.

Veronica met her father's angry gaze without flinching. "He's never asked me for a dime."

"This man is smart, all right. Smart enough to lull you into a sense of false security." Wen snorted. "Even going so far as pretending to convert to Christ. Despicable."

"You weren't there when he went up to the altar, Father. He's sincere about the Lord. I know he is. To judge someone when you don't know his heart is what's despicable." Veronica felt ire rising in her chest. "What we have is a friendship based on trust. In fact, I trust him more than some people I've known for years."

"How can you trust him?" Tess asked. "You still don't even know his last name."

Her mother had managed to hone in on the only

chink in Caspar's armor. He had revealed his devastation at the early death of his mother, his father's resulting bitterness, and his longing to reconnect with a brother living somewhere in Central America. Yet, he refused to discuss the circumstances that led to his arrival at A Place of Our Own. Determined not to let her mother win, Veronica searched for a response. "He's entitled to as much privacy as anyone else."

"Is that so? I would think one gives up the right to privacy when one chooses to sponge off of the church."

"Don't even bother to answer that, Veronica," Wen said.

She was just about to thank him when his voice stopped her.

"Because what you said is right. He has no business seeking romance, or really, even a friendship with a woman like you—at least not until he gets on his feet financially." Digging into his pile of Stroganoff, Wen scooped a large forkful and shoved it in his mouth.

"Father, I don't care how much money my friends have or don't have."

"Maybe not, but I don't like the direction this relationship is going," Wen said. "So until he has enough financial stability to leave the shelter, I don't want him in this house. In fact, I don't want him anywhere near you. Caspar is off limits."

As much as she wanted to respect her parents' wishes, Veronica felt her blood pressure rise upon being ordered around like a little girl. The time had come to show them she was an adult. In her anger, she threw her white cotton napkin beside her plate, where it made contact with her gravy-splattered knife and sent it careening to the floor. At that moment, Veronica didn't care that the blade had hit the white damask tablecloth or that the brown sauce was certain to stain her mother's treasured off-white carpet. "You can't tell me who is and who isn't off limits, Father! I'm a grown woman, and I'll make my own decisions."

"If that's the way you feel, fine. If you want to continue seeing this man, you'll do it without our help." His face grew hard. "That means living on your own, scraping by on the peanuts they pay you at that gallery."

Tess interrupted, "Wen, you don't mean she has to leave the house, do you?"

"And give her an excuse to move into the shelter with that man? Of course not. She stays here until she finds her own apartment."

A look of fright flashed in Tess's blue eyes. "You don't mean that."

"But I do. She's never had to face reality. When she does, she'll be back."

Veronica's passion overtook her common sense. "Well, that's just fine with me! I'll start looking for a place tomorrow." Rising from her seat, she squared her shoulders to show she meant her words. Spinning on one heel, she turned her back to her parents and exited the dining room.

"And don't expect any help from us in the future, either," her father yelled, his voice resounding up the stairs as she marched to her room. "You can kiss your trust fund good-bye!"

Six

T hanks for helping me move, Caspar." Veronica
handed him an unopened soft drink before pop-
ping open her own soda. "Sorry I don't have any
glasses washed yet. I'll try to do better next time."

"I plan to take you up on that." He took a sip of his
drink. Green eyes flashing over the top of the red can
reminded Veronica of Christmas. "Besides, helping you
was easy. It's not like you have a lot of furniture." He
gave her the lopsided grin she had come to love.

She rolled her eyes in agreement. "It doesn't take
much to outfit one bedroom. That's all I had at home."

Veronica placed her hands on her narrow hips and
surveyed the larger of the two rooms in the apartment,
an open area that served as kitchen, eating area, and
living room. Walls painted eggshell white begged for
pictures, but her lease included a provision against
damage. Empty corners called for a television and wing
chair, neither of which she possessed. A nook was supposed to house a dining room set, but that, too, was
bare. An old green couch her mother allowed her to
take from the attic looked lonely.

Veronica let out a labored sigh. "Looks like I'll be doing some shopping."

"Fun, huh?" Caspar asked. "I guess you had the itch to express yourself, to get your own place like this."

Veronica winced. "I hadn't planned to. At least not this way."

His eyes filled with a look that expressed a combination of concern and puzzlement. "What do you mean? Did something happen?"

Though tears threatened, Veronica told Caspar about the argument that led to her move.

Caspar took a few moments to absorb the story. "You gave up your trust fund for me?" The shock in his eyes was evident.

Veronica wasn't sure how to answer. "It was time to go."

"But Veronica, your parents mean everything to you. I know they feel the same. How could they not? You're the only child they have."

"Thanks for reminding me. As if I didn't already feel guilty enough." With the back of her hand, she wiped away a tear that spilled down her cheek.

"What do you have to feel guilty about? They're the ones who told you to go, not the other way around."

"Well, Mother didn't really want me to leave. I could tell, and I think Father's been having second thoughts. He seemed upset when I told him I'd found a place, but he's too stubborn to back down and ask me to stay."

His gaze searched her face. "Would you move back if he asked?"

She looked around the vacant room and wondered if she could ever make the apartment seem like home. Veronica felt her face flush hot. "I won't say the idea isn't already tempting, but I wouldn't."

Caspar tilted his head toward the sliding glass doors that led to a small balcony. "Come on. I've got something to show you."

Muggy air greeted them as they stepped onto a concrete surface. "I wish you hadn't suggested this, Caspar," she said only half-jokingly. "This just reminds me I need to buy a couple of chairs for out here, too." She groaned. "I can just see the smoke pouring off my credit card now."

"At least you'll have a few more things to take to your next place."

"My next place? I'll be lucky if I can keep up the rent here. It's amazing how a tiny apartment can be so expensive."

"Are you suffering a bit of buyer's remorse? Or should I say renter's remorse?"

"Not enough to move back with my parents, if that's what you mean." She leaned on the metal grate serving as the only obstacle between her and a fall of four flights. Below was an asphalt parking lot containing an assortment of vehicles. Most were typical first cars, ranging from newer small imports to behemoths eligible for license plates designating them as antiques. "Some view, huh?"

Caspar shrugged. "I've seen worse."

Worse. Like at the shelter.

A twinge of guilt reminded Veronica she shouldn't

be ungrateful. She was about to apologize for being so insensitive when Caspar withdrew a rectangular box from his pocket. It was wrapped in silver paper and topped with a matching silver bow. He handed it to her.

"What is this?"

"Take it. It's a housewarming gift."

"Caspar, your gift to me was helping me move. You certainly had no business buying me a housewarming gift. How could you afford a present, anyway?" As much as she hated herself for asking such prying questions, her conscience demanded an answer.

He shrugged. "I saved up from my job."

Curious, Veronica wondered what could be in the box. "What is this? A silver spoon?" she joked.

"Of course not. You already had that the day you were born," he quipped. Then a sheepish expression covered his face. "I know I should have gotten you something for the house. Like towels, a flower vase, or something equally useful. If you want to know the truth, I figured you'd be bringing plenty of furniture and stuff for the house from your parents' place."

Veronica winced. That would probably have been the case, had she vacated under more friendly circumstances.

"What are you waiting for? Open it!" Caspar's face was lit with anticipation.

"Oh, all right. Who can resist a surprise?" Tearing away the paper, she discovered a black velvet box. Inside was a tennis bracelet with brilliant stones that looked to be at least a quarter carat in weight each.

"Caspar, I can't take this."

"Of course you can."

"Look, I know cubic zirconia is pricey even in a pawnshop."

"It didn't come from a pawnshop. It's new." He seemed insulted.

Closing the box, she handed it back to him. "Then I definitely can't take it."

"Sure you can." Bowing his head, he muttered, "I want you to have it. I can afford it."

Opening the box, Veronica reexamined the bauble. The diamonds appeared genuine, but good cubic zirconia could fool jewelers on first sight. "If you say so. But Caspar, this is still a lovely bracelet. You shouldn't have spent even this much."

"Maybe I shouldn't have. But please don't ask me to take it back. Allow me to do this for you."

Realizing Caspar's dignity was at stake, she nodded. "All right. Thank you."

"Let me put it on you." He extended his hand to take the box.

Veronica looked down at the baggy brown T-shirt that said, "Knock Knock! Who's There? Matthew 7:7," coupled with a pair of khaki Capris. "I'm hardly dressed for it."

"Sure you are. Diamonds—even fake ones—go with everything." He fastened the clasp against her slim wrist. "There."

"It's beautiful—"

She felt his lips press against hers, his arms wrap around her waist. The shock of being taken by surprise gave way to a comfort she had never before felt, as though Caspar was meant especially for her.

A whistle and hoot from a group of young men in the parking lot broke the spell. Laughing, they rushed into a red Volkswagen and sped away. Suddenly feeling awkward, Veronica was grateful they offered a distraction. She wasn't ready to face Caspar. Or the feelings his kiss had ignited.

⚜

Later that evening, Caspar ran for protection under the lobby awning of the shelter. A brutal thunderstorm had developed, showering the city with rain. Thunderclaps added a backdrop not unlike cannon fire. Forked lightning provided a dramatic show.

Caspar shivered. *I'd hate to be out tonight.*

Even so, no amount of rain could take away the brightness he felt in his soul. His acceptance of the Lord was only the first step on what he hoped to be a long spiritual journey. Yet already, he felt energized and ready to take on anything.

"You there!"

Turning, Caspar spotted a figure running toward him. He seemed to be carrying something, a piece of cardboard, under his arm. With each step, the man took, water splashed upward, droplets hitting his pants. As he drew closer, Caspar could see the man's overgrown hair and graying beard. With no coat to shield him, his clothes had become drenched. He wore a knit hat that must have been blue at one time, but was now covered with layers of dirt. Locks of limp hair peeked out from underneath the hat, matting to his neck and forehead. A ragged red-and-black-plaid flannel shirt served as a makeshift jacket over a stained T-shirt. He wore khaki pants that probably served a businessman well on many casual Fridays before being donated to charity. Caspar was sure their previous owner wouldn't recognize them now that they sported a variety of unidentifiable spots. A pair of worn loafers completed the hodgepodge.

A glimmer of recognition hit Caspar. "Aren't you the guy that collects money near the plaza?"

His eyes shifted from side to side. "Well, I guess I can't hide it." He held up the piece of cardboard, which turned out to be the top of a pizza container. On the reverse was written in red magic marker: *Homeless Veteran. Please help.*

"Pleased to meet you. What's your name?"

"Darrin," he whispered. "That's all I'm gonna tell you."

As Caspar nodded, a stench entered his nostrils. Darrin obviously hadn't taken a shower for some time. The need to get away from the nauseating odor overcame Caspar's manners. He stepped back, a motion that lessened his exposure to the stink, but not enough to allow Caspar to breathe comfortably. "How can I help you?"

"Y'all take in people who ain't got nowhere to go, right?"

Caspar nodded. "Come on. Let's go in the office."

"Not yet." Darrin leaned toward Caspar as if sharing a confidence.

The smell of liquor from his breath filled the air. Reacting to the unexpected odor, Caspar pulled his face away. If Darrin noticed, he was undeterred. "I don't take to these places. I try to stay out on my own, you know. If I don't, they'll find me."

"Who will find you?"

"The Federal Bureau of Investigation. Also known as the FBI. They keep files on everybody, you know." He stared into Caspar's face. "You ain't from the FBI, are you?"

Caspar shook his head.

"Then you better be careful. They're always watchin' everybody."

At that moment, a robust thunderclap caused both men to look westward. They witnessed a fork of lightning dig into the earth a few miles off with the gusto of a chowhound devouring a porterhouse steak.

"You can see why I might like to be inside tonight, even no matter what they decide to record in my file." His voice dropped to an even lower whisper. "There ain't no video cameras set up in them rooms, are there?"

"I haven't seen any."

"Okay, I'll take your word for it. So, can you put me up?"

"I'd like to say yes, but I'm not in charge. Max runs the place. I think he's still here." Caspar tilted his head in the direction of the lobby door. "Let's go see."

"Thanks."

Upon being subjected to another whiff of liquor-soaked breath, Caspar remembered Max's cardinal rules: no drugs, no alcohol. Caspar reached into his pocket for a mint. "Here." He shoved the candy into his companion's hand. "Put this in your mouth."

Darrin grimaced, but accepted the mint. "You ain't got no money in that pocket, do you?"

Caspar would have offered Darrin his last dollar if

he didn't think it would find its way to a liquor store the next day. "Tell you what," he answered, "I'll buy you a good meal sometime."

He held open the door for Darrin to enter. Sitting behind a counter cluttered with papers, Max watched the news.

"We have a visitor," Caspar said to get Max's attention.

"A visitor?" Max swiveled his chair to face them and gave Darrin a grin of recognition. "I thought I might see you on a night like this, Joe."

"Shhhh!" Darrin put his fingers to his lips. "It's Darrin."

"All right, Darrin." Max's tone reminded Caspar of a teacher trying to be patient with a young child. "I wish you'd shown up sooner. There's no more room tonight. Every bed is taken. I'm sorry."

Darrin tensed. "You mean, I gotta go back out there?"

"I'm afraid so."

"No, you don't, Darrin," Caspar interrupted. "You can have my bed."

"You don't have to do that, Caspar. You were here first, and we're committed to keeping you off the street as long as you need us."

Caspar raised a surrendering palm to Max. "That's just it. I don't need you anymore."

Max looked at him quizzically. "How's that?"

"Don't worry about me. I have somewhere to go." He turned to Darrin. "Come on. I'll show you to your new room."

Trying to put on a casual facade, Veronica whistled a Maranatha tune as she entered the shelter the following Wednesday. Ever since the kiss, she had been unable to think of anyone, and barely anything, but Caspar. Her heart beat a rapid pace at the prospect of seeing him, gazing into his eyes, and sharing with him the non-events surrounding her shopping expeditions to procure furniture. The little incidents that, together, formed the essence of life.

For what must have been the zillionth time, her glance traveled to the bracelet. She hadn't taken it off since Caspar fastened the little gold clasp tightly around her arm. The faux diamonds captured beams from the fluorescent lights in the lobby. Prisms of light bounced off each facet, entertaining her with a colorful show.

"I wouldn't think you'd be wearing diamonds after what happened to you the first night you got here," Max observed from his perch behind the counter.

She stopped in midtune. "Oh, it's fake."

"They make those things realistic these days," he remarked, eyeing the trinket.

Not wishing to further her conversation with Max, she cast her gaze to the spot by the door where Caspar should have been waiting for her.

That's funny. He's not usually late.

Swaying back and forth on her heels, she clutched her Bible and waited by the door. Several of her students greeted her as they passed. A couple of them stopped to chat. Not wanting to show her anxiety about Caspar's absence, Veronica tried not to glance at the wall clock too often.

A few minutes later, Max asked, "Are you waiting for Caspar?"

Feeling heat rise to her cheeks, Veronica nodded.

"Didn't you know? He's not here anymore."

His words came as such a shock that Veronica nearly dropped her Bible. "What did you say?"

"He's not here anymore. He left a couple of nights ago."

"But that's impossible." Determined to discover more, Veronica marched to the counter.

"I'm telling you it is possible." Irritation colored Max's voice. "Caspar gave his bed to someone else. After that, he took off, and I haven't seen him since."

Veronica felt her heart beating in fear. "Is he all right?"

Max shrugged, though his expression wasn't unkind. "I think Caspar can take care of himself."

Veronica placed her Bible on the counter and withdrew a ballpoint pen and piece of scrap paper. "Tell me where I can find him."

"You mean, you want an address?"

"Yes." Her voice was curt.

"He has no address. That's why he's called *homeless*," Max said as if she were dense.

"But he must have gone somewhere." Despite her efforts to remain calm, Veronica heard her voice rise with frustration and helplessness.

"He said he had somewhere to go, but I couldn't tell you where. Try the other shelters." Pointing his index finger in the direction of the small room filled with students, he added, "But first, your public awaits."

Seven

S tanding in the executive office of Morton Construction Company, Veronica studied the painting she held in her hands. The picture of several joyous couples running in the rain reminded Veronica how much she longed for Caspar.

After weeks of searching proved fruitless, she had resigned herself to the fact she would never see him again. Yet hardly a moment passed when his image didn't cross her mind. She had so much news she wanted to share. What she wouldn't give for a few minutes at the diner, talking over a cup of coffee. Often she found herself speaking to him in her thoughts.

Even the victory of Jesse and Maria accepting Christ at the study last week is less exciting without you. You're the only one who would understand.

Still staring at the picture, she let out a sigh.

"Lovely, isn't it? But not as lovely as the woman holding it."

Veronica's heart lurched. *I know that voice. No, it can't be!*

Turning to the direction of the voice, she spotted

gold-shot brown hair and emerald green eyes. "Caspar?"

✦✦

"Yes, it's me."

Although he had expected to see her, he wasn't prepared for the slamming acceleration of his heartbeat. Ever since he'd left the shelter, he'd dreamed of returning, just to see her. The image of her beauty, the smell of her perfume, and the sound of her voice never left his mind. He had hoped he could move on. Forget her. But it was no use. If he had harbored any doubts, they melted as her presence confirmed that he could never claim victory over his love.

But she deserves someone better than I am. Someone honest. How can I tell her I betrayed her?

At that moment, his secretary hovered in the doorway. "Will there be anything else, Mr. Morton?"

"No, that will be all. Please hold my calls."

"Yes, Mr. Morton."

"Mr. Morton?" Veronica's mouth formed an astonished O. Her eyes scanned the well-appointed office, then returned to him. "You—you're a Morton? As in, the family who owns this company?"

He nodded, watching the changing emotions play across her beautiful face.

Distress filled her blue eyes. "I don't understand."

"It's a long story."

She set the painting down on the desk. "This painting is yours?"

"Correction: was mine. I donated it to your museum because I had to see you."

"You didn't have to do that. I've been trying to find

you for weeks." Her voice trembled.

He pursed his lips. "I can imagine. Only, as you can probably guess, I haven't been in any of the shelters."

"Or the hospitals." Folding her arms, she arched one eyebrow. "There were a lot of less expensive ways to secure an appointment with me than donating a piece of artwork to the museum, so you might as well use your time wisely. You paid for it." Expectation was evident by the stubborn set of her jaw. The time to tell the whole truth had arrived.

"All right. I'll tell you. Sylvester Morton, the owner of this company, is my dad. And my name isn't Caspar." Despite the confidence in his voice, his stomach did flipflops. Walking toward her with a smile, he extended his right hand. "I'm Ben Morton."

"If you think we can start over, you're mistaken." She kept her hands folded. "But I do want to know why you were living in the shelter."

Her clipped words sent his prepared speech sailing from his mind. "Never let it be said you don't come right to the point."

She looked at her watch and tapped her foot.

Ben had anticipated some resistance, but not for Veronica to turn into granite. He swallowed. "I know I shouldn't have taken a bed at the shelter. Nothing could make amends for what I did. I doubt if I'll ever forgive myself."

"Then why, Ben? Why did you do it?"

"You'll never believe it." Unable to look her in the face, he sent his gaze to his feet. "I have a couple of buddies who love to play pranks. We made a bet." He looked up in time to see her eyes narrow.

"What kind of bet?"

Ben cleared his throat. "You know they say money is a powerful aphrodisiac."

Her full mouth closed into a tight line. "Go on."

He swallowed. "I had just come out of a relationship where I'd pulled out all the stops. I couldn't spend enough money on this woman, but as soon as someone richer came along, she dumped me. After that happened, my friends dared me to romance someone without using my money. I don't know. Maybe they were trying to help."

"But to pose as a homeless man?" She seemed to be containing a fit of rage.

"I thought that was the easiest way to prove my point. Who would think a homeless man has money?" Feeling an overwhelming sense of disgrace, he nevertheless forced himself to continue. "It pains me to admit this, but I thought I'd snag the interest of one of the women there, introduce her to my friends, and that would be enough."

"So you were planning to woo some poor homeless woman just to win a bet?"

"I wish you wouldn't put it like that." He flinched. "But if you want to know the truth, I had every intention of doing something nice for her once she found out. A few good meals, enough money to buy new clothes, maybe even a job here."

"So you were going to buy her off to appease your conscience?" By this time, Veronica's breath was spewing in audible gasps. "Sort of like donating a picture to my museum?"

"No, I wanted you to have the picture. If you want to know the truth, I could donate a gallery full of pictures, and even that wouldn't be enough to make me feel better about taking such a stupid bet." He gazed into her blue eyes. To his horror, they gleamed with an accusing light. "What I did was unforgivable. Sometimes I lie awake, thinking about it. I wonder if I'll ever forgive myself. I see now how dishonest I was. The whole idea started out as a joke, but I can see now it wasn't funny at all."

"No. It wasn't." Veronica's nostrils flared.

"I never dreamed things would turn out like this— that I would find someone like you." He paused. "And I certainly never dreamed I would come to accept Christ."

"Then why didn't you act like it? Why didn't you tell me everything, instead of letting me go on thinking you cared about me?" Her chin shook as though she might begin to cry.

"But I do care about you." Gently, he placed one hand on each of her shoulders, determined to hold her in place long enough to listen to his explanation. "I want you to know, my plans never even began to materialize before I met you. The night you were robbed, I'd only been there a couple of days. After the moment I met you, I was never able to think about any other woman."

"Don't tell me you had no intention of going ahead with your bet," she said through clenched teeth. "Why else would you have asked me to go to the diner every week?"

"Do you really want to know the truth?"

"Are you capable of telling me the truth?"

Though he cringed, Ben was determined not to let her accusation stop him. "The truth is, I tried to convince myself I only asked you out so I could keep the bet; but the more time I spent with you, the more I realized I wanted to be with you. The bet didn't matter anymore."

"Didn't you win?"

"No. At least, I never admitted it. I just told them I wanted to call it off." He gave her an embarrassed look. "At great expense, I might add."

"Serves you right. I hope you don't expect me to feel sorry for you, Ben."

Never had he heard his name said in such an icy manner. "I'm the one who's sorry." In a desperate move to show he wanted her forgiveness, he tried to gather her into an embrace.

Instead, she took a step back. "I'm sorry, too. Sorry I fell for you. But I don't want this token for my trouble." She clawed at the clasp of the bracelet, unable to release it in her anger.

He reached for her wrist in hopes that his touch would calm her, but she jerked it from his grasp. "Veronica, that bracelet is not a token. It has much more meaning to me. Can't you see that?"

"No!" As her eyes narrowed, he could feel her erect a stone wall around herself.

He tried to chip through. "I'll have you know those diamonds are real."

"Great." Ripping the bracelet from her wrist, she

threw it in his face, ignoring the fact that it hit his nose before falling to the ground. "Give this to someone who needs an aphrodisiac!" Turning on one heel, she ran out of the door, slamming it behind her.

Eyeing the picture that still lay on the desk, he pursued her. "Don't forget the painting!"

He had just reached the outer door when a quizzical look from his secretary stopped him.

"Is anything the matter, Mr. Morton?"

Hunching his shoulders in defeat, he decided the only way to maintain any dignity was to let Veronica go. Without answering, he slunk back into his office. No way would he tell his secretary he had just let pride keep him away from the only woman he had ever loved.

❧

"So your homeless friend is really Ben Morton? That news is the best birthday present you could have given me," Tess told Veronica over escargot swimming in butter and garlic, her favorite appetizer at Chateau Robespierre.

Veronica slid her spoon across the surface of the pink lobster bisque she was in no mood to eat. "Apparently so, Mother."

A triumphant grin played across Wen's lips as he scooped up an oyster. "Well, well. This changes things."

"How?"

"Do you have to ask?" Wen wondered.

"Of course she doesn't, Dear." Tess speared a snail, pausing before placing the delicacy in her mouth. "So when are you planning to see him again? Maybe he can come to dinner at the house sometime soon?"

"I don't plan to see him ever again."

"But you must!" Tess protested. "You can't let the museum lose a perfectly good painting just because you decided to leave it sitting on his desk."

"Not to worry. He sent it by courier that same day."

"Too bad. There goes your excuse," Tess said. "You'll have to think of some other way to see him."

"No, I don't, Mother. If he wanted to see me, he would have brought the painting by the museum himself." An unexpected twinge of regret filled her at the thought that Ben didn't want to see her again, either.

"No doubt he was perturbed by your temper tantrum." The admonition in Wen's voice was obvious.

"Perhaps it's all for the best. At least I can end the relationship, knowing the real truth." Veronica meant what she said. Even though a week had passed since her encounter with Ben, the feelings of hurt and betrayal remained. She saw no alternative other than to forget Ben forever.

Tess patted her hand. "I can understand why you're a bit miffed now, but you'll get over it."

"You're amazing, Mother."

"I think she's pretty amazing." Wen gave Tess a wink.

His levity failed to put Veronica into a good humor. "So you like him now that you know he's a man of distinction." Her voice was flat. "When you thought he was penniless, you called him a con artist. Turns out, you were right about that."

"You think taking a little bet makes him a con artist?" Wen chuckled.

"When the bet means taking advantage of home-less people and volunteers running a shelter, then yes, he's a con artist."

"I'm sure he didn't think of it that way at the time, Veronica," her father assured. "You know how things get when a bunch of guys start daring each other. Things escalate, and before you know it, you've agreed to pull a prank you'd never think of under any other circumstances."

"Sort of like with your fraternity brothers?" Tess reminded him. "Like the time you replaced the American flag over the dome with the dean's underwear?"

Wen's face flushing red, he tried to recover by humming a few bars of "America the Beautiful."

Tess let out a musical laugh, her features softening into an image of what she must have looked like as a college coed. "If your father's fraternity brothers learned about the joke Ben played on you, they'd think it was a scream."

"In that case, I don't think I'd care to meet them," Veronica said.

"Oh, why not?" Tess chided. "Where's your sense of humor?"

"The whole situation might have been funnier if I didn't feel like I was being tested."

"An interesting thought," Wen observed. "Maybe God really was using Ben to test you."

"Really?" Veronica had never entertained such a suggestion, but since her father vocalized it, she gave it her consideration. "You know, I think you might be on to something. When he didn't take the money you offered him for rescuing me from the robber, he proved that money doesn't buy everything. Possessing wealth isn't a magical solution to all of life's problems."

"Although teaching you a lesson certainly wasn't his motive," Tess pointed out.

Veronica nodded. "God often uses people's ill motives for good. Remember Pharaoh's attitude toward Moses when he was trying to free his people from bondage? Yet the people were still freed."

"The situation probably would have turned out differently had Ben actually been homeless," Tess observed. "Otherwise, he might have taken the reward."

"And I would have gone on thinking that money can solve every problem." Stirring her soup, Veronica contemplated the significance of their relationship. "Without meaning to, Casper, I mean Ben, rescued me from the bondage of wealth. Suddenly, it's as clear as the handwriting on Belshazzar's wall."

"I remember that message." Tess raised her eyebrows. " 'Thou art weighed in the balances, and art found wanting.' "

"Oh, I'm sure that applies to me. But thankfully, I have something King Belshazzar didn't—the redeeming love of Christ."

"But you say Ben accepted Christ," Tess pointed out. "Aren't his mistakes covered by the blood of the Lord, as well as yours?"

A sense of shame washed over Veronica. "Yes, they are. I guess that's something I should remember."

❦

"Who's that coming up the walk?" The museum curator,

Beverly, peered out the picture window of the refurbished nineteenth-century mansion. "Doesn't he know we're closed for the day?" Adjusting her glasses, she craned her neck for a better look. "But I must say, whoever he is, he's quite handsome. If I were twenty years younger. . ."

"Must be Sonya's boyfriend. He probably doesn't realize she has the day off." From her position in the back of the foyer, Veronica couldn't resist a calculating grin as she hurried to stash the dust cloth she had been using in a drawer. "So you'd steal him away from Sonya, would you, Beverly?"

Bells tinkled as the door opened, followed by the sound of footsteps. Beverly ignored the bell. "Are you kidding? Sonya wouldn't stand a chance."

"Who's Sonya?"

No, it couldn't be. Heart thumping wildly, Veronica stepped forward to greet the owner of the voice she knew as well as her own. Upon seeing him again, she drew in a sharp breath. The snapshots she had preserved in her mind, revisiting them over and over as if she were looking at a beloved photo album, depicted but a shadow of the real man.

"Caspar, what are you doing here?" She realized her faux pas. "I'm sorry. It's hard for me to think of you as Ben."

"That's all right." A soft light danced in his eyes. "I'll answer to anything as long as it means you're talking to me."

Beverly interrupted by clearing her throat. Taking the hint, Veronica made the proper introductions.

Afterward, Beverly declined to leave. She watched the two of them as if they were appearing on a prime-time drama.

Feeling awkward, Veronica opted to remain behind the podium that housed the guest register and to act in her capacity as a museum worker. "I wish I could give you a tour, but we're just about to close."

"Too bad." He looked at his watch. "And right here at dinnertime, too." He let out an exaggerated sigh. "How lonely I'll be tonight at the diner. Unless of course, you'd care to join me." To her surprise, he brought his hand from behind his back and extended a bouquet of pink roses. "Fresh from my garden."

"Oh, how lovely!" Beverly threw Ben a flirtatious glance. "I envy you, Veronica," she added as she made her exit.

"They are beautiful," Veronica conceded as she inhaled their sweet fragrance.

Once the curator was out of earshot, Ben became more free with his words. "I know I was wrong. Can't you give me this one evening to make amends?"

Veronica hesitated.

"Please?"

Remembering her mother's pointed observation about forgiveness, Veronica decided to acquiesce. Besides, she never could resist his sparkling eyes. "All right, Ben. You win."

Moments later, as they made the trip to the diner in Ben's BMW convertible, he chatted about every topic except his apology.

For this, Veronica was grateful. She wanted to enjoy

the evening. Delaying the apology meant she could avoid deciding whether or not she could forgive him. Over a hot open-faced roast beef sandwich, she practiced calling him "Ben" until the name tasted sweet. Soon her mixed emotions melted and she felt at ease with him. As she had predicted, he understood her joy at the progress of the Bible study like no other. Even though he had betrayed her, Veronica could still see he continued to draw near to the Lord.

After dinner, she was glad when he suggested they drive into Georgetown and take a walk along the C & O Canal. The cloak of darkness, barely interrupted by the lights of Georgetown, created a romantic aura. Few other people were walking along the canal, conferring upon Veronica the sensation that she and Ben were alone.

"You know," he said as they strolled by the water, "I almost didn't go to the museum tonight. After you peeled out of the office the other day, I was afraid you wouldn't accept my invitation."

For the first time since dinner, Veronica felt chagrined. "I guess you did see quite a display of temper."

"I admit, that was unusual for you," he noted. "Not at all like the sweet Veronica I know—the Veronica I'm with tonight."

"Perhaps," she admitted. "But you must know how deep your betrayal was."

Through the shadows, she could see the regret written upon his face. "I do. It pains me to think about it. You don't know how many times I've kicked myself for taking the bet. Except, if I hadn't, I wouldn't have met you." Stopping his pace under a tree, he turned to the side to face her. "Veronica, I realize you might not be able to forgive me. Just know that, no matter what, I'll always be grateful to you for bringing me to Christ."

"I didn't bring you to Christ. You made that decision on your own."

"I do think our meeting was part of God's plan. God used my pride to bring me to the shelter."

"Your pride?"

"Of course. I took the bet wanting to prove that I didn't need money to attract a woman. My pride and vanity were greater than my common sense. I see now that winning an idle bet wouldn't have been a victory at all."

When he took her hand in his, she felt the warmth of his presence. Wanting to hold on to the feeling forever, she gave his fingers a gentle clasp.

"But it was more than the shelter experience that made me realize how foolish I was. Your study was the real key."

"I can thank you for encouraging me to continue it. After I was robbed, I was ready to give up on teaching."

"I'm glad you didn't."

As he gave her hands a soft squeeze, a mild current of warm air wafted the smooth scent of his cologne toward her. She inhaled, wanting to capture and possess his essence. Yet she could have no peace until all of her questions were answered.

"There's still one thing I want to know," she said. "Why did you leave the shelter?"

A guilty expression flickered upon his handsome

features. "A man who really needed the bed came to the shelter, and Max told him there was no room. I realized I was taking a bed from someone who really needed it, so I let him have the bed I was using."

"Really? Why, that was wonderful of you."

"I'm no hero for giving up what was never mine to begin with." He bowed his head for a moment, but then returned his gaze to her. "Veronica, I will ask you one last time, and if the answer is no, I'll accept that. But I beg your forgiveness. For the bet. For taking a place at the shelter. For deceiving you. For everything."

Recalling the dinner conversation with her parents, Veronica averted her eyes. "Through the love of Christ, I have been forgiven so much. How can I not forgive you?"

He put his arms around her. His closeness made her heart beat with anticipation. Taking her chin in one of his strong hands, he lifted her face so she could gaze into his eyes—the distinctive eyes that had brought him to Veronica's attention that first night they met. The ones that stood out among all the other eyes in the crowd.

"You have no idea how you rescued me from my own pride. Before I met you, I couldn't have ever asked forgiveness," he whispered. "Not even from the woman I love."

"Love?" Veronica could barely breathe the word. The moment the pledge escaped his lips, she realized how much she had been longing for him to say it.

"I loved you from the first night we met—even though the circumstances were hardly ideal."

"God does have a way of turning bad into good, doesn't He? And meeting you," she whispered, "is the best thing that ever happened to me."

This time, when Ben brought his lips near hers, she met them eagerly. For she knew they held the truth and the promise of a lifetime of love.

TAMELA HANCOCK MURRAY

Tamela is a Virginia native who is blessed with a wonderful husband and two daughters. She enjoys writing both contemporary and historical Christian romances. Her family activities include church youth group, Girl Scouts, choir, vacation Bible school, and Bible study. Tamela is a regular at step aerobics class, enjoys needlework and reading, and likes to exercise on the Stairmaster because she can read a book at the same time.

A Letter to Our Readers

Dear Readers:

In order that we might better contribute to your reading enjoyment, we would appreciate you taking a few minutes to respond to the following questions. When completed, please return to the following: Fiction Editor, Barbour Publishing, Inc., PO Box 719, Uhrichsville, OH 44683.

1. Did you enjoy reading *Rescue*?
   ❑ Very much. I would like to see more books like this.
   ❑ Moderately—I would have enjoyed it more if ——————
   ————————————————————————
   ————————————————————————

2. What influenced your decision to purchase this book? (Check those that apply.)
   ❑ Cover   ❑ Back cover copy   ❑ Title   ❑ Price
   ❑ Friends   ❑ Publicity   ❑ Other

3. Which story was your favorite?
   ❑ *Island Surprise*   ❑ *Wellspring of Love*
   ❑ *Matchmaker 911*   ❑ *Man of Distinction*

4. Please check your age range:
   ❑ Under 18   ❑ 18–24   ❑ 25–34
   ❑ 35–45   ❑ 46–55   ❑ Over 55

5. How many hours per week do you read? ——————————

Name ————————————————————————————

Occupation ————————————————————————

Address ——————————————————————————

City——————————— State ————— ZIP—————

If you enjoyed

RESCUE

then read:

Once Upon a Time

*Four Modern Stories with All the
Enchantment of a Fairy Tale*

A Rose for Beauty by Irene B. Brand
The Shoemaker's Daughter by Lynn A. Coleman
Lily's Plight by Yvonne Lehman
Better to See You by Gail Gaymer Martin

If you enjoyed

RESCUE

then read:

British COLUMBIA

*The Romantic History of Dawson Creek
in Four Complete Novels by Janelle Burnham Schneider*

River of Peace
Beckoning Streams
Winding Highway
Hidden Trails

Available wherever books are sold.

Or order from:
Barbour Publishing, Inc.
P.O. Box 719
Uhrichsville, Ohio 44683
http://www.barbourbooks.com

You may order by mail for $4.97 and add $2.00 to your order for shipping.
Prices subject to change without notice.

If you enjoyed

RESCUE

then read:

Montana

A Legacy of Faith and Love
in Four Complete Novels by Ann Bell

Autumn Love
Contagious Love
Inspired Love
Distant Love

If you enjoyed

RESCUE

then read:

LESSONS
of the
Heart

*Four Novellas in Which
Modern Teachers Learn about Love*

Love Lessons by Kristin Billerbeck
Beauty for Ashes by Linda Goodnight
Scrambled Eggs by Yvonne Lehman
Test of Time by Pamela Kaye Tracy

If you enjoyed

RESCUE

then read:

Gift
OF LOVE

Gifts are given in love in these four modern romance stories

Practically Christmas by Carol Cox
A Most Unwelcome Gift by Pamela Griffin
The Best Christmas Gift by Veda Boyd Jones
The Gift Shoppe by Darlene Mindrup